History Alive!®

America's Past

Teachers' Curriculum Institute

Bert Bower   Jim Lobdell

Managing Editor: Jeri Hayes
Project Coordinator: Pauny Rezai
Project Editor: John Bergez
Art Director: Tim Stephenson
Graphic Designer: Christy Uyeno
Photo Editor: Margee Robinson
Operations Manager: Ellen Mapstone

This book is published by Teachers' Curriculum Institute.

Teachers' Curriculum Institute
PO Box 50996
1170 East Meadow Drive
Palo Alto, CA 94303

Customer Service: (800) 497-6138
www.teachtci.com

ISBN 1-58371-052-3

1 2 3 4 5 6 7 8 9 10   03 02 01 00 99

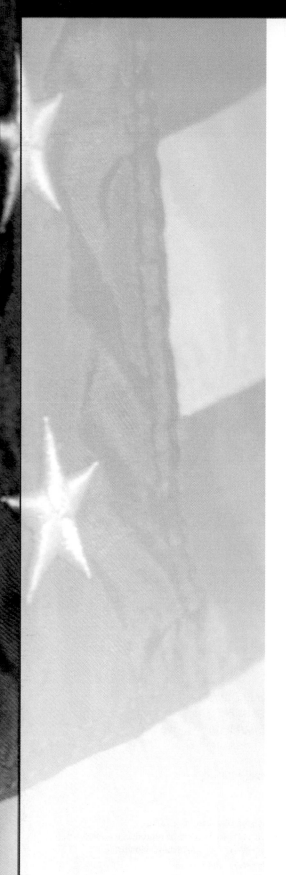

Authors

Bert Bower   **Jim Lobdell**

Contributing Authors
Joyce Bartky
Vern Cleary
Terry Coburn
Anne Maloney
Kelly Shafsky

Consultants
Diane Hart
Social Studies Specialist
Assessment Consultant
Menlo Park, California

Kate Kinsella, Ed.D
Reading and TESOL Specialist
Department of Secondary Education
College of Education
San Francisco State University
San Francisco, California

Scholars
Jeanne Barry
Readability Consultant
Jeanne Barry and Associates, Inc.
Incline Village, Nevada

Stanley J. Underdal, Ph.D
Scholar of Native American Studies, Ethnicity,
and Race in U.S. History and History of the West
San Jose State University
San Jose, California

James Young, Ph.D
Map Consultant
Appalachian State University
Boone, North Carolina

Teacher Reviewers
Ann Dawson, Wilson Hill Elementary, Worthington, Ohio

Nancy Einstein, Cynwyd Elementary School,
    Bala Cynwyd, Pennsylvania

Leslie Frizzell, Oakland Elementary, Bloomington, Illinois

Eleanor C. Jones, Otice Parker Intermediate, Houston, Texas

Joan Kinder, Ortona Elementary, Daytona Beach, Florida

Sharon Ratto, Colonial Heights Elementary, Stockton,
    California

We hold these truths to be self-evident, that all people are created equal, that they are endowed by their Creator with certain unalienable Rights, that among these are Life, Liberty and the pursuit of Happiness.

Contents

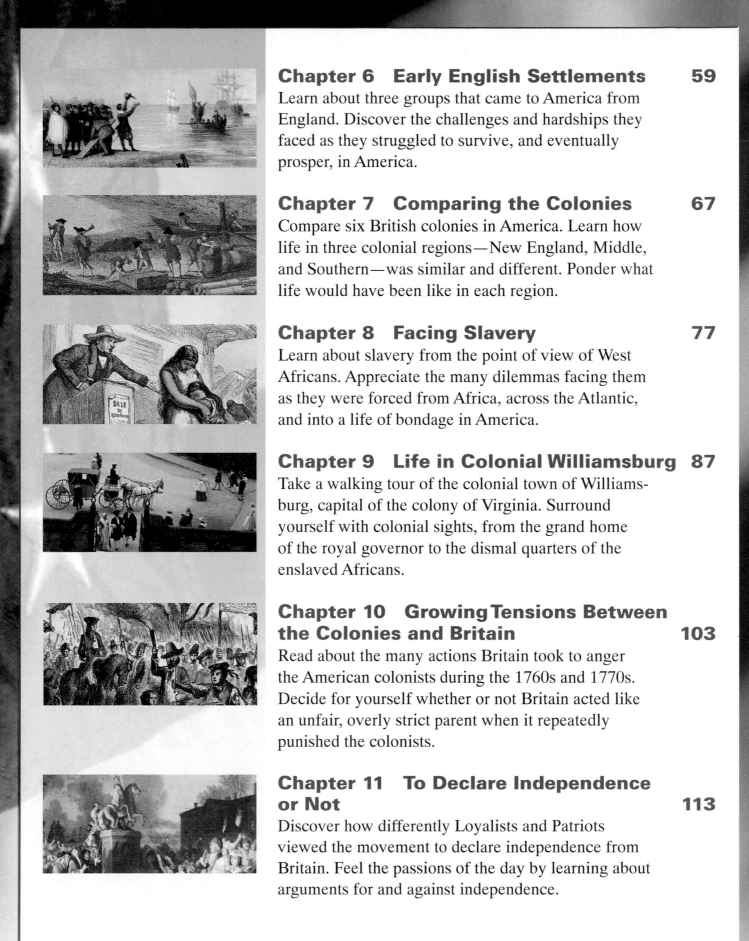

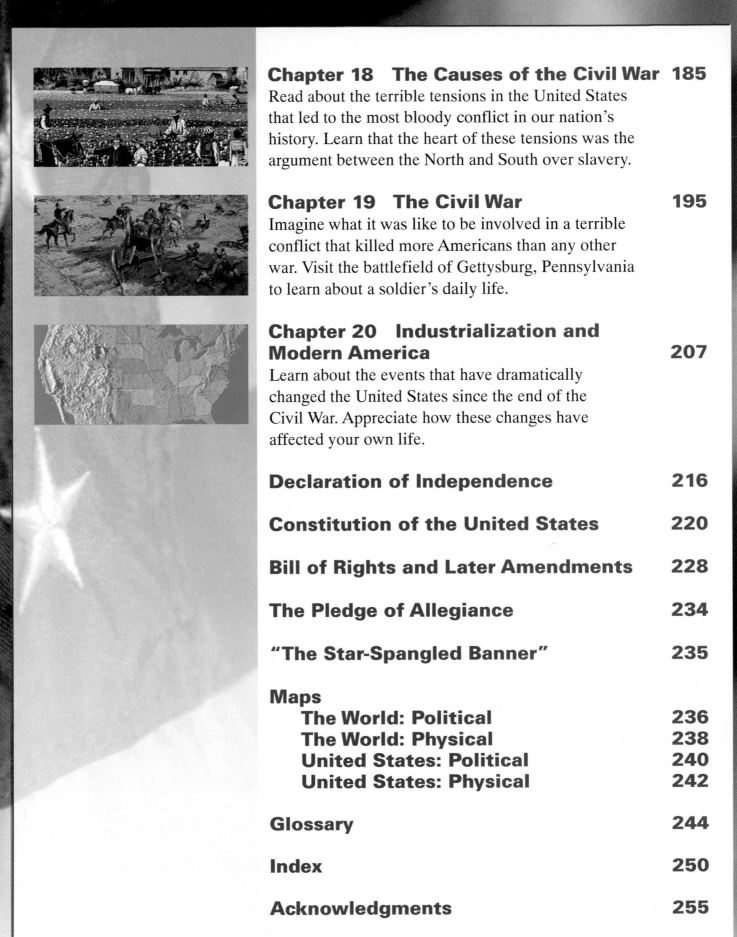

These lakes
are bordered
by which two
countries?

What state
is this?

chapter 1

Geography of the United States

1.1 Introduction

Before learning about the history of the United States, you need to know something about our country's **geography**. *Geography* comes from a Greek word that means "writing about" or "describing" the Earth. Geography is the study of our physical and cultural surroundings. Geographers study our natural surroundings. They tell us the locations of places and describe plants, bodies of water, and landforms.

Geography helps to explain how humans interact with their natural surroundings. For example, geographers study how mountains prevent people from moving easily from one place to another. Learning about the geography of the United States will help you to understand our country's history.

In this chapter, you will learn some geography skills for reading and understanding maps. You will begin by learning how to read a **globe**. A globe is the most accurate map of Earth. You will then learn how to use **latitude** and **longitude** to find any place on Earth. Next, you will learn 14 **geographic terms**. These terms are used to describe bodies of water, such as bays, and landforms, such as islands. Finally, you will learn about 15 **physical features** of the United States, such as the Mississippi River and the Great Plains.

Look at the picture of the globe on this page. This part of the globe shows the United States. As you read this chapter, look back at this globe. How can you use a globe to find places? How does a globe help you to better understand the United States?

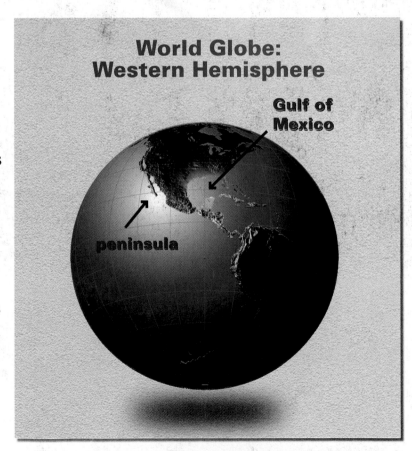

World Globe: Western Hemisphere

Gulf of Mexico

peninsula

World Globe: Hemispheres

Northern Hemisphere

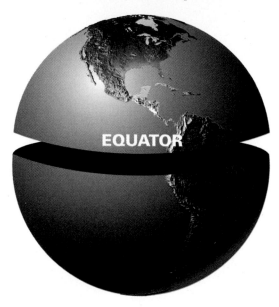

EQUATOR

Southern Hemisphere

Western Hemisphere   **Eastern Hemisphere**

PRIME MERIDIAN

The four main points on this compass rose (in blue) are *cardinal points*. Points in between them (in red) are *intermediate points*.

compass: An instrument (tool) for finding directions. A magnetic compass has a needle that always points north.

1.2 Understanding the Globe

Earth is a huge sphere, like a ball. Most maps that show Earth's surface are flat. A globe, though, is a sphere. Only a globe is a truly accurate map of Earth.

The most northern point on Earth is the North Pole. The most southern point is the South Pole. No matter where you are on Earth, north is always in the direction of the North Pole. South is always in the direction of the South Pole. When you face north, east is to your right and west is to your left. These directions are the four main points on a **compass**. They are called *cardinal points*.

Points in between the cardinal points are called *intermediate points*. These points include northeast, northwest, southeast, and southwest. Many maps have a symbol that shows all or some of these directions. This symbol is called a *compass rose*.

An imaginary line circles Earth halfway between the North Pole and the South Pole. This line is called the *equator*. The equator divides Earth into two half-spheres called *hemispheres*. The half of Earth that is north of the equator is the Northern Hemisphere. The southern half is the Southern Hemisphere.

Another imaginary line cuts Earth in half from the North Pole to the South Pole. This line is called the *prime meridian.* (You will learn more about meridians in the next section.) The half of Earth that is east of the prime meridian is the Eastern Hemisphere. The half to the west is the Western Hemisphere.

A globe of the world shows that we live on a watery planet. More than 70 percent of Earth's surface is covered by water, mainly the water of oceans. Oceans are the largest bodies of water on Earth. The four oceans, from largest to smallest, are the Pacific Ocean, the Atlantic Ocean, the Indian Ocean, and the Arctic Ocean.

Oceans surround large masses of land called *continents.* The seven continents on Earth, from largest to smallest, are Asia, Africa, North America, South America, Antarctica, Europe, and Australia.

World Map: Continents and Oceans

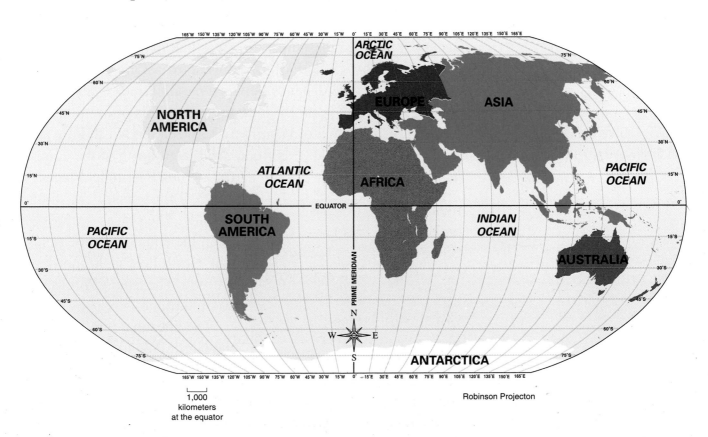

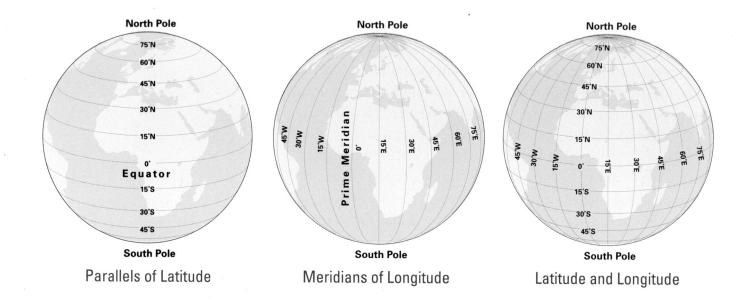

Parallels of Latitude | Meridians of Longitude | Latitude and Longitude

1.3 Understanding Latitude and Longitude

Geographers begin to study a place by finding its location. To do this, they use two types of measurements, called *latitude* and *longitude*. With these lines, they can pinpoint any spot on Earth. Distances between these lines are measured in degrees (°).

The lines that circle Earth from west to east are called *parallels of latitude*. The distance between parallel lines is always the same. The starting point for measuring parallels of latitude is the equator. The equator is halfway between the North Pole and the South Pole. It is at 0° latitude. All places north of the equator are north latitude. Places south of the equator are south latitude. The places farthest from the equator are the poles. The North Pole is 90º north latitude. The South Pole is 90° south latitude.

The lines that run from the North Pole to the South Pole are called *meridians of longitude*. These lines are half-circles. They are not parallels because they are not always the same distance apart. They are farthest apart where they cross the equator, and they meet at the two poles.

Any spot on the globe can be pinpointed exactly by using latitude and longitude. For example, this boat is in the middle of Earth's largest ocean at 15°S, 150°W. Can you find that spot on the world map on page 15?

The starting place for measuring longitude is the prime meridian, or first meridian. It is numbered 0°. All lines to the east of the prime meridian are east longitude. Lines to the west of the prime meridian are west longitude. There is one line that is the same distance east and west of the prime meridian. It is exactly halfway around the world from the prime meridian. This line is at 180° longitude. It is called the *international date line*.

You can locate any place on Earth by using parallels of latitude and meridians of longitude. To note the location of a place on Earth, first name its latitude, including north or south. Then name its longitude, including east or west. For example, one location on Earth's surface is at 30°N, 90°W. Can you find this location on the map below?

This is an aerial photograph of the world's largest rainforest. Can you find this spot at 15°S, 60°W on the world map below?

World Map: Latitude and Longitude

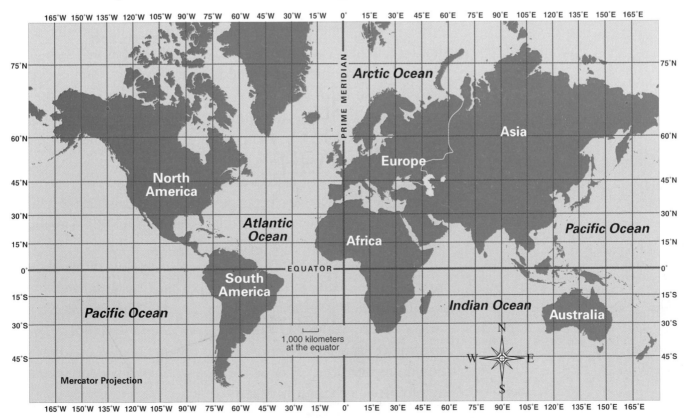

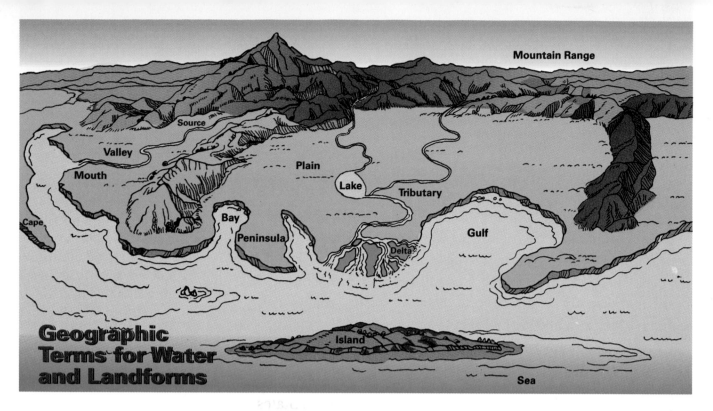

Geographic Terms for Water and Landforms

1.4 Using Geographic Terms for Water and Landforms

Geographic terms, or names, help us describe different **landforms** and bodies of water. You already know that most of Earth's water is in the four oceans. A smaller body of salt water is called a *sea*. Sometimes part of a sea or an ocean cuts into a mass of land. A body of water like this is called a *gulf*. An example is the Gulf of Mexico, near the southeastern part of the United States. A *bay* is similar to a gulf, but usually it is smaller and has a wide opening to the sea. A body of fresh water that is surrounded by land is called a *lake*.

Water also flows in rivers. A river has a *source,* where the river begins. It also has a *mouth,* where the river empties into a larger body of water like an ocean or a lake. A smaller stream that feeds into a river is called a *tributary*.

The major types of landforms are mountains and plains. Mountains usually have steep sides and rise at least 2,000 feet above sea level. A row of connected mountains is called a *mountain range*. *Plains* are land that is mostly flat, with few trees.

You can see other landforms in the illustration above. A *cape* is an extension of land jutting out into the water that is usually smaller or thinner than a peninsula. A *peninsula* is surrounded by water on three sides. An *island* is completely surrounded by water. A *valley* is the low area between ranges of mountains or hills. A *delta* is formed when soil is deposited at the mouth of a river. It is usually shaped like a triangle.

1.5 Physical Features of the United States

The United States is located on the continent of North America. It is the world's third largest country. (Russia is the largest, Canada the second largest.) The United States is bordered on the west by the world's largest ocean, the *Pacific Ocean*. On the east, it is bordered by the world's second largest ocean, the *Atlantic Ocean*. To the southeast, it is bordered by the *Gulf of Mexico*.

Imagine riding in a space shuttle and looking down at the United States. You would immediately see huge mountain ranges that run from north to south. In the western part of North America, the *Rocky Mountains* stretch about 3,000 miles from New Mexico to Alaska. The Rockies are the largest mountain system in North America. The *Appalachian* mountain range is the second largest mountain range in the United States. The Appalachians stretch about 1,600 miles across the eastern United States, from the St. Lawrence River to Alabama. The *Sierra Nevada* mountain range, in the far western part of the

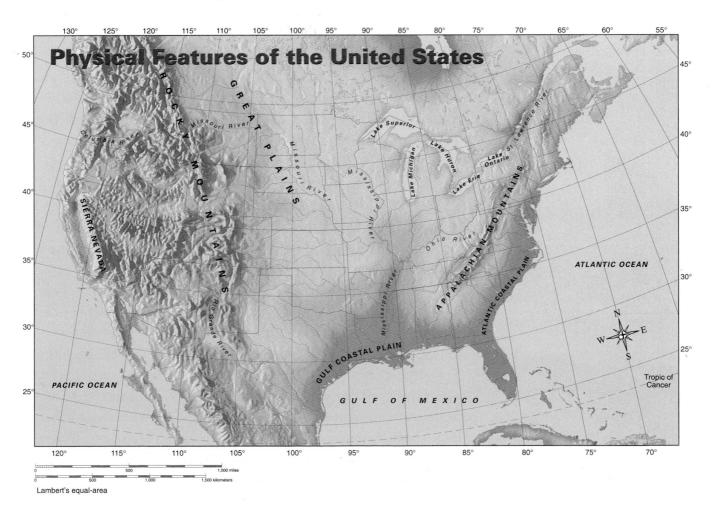

Glacier National Park is in the Rocky Mountains in northern Montana. The Rockies are the largest mountain system in the United States.

United States, is about 400 miles long. The Sierra Nevada includes Mount Whitney, the tallest peak in the United States, outside of Alaska and Hawaii.

While observing Earth from space, you would also see areas covered by huge plains. The largest of these areas is the *Great Plains.* The Great Plains stretch all the way from Canada to Texas. At one time, they were a huge natural grassland where buffalo roamed. Today, farmers in the Great Plains grow much of the world's wheat.

The other large area of flat land is the *Gulf Coastal Plain* in the southeast. This land sometimes experiences flooding. The floods bring rich soil down from the mountains, making the land ideal for farming.

One of the most striking features of the United States is its system of mighty rivers and lakes. These waterways have provided routes for ships and power for industry. In this way, they have helped the United States to become a wealthy nation. The largest river in the United States is the *Mississippi River.* The Mississippi has its source in Minnesota and runs 2,350 miles before emptying into the Gulf of Mexico. Two of its largest tributaries are the *Ohio River* and the *Missouri River.*

Another key river in the eastern United States is the *St. Lawrence River.* It flows from one of the Great Lakes, Lake

Ontario, in the north, into the Atlantic Ocean. The St. Lawrence forms part of the border between the United States and Canada. In the south, much of the border between the United States and Mexico is formed by the *Rio Grande* (Spanish for "large river"). Finally, the *Columbia River* is the largest river on the West Coast of the United States. It forms part of the border between the states of Oregon and Washington. The Columbia empties into the Pacific Ocean near Portland, Oregon.

1.6 Chapter Summary

In this chapter, you learned about the geography of the United States. Geography helps us to understand how our physical surroundings affect our lives. In learning about America's geography, you used a picture of part of a globe to learn about maps and how to use them.

Geographers use special tools to describe Earth. A globe shows the shape of Earth, as well as features like oceans and continents. Points of the compass show directions. Imaginary lines of latitude and longitude allow geographers to locate any place on Earth.

Geographic terms such as *mountain* and *ocean* are useful for describing landforms and bodies of water. In this chapter, you used a number of these terms to study geographic features of the United States. In later chapters, you will learn how features like mountains, plains, and rivers played an important part in the history of the United States.

The story of the United States begins with the first people to come to North America. Who were these people? Where did they come from? How did their physical surroundings affect their lives? You will find out in the next chapter.

Imagine you are in a spaceship looking down at this view of Earth. What continents do you see?

What might this have been used for, and how was it made?

What might this dog be carrying?

What type of animal skin might this coat be made from?

chapter 2

Native Americans and Their Land

2.1 Introduction

In this chapter, you will learn about Native Americans, the first people to live in North America. You will learn where Native Americans came from, where they chose to live, and why they established different ways of life.

Most Native Americans tell **origin stories** to explain where they came from. In this chapter, you will read one of these stories.

Another idea about the origin of Native Americans is the theory of migration. Scientists believe that Native Americans first migrated (moved) into the Americas from the continent of Asia thousands of years ago. Over hundreds of years, they followed several **migration routes** into different parts of the Americas.

Native Americans migrated into many different **environments**. You will read about four of the environments in which they lived. One of these, the ice fields of the Arctic, was home to the Inuit people. You will discover how these Native Americans learned to **adapt,** or adjust, to that environment.

Have you ever looked through the zoom lens of a camera? A zoom lens lets you look more closely at the parts of a scene. The drawing below shows how reading this chapter is like looking through a zoom lens. You will begin with a view of Native Americans' migration to North America. Then you will zoom in on four environments in North America. Finally, you will take a close-up look at how the Inuit adapted to life in the Arctic.

Native Americans Adapted to the Environments of the Americas

goddesses: female spirits of gods who control parts of the world

2.2 Native American Origin Stories

Storytelling has always been important to Native Americans. Native Americans told stories to entertain one another and to teach about their beliefs and ways of life.

Some of these stories, called *origin stories,* told how the Earth and its people came to be. Here is an origin story from the Hopis. This group of Native Americans lived in the Southwest, in what is now the state of Arizona.

Hopi women gather at a watering hole in the dry southwestern desert. The Hopi believe the Earth was created by goddesses.

Hopi Origin Story

In the beginning, the Earth was covered with water. There were no animals or birds. Only spirits, gods, and **goddesses** lived inside the dark Earth. One day, the goddesses of the East and West decided to create a living creature. They made a bird from clay. The bird flew all around the Earth but could find no other life. Seeing how lonesome the bird was, the goddesses made humans to keep it company.

At first, the people lived happily inside the Earth. After a while, however, the rains stopped, and the crops failed. People began to argue with one another. The worried chiefs decided the people needed to leave the Earth's dark inside. One leader found a ladder that led to a hole in the Earth's crust. The chiefs guided their people up the ladder to the Earth's surface.

Once there, the people did not know where they should settle, so each chief set out in a different direction with his followers. They traveled east, west, north, and south until they found good land upon which they could grow crops and build villages. This is how it all began for the Hopis.

2.3 Migration Routes of the First Americans

Today, most scientists agree that the first people in North America came from the continent of Asia at least 15,000 years ago. This **migration** happened during the last Ice Age. An Ice Age is a long period when much of the Earth's surface is covered with ice.

The last Ice Age began about 30,000 years ago and ended about 10,000 years ago. During that time, Asia and North America were not separated by the Bering Sea, as they are today. Instead, they were connected by a bridge of land almost 1,000 miles wide.

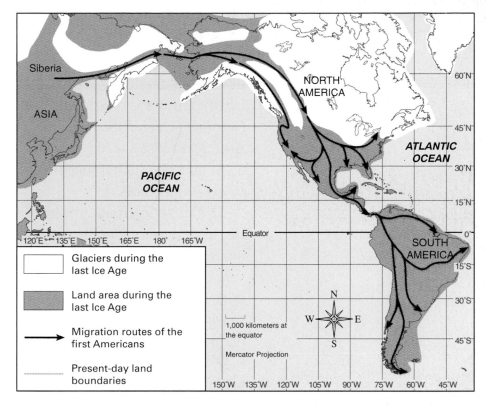

Scientists believe that people followed these migration routes from Asia into the Americas at least 15,000 years ago.

Most scientists believe that the first **migrants** were people from Siberia, called Siberians. The *Siberians* lived in northeastern Asia. They hunted **big game** such as mammoth (a large elephant-like animal), bison (also called *buffalo*), and caribou (reindeer).

Scientists believe that these large animals fed on the grassy surface of the land bridge. Over many years, they eventually wandered across it. Small groups of Siberian hunters followed the animals. In time they moved all the way to North America. Other Siberians may have reached North America by traveling along the southern coast of the land bridge in small boats.

For hundreds of years, Native Americans continued to hunt big game, following the animals south into North and South America. Some groups settled in different parts of these continents. Some Native Americans kept moving until they reached the southern tip of South America. The migrants' paths to their new homes are called *migration routes*.

migration: a movement of people from one country or area of the world to a new home in another country or area

migrants: people who move (migrate) from one country or area of the world to a new home in another country or area

big game: Large animals that are hunted for their flesh, skins, and other valuable body parts. ("Game" is another word for hunted animals.)

2.4 Native Americans and the Environment

In the hundreds of years following the last Ice Age, groups of Native Americans eventually stopped migrating and settled in different areas. During this time, changes in climate (weather) created many kinds of natural environments in North America. A natural environment is everything that surrounds us. It includes such things as sunlight, air, water, land, animals, insects, and plants.

Different environments have different climates and plant life, called *vegetation*. Every environment also has its own natural resources. Natural resources are things that help to support life. They include features of the land, such as mountains and rivers, as well as useful materials like timber from trees and minerals such as copper. They also include everything that people and animals use for food.

As Native Americans spread across North America, they settled in many types of natural environments. Look at the four natural environments pictured below. What do these images tell you about each environment's climate, vegetation, and natural resources?

As Native Americans spread across North America they settled in many types of environments, including the four pictured here.

GRASSLANDS

DESERTS

One environment Native Americans settled in was the grasslands. Most grasslands in North America get only enough rain to support huge areas of grass and small bushes.

A second type of environment Native Americans settled in was the deserts. Deserts get very little rain. People living in desert areas must often dig wells and ditches to get enough water for drinking and raising crops.

A third environment Native Americans settled in was the mountains. The mountains of North America receive lots of rain and snow. The lower parts of mountains are often covered by forests of pine, fir, and spruce trees.

A fourth environment settled by Native Americans was the ice fields of the Arctic. Near the North Pole, the Arctic is made up of huge ice sheets that permanently cover the land.

Most Native Americans chose to settle in areas that had the most natural resources. These environments had mild climates and plenty of food and water. Fewer people chose to live in areas where there were fewer resources to support life, such as the desert environment of the Southwest and the icy environment of the Arctic.

MOUNTAINS

ARCTIC ICE FIELDS

Here, an Inuit family sits in front of their camp at Plover Bay in northern Alaska. Inflated seal skins hang from the wooden poles on the tent frame. The Inuit attached inflated seal skins to harpoons and used them as floats.

adaptations: changes in a way of life that allow people to survive in a particular environment

2.5 Native American Adaptations to the Environment

Native Americans had to adapt their way of life to their surroundings. Each group had to find ways to use the available natural resources wisely so that it could survive in its particular environment.

One group that lived in a very harsh environment was the Inuit (IN-oo-it), who are also known as Eskimos. Like many Native Americans, the Inuit called themselves by a name that means "the people." The Inuit lived in northwestern Alaska, northern Canada, and Greenland, places that are part of the Arctic. The Arctic ice fields are a place of long, cold winters and land that is frozen most of the year.

The Inuit had to make special **adaptations** to their harsh environment. They hunted animals such as whales, walruses, seals, salmon, caribou, polar bears, Arctic foxes, squirrels, and birds. The Inuit did not waste any part of the animals they captured. They ate the meat. They sewed animal skins together to make clothing, blankets, and tents. They burned animal fat for fuel. They used bones to make dogsleds and tent frames.

They also carved bones into tools such as knives and harpoons (long spears).

The Inuit even learned to fill seal skins with air so that they would float. They attached the skins to walruses or whales that they had harpooned. These "floats" helped to tire out the animals when they tried to escape by diving under water.

To build shelters, the Inuit used the materials that they found around them. In the summer, they made tents by stretching the skins of caribou or seals over **driftwood**. Sometimes they placed heavy stones or pieces of bone at the bottom of a tent to keep it in place. In the winter, they built houses, called *igloos*, out of snow and ice.

To keep warm, the Inuit dressed in animal skins and furs. To protect their eyes from the bright glare of the sun shining on snow and ice, they made snow goggles. Snow goggles were made from bone or wood and had narrow openings to look through. The Inuit spread black soot (ashes from fires) on the inside to keep light from shining in their eyes.

driftwood: wood that has washed up onto the shores of rivers or oceans

2.6 Chapter Summary

In this chapter, you learned about the first people who lived in North America. You used the idea of a zoom lens to take a closer look at Native Americans and their surroundings.

The first Native Americans came to North America from Asia during the last Ice Age. Over hundreds of years, Native Americans migrated to many different environments in North and South America.

Wherever Native Americans settled, they had to adapt to their environment. You "zoomed in" on four environments to compare their climates, vegetation, and natural resources.

The Inuit were a group of Native Americans who lived in the Arctic environment. Using the natural resources they found around them, the Inuit made several adaptations to this harsh environment in order to survive.

For thousands of years, groups of Native Americans were the only people in North America. How were their ways of life similar and different? How were they able to adapt to the very different environments you read about in this chapter? You will find out in the next chapter.

How did the environment affect the clothes these people wore?

How did the environment affect the houses these people built?

How did the environment affect the food these people ate?

chapter 3

Native American Cultural Regions

3.1 Introduction

In Chapter 2, you read about how the first people settled the Americas. You learned ways that one group, the Inuit, adapted to the Arctic environment. In this chapter, you will see how several other Native American groups adapted to different geographic areas.

By the 1400s, Native Americans had developed a wide variety of **cultures,** or ways of living. Many groups lived in villages. Most were **nomadic,** moving from place to place as changes in seasons made food available in different areas. Historians call the areas where similar cultures developed **cultural regions**. Native Americans lived in seven cultural regions. These regions were the Northwest Coast, California-Intermountain, Southwest, Plateau, Great Plains, Eastern Woodlands, and Southeast.

Historians identify the cultural regions of Native American groups by looking at their **artifacts**. Artifacts are objects made by humans. Each Native American group created clothes, tools, and whatever else they needed from the natural resources around them. For example, Native Americans living along the forested Northwest Coast used wooden boxes for food storage. Native Americans living in the treeless Southwest kept food in pots made from local clay.

Look at the annotated map to the right. It shows the seven major Native American cultural regions. As you read this chapter, locate each region and use this map to remember information about different Native American groups. What was the environment like in each region? How did these environments affect Native American cultures?

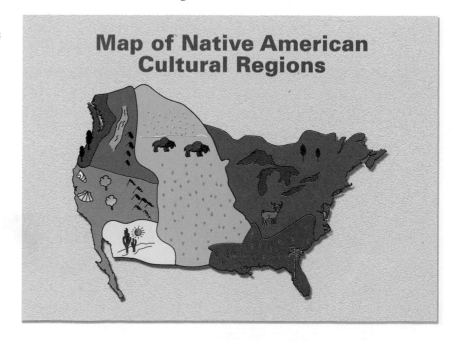

Map of Native American Cultural Regions

3.2 Native Americans of the Northwest Coast

In the Northwest cultural region, Native Americans settled on rocky beaches that were surrounded by thick forests.

South of the Inuit, on a narrow strip of land along the Pacific Coast from Alaska to California, lived the Northwest Coast Native Americans. Dense fir, pine, and cedar forests grew right to the ocean's shore. So, people could settle only on the few flat, rocky beaches. The climate was mild, but the area received heavy rain almost all year. Many tribes, including the Tlingit, Chinook, and Kwakiutl, called this region home.

Wildlife was plentiful in the area. Fish, especially salmon, filled the streams. Migrating whales swam up and down the coast. Deer, elk, mountain goats, bears, and wolves lived in the forests.

The Kwakiutl (KWAH-kee-oo-tel) used wood from the forest for housing. Their homes were huge wooden structures meant for several families. Outside each home they placed totem poles. On these cedar poles, the Kwakiutl carved figures of animals, humans, and spirits. These carvings told about important events in the family's history and indicated the family's social position.

Clothes made from cedar bark protected the Kwakiutl from the wet climate. Women removed the bark's soft inner core to make thread. They wove the thread into warm, waterproof coats and hats.

The Kwakiutl turned other pieces of cedar bark into equipment they needed for survival, such as fish traps. They shaped each trap like a cone. Salmon swam into the cone and could not escape.

3.3 Native Americans of the California-Intermountain Region

The California-Intermountain cultural region extended from the Pacific coast of California inland over the Sierra Nevada mountains and into the Great Basin. This region contained a wide variety of environments. For example, the Great Basin was a desert. Because of the extreme heat and cold and little rainfall, it held few plants and animals. Native Americans who lived here were nomadic, moving on after using up available food such as rabbits, ants, and berries. The Shoshone and Paiute and many other tribes made this area their home.

Unlike the Great Basin, California had many different landscapes and a mild climate that provided plentiful resources. Huge redwood trees covered the coastal mountains. Oak trees, grasses, and berries grew inland. The land was rich with deer, rabbits, and birds. Streams were filled with fish, and clams and other shellfish lay along the seashore. Among the many tribes who lived here were the Miwok and Pomo.

Along the California coast and a little inland lived the California Pomo (PO-mo). Coastal Pomos used the giant redwood trees that grew in the area to build their homes. They piled long strips of redwood bark against a center pole to make a house that looked like an inverted ice cream cone.

The sea provided resources from which the Pomo created jewelry. Artisans used clamshells to make necklaces. They broke the shells into pieces, shaped the pieces into beads, and strung them on cords.

The Pomo used the natural materials around them to create practical and artistic crafts. For instance, to hold food, they wove beautiful baskets from the native grasses. They decorated the baskets with shells, beads, and feathers.

The ocean provided many resources for Native Americans living in the California-Intermountain region.

Some Native Americans made their homes on dry, treeless mesas in the Southwest.

3.4 Native Americans of the Southwest

The driest cultural region was the Southwest. This region stretched from the southwestern United States to northern Mexico. It contained mountains, flat-topped **mesas,** canyons, and deserts. These varied places shared a similar climate. They received very little rainfall, and they had extreme temperatures. Days were hot, and nights were cold. Summers were scorching, and winters were freezing. So, the Southwest had few trees or other plants.

Some of the Native American tribes who lived here were nomadic, like the Apache. Others, like the Hopi, found ways to farm with little water. They raised crops like corn, beans, squash, and cotton, and they established villages.

The climate of the Southwest greatly influenced the way people lived. For example, since trees were scarce, the Hopi (HO-pee) did not use wood to build their homes. Instead, they used stone and adobe, a type of clay that hardens like cement. They built apartment buildings called *pueblos*. These pueblos were four to five stories high. To move from one story to another, the Hopi used ladders.

To dress themselves during the scorching summer heat, Hopi women wrapped cool cotton cloth around their bodies. They used plants and minerals to dye fabric. Then they wove yellow, red, blue, and green stripes into the material.

The Hopi also created clay pots in which they stored their limited water. Potters painted black geometric designs and images of living creatures to make these containers beautiful.

mesa: a flat-topped hill area with steep sides

3.5 Native Americans of the Plateau

The Plateau cultural region lay between the Cascade and Rocky Mountains. This region included parts of the northwestern states and British Columbia. It featured flatlands, rolling hills, and steep **gorges**. Like the Southwest, rainfall was light. Summers were hot, but winters were very cold. However, the Plateau had plenty of water, provided by the large Columbia and Fraser Rivers. Many tribes, such as the Nez Percé, Spokane, and Yakima, lived in the Plateau region.

Various types of plants and animals survived on the Plateau. Forests grew near the mountains. Other areas had only thick grasses, berries, or camas, a type of lily. The camas root was an important food for people on the Plateau, since few animals lived here. Some deer and bear roamed the forests. Jackrabbits made their homes in drier sections.

Yakima (YA-kuh-muh) artifacts show the culture that developed as people adapted to the harsh climate and available resources. For instance, the Yakima built their winter homes partially underground to protect themselves from the cold. Each house was a three-foot-deep circular hole with a grass-mat roof. To help keep heat inside, the Yakima covered the mat with earth.

Yakima women also wove local grasses into distinctive clothing, such as basket hats. These hats were cone-shaped but flat on top, and they were decorated with designs.

To harvest camas and other roots, the Yakima developed a digging stick. They used a hardwood stick that was curved and pointed at the end. They attached a short handle of animal horn to the stick. Women pushed a digging stick under a root, and then lifted it out of the ground.

Large rivers provided water and salmon for the dry Plateau region.

gorge: a narrow, deep valley with steep sides

When Europeans introduced the horse to Native Americans, the Sioux moved to the treeless grassland of the Great Plains.

3.6 Native Americans of the Great Plains

East of the Plateau lay the Great Plains region. The Great Plains extended from the Rocky Mountains to the Mississippi River Valley. From north to south, it stretched from Canada to Texas. Among the many tribes who lived on the Great Plains were the Cheyenne, Pawnee, Comanche, and Sioux.

The Great Plains region was mostly treeless grassland with cold winters and hot summers. It was home to many animals, including pronghorn antelope, deer, and bears. To Native Americans, the most important creature on the plains was the buffalo.

The Western Sioux (SUE) felt that the buffalo was so valuable that they considered it sacred. They created many everyday objects from parts of this animal. For example, the Sioux made their homes, called *teepees,* from buffalo hides, or skins. To build a teepee, women sewed together 6 to 20 buffalo hides. They then constructed a cone of long poles and covered the cone with the hides. Men painted the outside of the teepee with scenes from daily life.

Sioux also used buffalo hides to make warm blankets to wear in the winter. They decorated the flesh side of hides and placed the fur next to their skin.

Warriors even made shields from buffalo skins. The skin of the shield was only one-quarter-inch thick, but it was strong enough to stop an arrow or a spear. Men painted their shields with scenes from their dreams. They believed these images came from heaven and protected them from harm.

3.7 Native Americans of the Eastern Woodlands

The Eastern Woodlands cultural region stretched from the Mississippi River to the Atlantic Ocean. It ran from the Great Lakes to the Ohio Valley. Native Americans settled among its hills and mountains, in valleys, and along seacoasts. Most Native Americans in the Eastern Woodlands belonged to tribes who spoke either Iroquois or Algonquian. Iroquois tribes included the Mohawk and the Seneca. The Mohegan and the Delaware were two of the many Algonquian tribes.

The area had four quite different seasons, including cold winters and hot summers. Plentiful rain created streams and rivers. The rich woodland forests included birch, oak, and maple trees. The forests provided homes for many animals, such as turkeys, deer, and beavers.

In the region's forests, the Algonquian (al-GON-kwee-in) tribes found the materials for houses. Their houses were called *wigwams*. To make them, the Algonquins (al-GON-kwins) bent small trees into a dome-shaped frame. They covered this frame with mats made from the bark of birch trees.

Animals provided materials for clothing. Deer hide was commonly used. On special occasions, Algonquian men wore capes made of wild turkey feathers. They sewed together overlapping turkey feathers to create a sleeveless cape.

Many Algonquian objects combined more than one resource. For instance, the Algonquins used several types of trees to make amazingly fast, light canoes. First, they constructed a cedar frame. Then they covered the frame with bark from birch trees. The canoe was so light that a man could carry it from one stream to another.

In the Eastern Woodlands, dense forests of birch, oak, and maple trees protected deer, beavers, and other wildlife.

Razor-sharp saw grass and palmetto trees grew in the Everglades swampland of the Southeast.

3.8 Native Americans of the Southeast

The Southeast cultural region extended south from the Ohio Valley to the Gulf of Mexico. It reached from Texas to the Atlantic Ocean. The territory included river valleys, mountains, coastal plains, and swamps. In both dry and wet areas, weather was usually hot. Many tribes, such as the Creek and Choctaw, lived in the Southeast cultural region. The Seminole lived in the Everglades swampland in southern Florida.

These swamps were particularly hot and steamy. Shallow streams crisscrossed the land. Tall, razor-sharp saw grass sprang from the waters. Giant ferns, cypress, and palmetto trees grew in the humid jungle. While deer roamed the forest, fish, alligators, and snakes lurked in the swamp waters.

The Seminole (SEH-meh-nol) developed a culture suited to swamplands. For example, they built their homes, called *chickees,* on wooden platforms three feet above the ground. The platform protected the houses from the swampy ground. Wooden posts supported a slanted roof constructed of palmetto leaves. To allow breezes to blow through, the chickee had no walls. This made it especially practical in the hot climate.

The swamp environment sometimes forced the Seminole to wear clothing that was unusual for such a warm climate. For instance, to protect their legs from sharp saw grass and mosquitoes, Seminoles wore leggings. They made the leggings of deer hide.

To move along the shallow streams, the Seminole developed flat-bottomed canoes. They constructed each canoe from a fallen cypress tree that they hollowed out using seashells.

3.9 Chapter Summary

In this chapter, you learned about a variety of Native American cultures. You used a map to locate the seven Native American cultural regions and to connect the environment of each region with cultures that developed there.

Native Americans in each area used the available natural resources to make their houses, clothing, tools, and art. In the heavily wooded Northwest, Kwakiutl built wooden homes. In the dry Southwest, homes were made of clay.

Each group also adapted to fit its environment. For instance, in the cold Plateau winters, the Yakima built their homes partially underground. In the hot and humid Southeast, the Seminole built houses without walls.

In the next chapter, you will learn why Europeans decided to come to the continent that the Native Americans had already settled. What pushed the Europeans out of their own cities and villages? What did they hope to find in America? Soon you will find out.

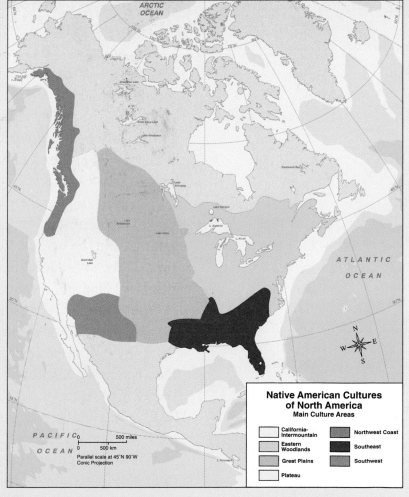

Native American Cultures of North America
Main Culture Areas

- California-Intermountain
- Eastern Woodlands
- Great Plains
- Plateau
- Northwest Coast
- Southeast
- Southwest

What might this diver be doing?

What is the device this diver is holding? What is she doing with it?

What do you think these white plastic tubes are used for?

chapter 4

Why Europeans Left for the New World

4.1 Introduction

In Chapter 3, you read about Native American cultural regions. In this chapter, you will learn why Europeans sailed to the Americas, which they called the **New World**. Of course, to Native Americans this was not a "new" world. They had lived here for thousands of years.

The 1500s were the **Age of Exploration** for Europeans. Prior to this time, only a few people had traveled very far from Europe. Beginning with Columbus's famous voyage to North America in 1492, Europeans wanted to search lands unknown to them. **Explorers** sailed small ships across large oceans that few had crossed before.

Ocean storms and rocky shores sometimes destroyed their ships. Today, people find and excavate, or dig up, such sunken ships. They look for artifacts, such as tools and gold coins, on the nearby ocean floor. These objects reveal why explorers sailed to "new" lands and what they found there.

Look at the drawing of the sunken ship to the right. As you read this chapter, imagine that you are a diver investigating a sunken ship to learn about European exploration. What objects might you find? What clues do they give about why Europeans came to the continent of North America?

Archeologists Investigate a Sunken Ship

4.2   Underwater Archeology

Archeologists often look for sunken ships in order to understand the Europeans who first explored the Americas. To find a sunken ship, archeologists examine old ship records kept by European merchants. They read tales from shipwreck survivors. Sometimes, they use machines to help find a ship's anchors or cannons. For example, *sonar* is a technology that uses sound to locate sunken objects.

Archeologists need to know the location of each artifact on a sunken ship. So, divers mark off the site in squares with cables or plastic tubing. Using this grid, they can carefully record each object's location. This information will help archeologists decide who probably used the objects and for what purposes.

Each artifact must be photographed, brought to the surface, tagged, recorded on a list, and cleaned. Metal artifacts usually survive longest. Objects made of plants or animal products may disappear. After studying hundreds of artifacts, archeologists may be able to tell the name of the ship, where it was going, and why—perhaps even who was on it!

Finding a sunken ship often takes many years. Bringing up the remains can take weeks or even years. Understanding what the objects mean takes even longer. Read on to learn about artifacts that give clues about why Europeans sailed to the New World.

A team of archeologists tags, measures, and cleans ancient pottery that divers have brought to the surface.

4.3 Bible

The Christian Bible is the sacred book of Christians. In the Bible, the Old Testament contains writings from the Jewish religion. The New Testament contains writings by the followers of Jesus Christ.

Christianity began in the Middle East. It spread to Europe almost 2,000 years ago, in the time of the Roman Empire. Later, Europeans spread Christianity to many other parts of the world.

European Christians belonged either to the Roman Catholic Church or to Protestant churches. Many of them believed that everyone in the world should become a Christian. Christian nations sent priests and armies to teach or to force people in other lands to join their churches. European explorers took the Bible wherever they went because it contained the stories and teachings of their faith.

European explorers brought along Bibles. This one was written in Latin and published in 1455.

4.4 Flag

Flags are symbols of the power of countries and rulers. They were probably invented in ancient China or India and were brought to Europe by traders from the Middle East.

In the 15th and 16th centuries, explorers carried flags or banners to honor the kings and queens who permitted them to go exploring. Sometimes, rulers also paid for their ships and crews. Spanish ships often flew a flag that showed a cross. Their flags also had the letter "F" for King Ferdinand and "Y" for Queen Ysabel (Isabella).

A flag is a proud signal to people on land and to other ships at sea. Planting a flag on a new land means, "My country and my ruler now own this land." When mapmakers drew maps of newly claimed land, they usually decorated them with that nation's flag.

4.5 Gold and Silver

Europeans counted wealth in gold and silver. They made their most valuable coins from these metals. In the late 1400s, Spain fought an expensive war. So, its king and queen wanted to build up their treasury (gold and silver owned by a country). They were happy to learn that the New World might have gold.

In Mexico and South America, the Spanish found gold and silver. They forced Indian slaves to work in the mines. Slaves made gold and silver **ore** into bars, coins, and other objects. They stamped a special number on each gold bar and a date on each coin. The Spanish kept track of each numbered bar, making sure it wasn't stolen and was put on the right ship. Ships carried this wealth back to Spain.

ore: rock or earth from which metal can be taken

4.6 Food

Each continent has its own native plants. Many New World plants provided new foods. All over the Americas, Indians were growing many types of corn, for roasting, boiling, popping, and grinding into flour. The Spanish were delighted by this new food. It was as healthful and versatile (useful) as wheat, but its seeds were much bigger and tastier.

Spanish explorers brought back tomatoes from Central American Indians. At first, some Europeans wouldn't eat tomatoes because they are related to *deadly nightshade,* a poisonous plant. Italians were the first to grow tomatoes as a food crop.

The Spanish also found another fruit, which looked like a giant pine cone. They called it "piña de Indias." The English later added "apple" to the name and called the fruit *pineapple*. Portuguese traders spread pineapple farming to other tropical parts of the world.

Corn is a New World plant. The Spaniards were amazed by its seeds, which are much larger than seeds of wheat.

4.7 Tobacco

Throughout the Americas, explorers found people growing a tall, leafy plant called *tobacco*. Native Americans dried the leaves and smoked them in pipes or in cigars. Others chewed tobacco or inhaled it as a powder, which Europeans called *snuff*. In almost every tribe, men were addicted to tobacco. They thought it was good for their health and made it part of religious and peacemaking ceremonies. Native American women did not generally use tobacco.

Thinking tobacco was a medicine, explorers took it back to Europe. They, too, became addicted to it. Because tobacco grew better in the New World than in Europe, American colonists planted huge fields of it and sold it to Europeans. Tobacco became an enormous **cash crop** that helped colonists buy goods from Europe.

Tobacco is a New World crop that Europeans soon became addicted to.

cash crop: a crop that is grown in large quantities for sale to other people

4.8 Astrolabe

When sailors cross the ocean, they need a way to stay on course. They have no landmarks to guide them in the open sea. Explorers in the 15th and 16th centuries used an *astrolabe* (AS-tro-layb) to find their position.

The astrolabe was a circular piece of metal with marks around its edges. A bar attached to it could be rotated about the center as a pointer. The sailor held the astrolabe on its edge. He then tilted the bar so it pointed to the sun, the North Star, or another known star. He could measure the latitude of his ship by measuring the angle of the star above the horizon (where the Earth and sky meet). The angle told him how far north or south the ship was from the equator. Astrolabes enabled explorers to sail accurately by day or night.

4.9 Compass

European explorers used another tool for figuring direction: a compass. This tool has a magnetic needle balanced on a small metal post. The needle is allowed to spin freely. The needle's point is attracted by the powerful magnetic field that lines up close to the North Pole. So, the compass needle always points north.

Once a navigator knew north, he could tell the other directions, too. South is the opposite of north. When facing north, east is to the right and west is to the left. A compass didn't tell a ship's navigator where he was. But it did show which direction the ship was heading, even when it sailed through fog or in total darkness.

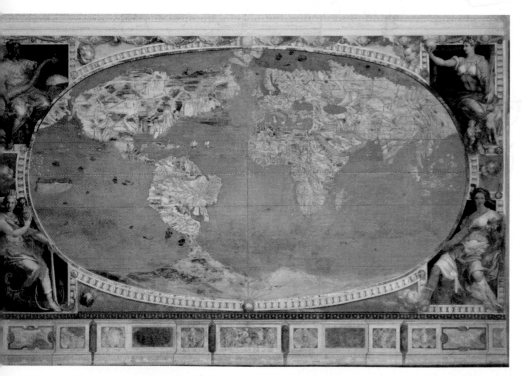

This world map is actually a mural painted in 1574 on an entire wall of an Italian palace. Can you find North America? South America?

4.10 Maps

Maps are drawings of the shapes of bodies of land and water. They also show the locations of important physical features. Ocean maps include such features as rocky shores and safe ports. Maps for navigation also show where winds blow and ocean currents flow. European explorers carried maps of the ocean and maps of the territories to which they journeyed.

European mapmakers got new information from sailors, explorers, and scientists. They then added this information to their maps. In the 15th century, mapmakers understood that the world was round. But before Columbus, they didn't know about the "New World." And no one knew how wide the Atlantic Ocean was. For centuries after Columbus, maps of the Americas still had many blank spots for places that remained unknown. Many maps also had drawings of imaginary sea monsters, such as undersea dragons.

PLATE CXLVI.

4.11 Chapter Summary

In this chapter, you read about artifacts that might have been found on the ships of European explorers. They provided clues about why Europeans came to the New World.

The artifacts you read about included a Bible, which the Europeans brought along to help them spread Christianity. You also learned about navigation tools that helped explorers reach the New World. Finally, you learned about New World plants, such as tobacco and corn, which explorers brought back to sell in Europe.

In the next chapter, you will read about European explorers who made this journey across the Atlantic. Did they find what they wanted in the New World? Read on to find out.

European artists were fascinated by the New World plants and animals they heard about from explorers. This painting shows an armadillo and cactus from the American Southwest.

The 15th-century map of North America on the left has been turned upside down so that north is at the top of the map. By looking at the map on the right, can you tell which part of the coastline the 15th-century map represents?

Routes of Exploration to the New World

5.1 Introduction

In Chapter 4, you read about why Europeans crossed the Atlantic Ocean and sailed to the Americas. In this chapter, you will read about eight European explorers. You will discover why these explorers came to the New World and how their arrival affected the native peoples.

In 1492, Christopher Columbus landed on a Caribbean island and claimed it for Spain. Columbus's voyage prompted others to explore the Western Hemisphere. **Conquistadors** (cone-KEES-tah-dors), or Spanish explorers, planted the Spanish flag throughout the Caribbean and throughout Central and South America.

Explorers from England, France, and Holland also came. They wanted to find a **Northwest Passage,** a shortcut from Europe to Asia through North America. The explorers never found such a passage. But they quickly claimed North American land for their European sponsors—the countries that paid for their voyages.

Some people call the explorers great men. Certainly their accomplishments were great. Their voyages established new trade routes and produced better world maps. However, as you will learn, they also killed many native people who opposed them. They also infected them with **contagious diseases,** sicknesses that spread quickly.

Look at the matrix on this page. A matrix is a chart with rows and columns, useful for organizing and comparing information. As you read this chapter, think about how you can use this matrix to compare the explorers with one another.

Comparing New-World Explorers

	Columbus	Cabot	Ponce de León		
Personal Background		?	?		
Sponsor		?	?		
Motives		?	?		
Dates	?	?	?		
Route of Exploration	?	?	?		
Impact	?	?	?		

The route of Christopher Columbus's first voyage to the New World

5.2 Christopher Columbus

Christopher Columbus was born in 1451 in Genoa, a busy seaport on the coast of Italy. As a child, Columbus had read about the travels of Marco Polo. In the late 1200s, Polo had journeyed to Asia and brought back gold, jewels, and spices from China. Columbus was also interested in exploring these faraway lands.

So, around the age of 15, Columbus became a sailor. He sailed on ships that went south along the coast of Africa and north to Ireland. They may have gone to Iceland. Viking sailors from Norway had already explored as far as Greenland and the eastern Canadian shores. But Columbus and others did not know about these voyages.

The Portuguese were trying to get to Asia by sailing south around the southern tip of Africa. In the 1400s, people knew much less about the world than is known today. Columbus thought the Earth was much smaller than it is. He also believed it had just one ocean. He thought that he could reach Asia faster by sailing west across the Atlantic.

Columbus tried to find someone to pay for his voyage. The kings of Portugal, France, and England turned him down. Their advisors thought that the route around Africa was shorter. Finally, after almost 13 years, Columbus convinced Queen Isabella and King Ferdinand of Spain. They gave him three small ships and about 90 men. Columbus promised to return with gold and spices to make Spain rich.

On August 3, 1492, Columbus left Spain with three ships, the *Niña*, the *Pinta*, and the *Santa Maria*. They sailed southwest past the Canary Islands and then west across the Atlantic Ocean. Early on the morning of October 12, a sailor spotted an island with white beaches and dense green forests.

Columbus named the island San Salvador, which means "Holy Savior" in Spanish. He claimed it for Spain. Friendly people greeted him. Columbus called them *Indians,* because he thought that he had reached the **East Indies**. Columbus captured some Indians as prisoners. He made them take him to the island of Cuba, where he found people wearing gold ornaments and pearls.

For three months, Columbus searched for gold and spices. In 1493, he sailed back to Spain, carrying a few gold ornaments and Indian captives. Queen Isabella and King Ferdinand rewarded Columbus and agreed to pay for more voyages.

East Indies: Southeast Asia, including India, Indonesia, and Malaysia

Columbus promised to bring them "as much gold as they need…and as many slaves as they ask."

Columbus made three more voyages, exploring more islands around Cuba and the coasts of South and Central America. He found very little gold. In fact, when he died in 1506, he didn't know that he had reached the New World.

Other Spanish and Portuguese explorers did find gold. They also found the perfect climate for growing crops, such as sugar cane and tobacco. These discoveries helped them establish wealthy **colonies** in the New World. But to do this, they forced the Indians to work in fields and mines. They hanged or burned those who resisted.

colonies: places ruled by another country, not by their own people

Early on the morning of October 12, 1492, Christopher Columbus landed on the island of San Salvador in the Caribbean Sea.

5.3 John Cabot

The trading that interested Columbus caught the attention of other explorers as well. Giovanni Caboto, later called John Cabot, was a young merchant (shopkeeper) in Venice, Italy. He was a skilled navigator who wanted to explore the world. Also, he had seen the spices and silks that were being traded from Asia. He wanted to find the place these goods came from. So, he set out to find the East Indies. Like Columbus, he thought the fastest route to Asia was to sail west.

In 1496, some merchants in England agreed to pay for his voyage. King Henry VII gave Cabot permission to explore any "unknown land." Cabot left Bristol, England, in May 1497, with one small ship and 17 men. They sailed around the coast of Ireland and then north and west across the Atlantic. They sailed north of Columbus's route to avoid territory claimed by Spain.

John Cabot, standing near the bow of the ship, leaves the coast of Labrador, Canada, to return to England.

John Cabot's first voyage to the New World in 1497

On June 24, Cabot reached the eastern coast of Canada and claimed the land for England. He saw thick green forests and plentiful fish, but no golden Chinese cities. Cabot returned to England to tell the king that he had found Asia and would soon find its wealth.

The next year, Cabot sailed back to North America. This time he explored at least as far south as Chesapeake Bay, near modern-day Maryland. But his ship sank, and he never returned to England.

Like Columbus, Cabot never realized that he had discovered a new continent. He did not know that his voyage opened the way for English settlers to come to North America.

5.4 Juan Ponce de León

When Columbus left for his second voyage to the New World, a young soldier named Juan Ponce de León came along. Once in the New World, he settled on a Caribbean island named Hispaniola. (Today, this island is divided into the countries of Haiti and the Dominican Republic.) On Hispaniola, he became a military commander under the governor.

In 1506, Ponce de León discovered an island named Borinquin (later renamed Puerto Rico). There, he met an Indian carrying a large nugget of gold. Hoping to discover more gold, Ponce de León led soldiers to conquer Puerto Rico. Although Ponce de León killed many Native Americans, King Ferdinand of Spain made him governor of the island.

Ponce de León soon heard stories of another island, one with a magic fountain. This was the "fountain of youth" whose waters were said to make old people young again. Ponce de León asked permission to search for this island. He wanted the glory of finding such a wonderful spot.

Ponce de León sailed from Puerto Rico in 1513. After a month, he reached a coast with palm trees, sweet-smelling flowers, and beautiful birds. That day was the feast day of the Easter of Flowers, called *Pascua Florida* in Spanish. Ponce de León named the land Florida and claimed it for Spain. He sailed up and down the coast, but he didn't find the fountain of youth. So he went back to Puerto Rico.

In 1521, he returned to Florida to start a settlement. He brought 200 men with horses, cattle, and seeds. The Indians resented the invasion. They attacked, and an arrow struck Ponce de León. Wounded, de León sailed to Cuba and died soon after. He never knew that Florida was not an island but part of a vast continent.

The route of Juan Ponce de León

Can you find Florida on this 1555 map of North America?

5.5 Hernán Cortés

Spaniards looking for gold heard stories of a rich Mexican empire. In 1519, Hernán Cortés, a Spanish nobleman living in Cuba, sailed to Mexico to conquer a native people called the *Aztecs.* He wanted adventure, gold, and silver.

Cortés first met the Aztecs on the exact day that the Aztecs believed a god would attack them. Thinking Cortés was this god, they sent gold to convince him to leave. The gold just made Cortés more determined to conquer them.

Cortés marched to the Aztec capital, a beautiful city on an island in a lake where Mexico City is today. When the emperor invited him in, Cortés took the emperor prisoner.

For six months, Cortés quietly held the Aztec emperor prisoner in his own city. Then, after a short trip away from the Aztec capital, Cortés returned. As he entered the city, the Aztecs attacked. Cortés and his army were surrounded by fierce Aztec warriors. The Spaniards fled the city. Before leaving, they stuffed their pockets with gold. Many of them were so heavily weighed down with gold that they drowned in the dark waters of the lake.

After their defeat, the Spaniards surrounded the Aztec capital for nearly a year. Many of the Aztecs had been weakened or killed by smallpox (a European disease) and began to starve to death. When Cortés and his army attacked, the Aztec warriors put up a strong defense; nevertheless, they were finally defeated in 1521.

The Spaniards now ruled all of Mexico. The mighty Aztec Empire lay in ruins. An Aztec poet wrote a sad poem about the mistreatment of his people:

We are crushed to the ground; we lie in ruins.

There is nothing but grief and suffering in Mexico, where once we saw beauty and valor.

The route of Hernán Cortés from Cuba to Mexico City

Hernán Cortés sits in a chair (on the right) with his translator at his side. He is talking with a group of Native Americans he hopes will join him in conquering the Aztecs.

Tenochtitlan.

5.6 Jacques Cartier

In 1521, Spain reached Asia by sailing around the southern tip of South America. Explorers had learned that the Americas lay between Europe and Asia. But people still thought that China was not far beyond the west coast of North America. King Francis I of France hoped to reach China's riches by sailing across North America. But no one had looked for such a water passage.

In 1534, the French king sent an experienced sailor and navigator, Jacques Cartier, to find this Northwest Passage. Cartier sailed west to Newfoundland, in present-day Canada. He entered a large gulf through a strait (a narrow waterway between two large land areas). He claimed the surrounding land for France. Then, he saw a waterway leading west. But his ship was low on food, so he had to return to France.

The next year, King Francis sent Cartier back to explore and map the waterway. Cartier reached its mouth on the feast day of Saint Lawrence. He named the river the *Saint (St.) Lawrence*. With Indian guides, he sailed almost 1,000 miles up river, until his boat could go no farther. He visited an Indian village, and brought its chief back to France. The chief told the king of great riches farther west.

In 1541, the king sent Cartier on a third voyage to set up a French empire in North America. He took more than 100 settlers. After enduring two harsh winters, Cartier and the settlers gave up. In 1542, they returned to France. Still, Cartier had staked France's claim in North America. Sixty years later, "New France" had its first settlers.

Jacques Cartier sails up the St. Lawrence River in 1534.

The route Jacques Cartier followed up the Saint Lawrence River

Francisco Vásquez de Coronado and his men searched for one of the Seven Cities of Gold in Cibola.

5.7 Francisco Vásquez de Coronado

Spain's rulers gained wealth and power from their land claims in Mexico and South America. So, they wanted more land in North America. In 1540, hundreds of Spanish conquistadors marched north from Mexico under the command of Francisco Vásquez de Coronado.

Coronado had come to America to seek glory and fortune. Although he was a nobleman by birth, his brother had inherited most of the family wealth. Coronado paid for his expedition with money from his rich wife and the viceroy, or governor, of Mexico.

A priest had told Coronado that he had seen one of the Seven Cities of Gold in Cibola (modern-day New Mexico). The Spanish had heard that the Seven Cities were as rich as the Aztec in gold. Coronado marched to Cibola. He found Indian pueblos but no gold. Scouts looked further. They found the vast Grand Canyon and the fertile Rio Grande valley, but no gold.

Still dreaming of gold, Coronado listened to an Indian slave. The slave told of a land where boats with golden eagles sailed past trees hung with golden bells. To find this land, Coronado marched across the plains to what is now Kansas. Again he found no gold. Angry, Coronado had the Indian strangled before heading home.

Coronado and his men returned in disgrace to New Spain in 1542. Representatives of the Spanish king later charged him with bad leadership of the expedition and treating the Indians cruelly. Only the Spanish missionaries considered Coronado's expedition successful. It gave them a chance to convert Indians in the southwestern part of North America to Christianity.

The route of Francisco Vásquez de Coronado through the American Southwest between 1540 and 1542

5.8 Henry Hudson

Holland and England kept searching for a northern sea route to Asia. In 1609, the Dutch East India Company in Holland hired Henry Hudson, an English sea captain. He set out to reach China by sailing across the top of Europe, near the Arctic Circle. His crew grew tired of ice and cold. They rebelled against their captain. Hudson agreed to change course and sail west across the Atlantic instead.

In July, Hudson and his men reached Maine and sailed south to Chesapeake Bay. Returning north, the ship entered a narrow harbor. Hudson saw a large body of water leading north. Believing this was the North-

Henry Hudson's ship along the shores of the Hudson River during his first voyage in 1609

west Passage, Hudson sailed up the waterway. When the water became too shallow for his boat, Hudson realized that it was only a river. (Today this is called the Hudson River.) But his voyage gave Holland a claim in North America. By 1624, the Dutch had settled in the Hudson Valley.

A year later, in 1610, English merchants paid for Hudson to cross the Atlantic again. Sailing farther north, Hudson reached Canada. He passed through a long, narrow strait into a large body of water. Hudson was sure that he had reached the Pacific Ocean. But, sailing down the coast, he found no opening. Then the waters froze, trapping the ship for the winter. In fact, Hudson had not reached the Pacific. The large body of water was a bay, now called *Hudson Bay*. He drew the first map of Hudson Bay.

In spring, the crew rebelled again. They set Hudson, his son, and seven others afloat in a small boat with no food. He was never seen again. But his voyage did give England a claim to eastern Canada.

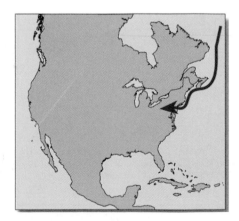

Henry Hudson's first voyage to the New World

5.9 Robert de La Salle

Robert de La Salle claimed the Mississippi River for France in 1682.

The French began to settle their territories also. In 1667, Robert de La Salle, a French nobleman, sailed to "New France." As a fur trader along the St. Lawrence River, La Salle learned Indian languages and explored the Ohio River. The Indians told him about a great river that flowed all the way south to the Gulf of Mexico.

La Salle dreamed not only of personal wealth but of a French empire of trading posts, forts, and settlements. In 1681, he set out in canoes to travel the Mississippi River. King Louis XIV of France liked the plan, but he wanted La Salle to pay for the journey himself. The governor of Montreal and a wealthy friend agreed to support him. When La Salle reached the mouth of the Mississippi River, he named the vast region Louisiana, for the French king.

La Salle then planned to establish a sea route from France to the Mississippi River. He went to France and received the king's permission. In 1684, he sailed to America with more than 200 settlers. After six months crossing the Atlantic, the ships missed the mouth of the Mississippi. They landed 400 miles to the west.

La Salle founded a colony there, on the coast of what is now Texas. Soon, everyone was starving. La Salle set out on foot for help. Convinced that La Salle was crazy, his own men murdered him. Most of these colonists died, but La Salle had given France claims to the entire Mississippi Valley.

Robert de La Salle's route in the New World

Spanish explorer Ponce de León was one of eight European explorers you read about in this chapter.

5.10 Chapter Summary

In this chapter, you learned about eight early European explorers of the Americas. You used a matrix to keep track of information about these explorers.

Europeans wanted a shortcut to the riches of Asia. Christopher Columbus sailed west and reached land. His success inspired others. Early explorers like Columbus thought they had reached Asia. Eventually, explorers realized that this land was not Asia but the Americas. Some, such as Cartier and Hudson, kept searching for a shortcut to Asia. Instead, the real treasure that made European countries richer was the American territory they claimed.

Unfortunately, Native Americans suffered as a result of European exploration. The explorers killed native people who opposed them. They also infected them with contagious diseases.

In the next chapter, you will learn what happened when people from England decided to settle in America. What difficulties did the first settlers face? Read on to find out.

John Gadsby Chapman, *Good Times in the New World (The Hope of Jamestown)*, 1841, Oil on panel, 7 7/8" H x 11 3/8" W
Virginia Museum of Fine Arts, Richmond. The Paul Mellon Collection. © Virginia Museum of Fine Arts.

Why do you think this man has come to the New World?

What is this man doing?

How do you think these Native Americans feel about the new visitors to their country?

Early English Settlements

6.1 Introduction

In Chapter 5, you read about eight European explorers who claimed land in the Americas for their own countries. In this chapter, you will learn about three groups that came to America from England. These people made the dangerous voyage across the Atlantic Ocean in order to create small communities, or **settlements**. You will learn about the challenges and hardships they faced.

The first English settlement was at **Roanoke**. Roanoke is an island off the coast of North Carolina. No one knows what happened to the people who settled there. That is why today Roanoke is called the "lost colony."

Shortly after Roanoke, 105 Englishmen arrived in present-day Virginia. They hoped to make money by finding gold and other natural riches. This group started a settlement they called **Jamestown**. Despite many hardships, Jamestown became the first successful English settlement in America.

A few years after Jamestown was settled, 102 Englishmen arrived in the area known now as New England. They built a town called **Plymouth** in present-day Massachusetts. Most of these people left England seeking freedom of religion. They became known as Pilgrims. (Pilgrims are people who go on a religious journey.)

Look at the three English settlers to the right. As you read this chapter, think about the hardships they faced. Why did some settlements in this strange new world survive while others did not?

Early English Settlers

I went to Roanoke because I thought I would have a better life there.

I went to Jamestown in search of gold and other riches.

I went to Plymouth to find religious freedom.

The only clue about what happened to the settlers at Roanoke was the word CROATOAN carved into a gatepost.

6.2   The Lost Settlement of Roanoke

In the 1500s, Spain was one of the world's most powerful nations. Spanish ships ruled the ocean and brought gold and silver from Spain's colonies in the Americas.

In England, Sir Walter Raleigh believed that colonies in North America could make his country richer and more powerful, too. In 1584, he sent two ships to explore the coast of North America.

The ships landed on an island near present-day North Carolina. The sailors named the island Roanoke after the Native Americans who lived there, the Roanokes. When they returned to England, they told Raleigh that the island had fish, animals, fruits and vegetables, and friendly people.

The next year, Raleigh sent a group of men to start a colony. Few of the settlers were farmers. Supplies ran short because they were unable to raise food. When fighting broke out between the English and the Roanokes, the settlers gave up and returned to England.

In 1587, Raleigh sent about 115 new settlers to Roanoke, including farmers and skilled workers. The settlers realized that the Roanokes would not give them food. So, they sent Captain John White back to England for supplies. Unfortunately, England was fighting a war with Spain, and White's ships could not leave England again.

Three years later, White finally returned to Roanoke. There was no sign of the settlers. Even their houses were gone. The letters CROATOAN were carved on the gatepost of a ruined fort. White thought that the settlers had moved to the island of Croatoan. Before he could find out, the weather turned bad, and he could not search the area. No one has ever discovered what happened to the colony.

6.3 Jamestown Colony

In 1606, King James gave permission to a group of wealthy men to start a colony in North America. The group sent settlers to Virginia, hoping to make money from the colony.

In April 1607, 105 settlers arrived in Virginia. Most of them hoped to become wealthy by finding natural riches like gold. They picked a spot near a wide river and built a settlement. In honor of King James, they called it *Jamestown*.

Unfortunately, the settlers built Jamestown on a marsh. A marsh is a low area of wet land that is sometimes unhealthful for people. The water around Jamestown was dirty and salty. The land was not good for farming. And mosquitoes carried a deadly disease, malaria.

Within eight months, disease killed most of the settlers. By January 1608, only 38 of them were still alive.

In late 1607, one of the settlers, Captain John Smith, was captured by some Native Americans. They took Smith to their chief, a man named

Powhatan (pow-uh-TAN). Powhatan ordered Smith to kneel and lay his head between two stones. Several men raised their clubs in the air. Smith believed that he was about to be killed.

At that moment, Powhatan's young daughter, Pocahontas, laid her head on Smith's. Smith believed that she saved his life. Historians, though, think that Smith may have misunderstood a Native American ceremony.

Later, Pocahontas visited Jamestown several times, bringing food to the settlers. Powhatan's people also taught the settlers to hunt, plant crops, and fish.

Meanwhile, more settlers kept arriving from England. In 1608, John Smith was elected president of the colony. Many of the settlers were "gentlemen" who were used to having servants do all the work. Smith knew that the settlement needed everyone's help in order to survive. He said firmly that any man who would not work would not eat. Smith's leadership helped to save the colony. That winter, only 18 **colonists** died.

In order to survive, the early settlers at Jamestown quickly learned that everyone had to work, even "gentlemen" who were used to having servants.

colonists: people who settle in colonies

Ætatis suæ 21. Aᵒ 1616.

Pocahontas is the Native American woman who helped the Jamestown settlers survive. Pocahontas eventually traveled to England, where she met King James. She is shown in this portrait dressed as an Englishwoman.

tobacco: a plant whose leaves are dried and turned into material for smoking, sniffing, or chewing

The next year, Smith returned to England after being badly burned by an explosion of gunpowder. The colonists had lost a strong leader, and Powhatan was no longer helping them. The winter of 1609–1610 was known as the "Starving Time." Many settlers had to eat horses and dogs. Hundreds of them died. Only about 60 settlers survived.

The Jamestown settlers never found any gold. They needed a way to support their colony in order to stay in America. Then, a man named John Rolfe found a way to grow a sweet-tasting kind of **tobacco**. People in England loved the new Virginia tobacco. Now the settlers had something that they could trade for money and supplies. Tobacco became Virginia's "gold."

By 1619, Jamestown was growing. Each settler was given 50 acres of land to farm. A ship brought about 200 women to Virginia so that settlers could marry and raise families. That year, settlers also elected representatives to make laws for the colony. They called this group the _House of Burgesses._ (_Burgesses_ was an English word for elected representatives.) Only wealthy men could be elected to this group. Even so, Virginia now had a more democratic government than England.

Meanwhile, Powhatan's people worried about so many settlers coming to their land. In 1614, John Rolfe married Pocahontas, and for a time the settlers and Native Americans were at peace. Pocahontas even went to England and met King James. But in 1617, she became ill and died before she could return home.

Soon after, Powhatan died, and his brother became chief. In 1622, the new chief and his followers attacked Jamestown and killed 347 colonists. But Jamestown survived and became the first successful English settlement in North America.

6.4 The Settlement of Plymouth

The third English settlement in North America was started by people who were looking for religious freedom.

King James said that everyone in England had to belong to the Church of England. Some people refused. Among them were people called *Separatists*. The Separatists wanted to have a separate, or different, church.

The Separatists decided to move to a place where they could be free to have their own religion. In time, they came to be known as the Pilgrims.

In September 1620, the Pilgrims sailed from England on a ship called the *Mayflower*. After more than two months at sea, they landed on the tip of Cape Cod in what is now Massachusetts. Before going ashore, the Pilgrims drew up a plan of government to help them live together peacefully. Most of the men signed the agreement, which is known as the Mayflower

Before the Pilgrims landed at Plymouth, they signed the Mayflower Compact. This agreement described the way the Pilgrims planned to govern themselves in the New World.

The Pilgrims, searching for a place where they could practice their religion, landed at Plymouth in winter. Almost half of the new settlers died during this first, terrible season.

Compact. (*Compact* means "agreement.") Then they elected a governor.

After exploring the area, the Pilgrims decided to sail the *Mayflower* across the bay and land at a place they named Plymouth. In late December, they started building houses and a meeting hall, called the *Common House*.

The first winter was very hard. The Pilgrims had landed too late in the year to plant crops. The climate was cold and harsh. Nearly half of the 102 Pilgrims died before spring. Only six or seven of them were strong enough to help care for the others.

In March 1621, a Native American named Squanto from the nearby Wampanoags (wam-puh-NO-ags) visited the Pilgrims. Sailors had taken Squanto to England, where he learned English. Squanto stayed with the Pilgrims and taught them how to plant corn, catch fish, and get sweet syrup from maple trees. The Pilgrims were so grateful that they thought Squanto had been sent by God.

Squanto also told the Pilgrims about the many Native Americans who had died from a disease that they caught from English and French fishermen. Squanto's entire tribe had died while he was overseas in England.

Another Native American who visited the Pilgrims was Massasoit (MAS-uh-soit), the chief of the Wampanoag people. Squanto helped to arrange a peace treaty, or agreement, between Massasoit and the Pilgrims. The Wampanoags and the Pilgrims promised not to attack each other. They also said that they would help protect each other against attacks by other Native Americans.

The Pilgrims' corn ripened during the summer. In the fall, they decided to celebrate the harvest (the food they collected from the plants they had grown). They invited Massasoit to come to a feast of thanksgiving. The Wampanoags brought deer to cook and eat. The Pilgrims had goose, wild turkey, lobster, and corn bread. The feast of thanksgiving lasted three days. Today, Americans still celebrate Thanksgiving Day.

In 1621, William Bradford was elected governor of the colony. He served as governor for more than 30 years.

In the next few years, ships brought more and more settlers to Plymouth. In time, other groups would join the Pilgrims in the area we now call New England.

6.5 Chapter Summary

In this chapter, you learned about the first English settlements in North America. You used three figures of early English settlers to think about the problems of these settlers and why some settlements survived while others did not.

The early settlers faced many challenges and hardships. One settlement, on the island of Roanoke, disappeared. A second settlement, Jamestown, survived only after many difficult times. Settlers often did not have enough food, and they became sick from unhealthful surroundings. At times, local Native Americans helped them. At other times, the settlers and Native Americans fought with each other.

While earlier settlers came to America looking for riches, the Pilgrims were looking for religious freedom. Their settlement at Plymouth survived with the help of Native Americans.

These early settlements were the start of 13 English colonies in North America. Why did more people keep coming to America? Who were they, and where did they settle? You will find out in the next chapter.

What do you think this building is?

What do you think these men are doing?

What do you think this boat is used for?

Comparing the Colonies

7.1 Introduction

In Chapter 6, you read about the first English colonies in America. In this chapter, you will learn about the other colonies that were established in the part of the New World that later became the United States.

By the mid 1700s, there were 13 **British** colonies in America. Most of them were located along the Atlantic coastline. They can be divided into three large areas, or **colonial regions:** New England, Middle, and Southern Colonies.

The colonies were different in important ways. They were founded for different reasons. The climate and geography of each was different. The **economy** of each colony varied. And the way the government was run in the colonies differed. Some colonial governments were more **democratic** than others.

Look at the map and matrix below. The map shows the three colonial regions. As you read this chapter, use the map and matrix to remember information about the colonial regions.

British Colonies in America: A Comparison

	Reason for Founding	Geography and Climate	Jobs	Government
New England Colonies				
Middle Colonies				
Southern Colonies				

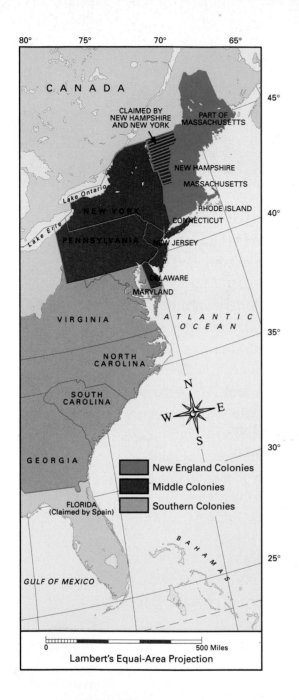

7.2 The New England, Middle, and Southern Colonial Regions

The three colonial regions in America each had a different climate and geography. In addition, people settled these regions for different reasons. As a result, each region developed its own opportunities and ways of life.

The New England region included the colonies of Massachusetts, Rhode Island, Connecticut, and New Hampshire. This region had rocky soil, plentiful forests, and easy access to the sea. Consequently, New England colonists built an economy that was based on small farms, lumbering, fishing, shipbuilding, and trade.

Most New England colonists were Puritans. Puritans wanted to make the English (or "Anglican") church simpler, or more pure. Religion was very important in their daily lives.

The Middle Colonies included New York, Pennsylvania, New Jersey, and Delaware. The rich soil in this region allowed farmers to raise a wide variety of crops and cattle. Farmers sold pork, beef, wheat, and rye (a type of grain) to people in other colonies.

The strong economy of the Middle Colonies attracted people from European countries, such as Germany and Ireland, as well as from England. These people also came from different religious groups. As a result, the Middle Colonies had a **diverse** population.

The Southern Colonies included Maryland, Virginia, North Carolina, South Carolina, and Georgia. This region's climate and geography favored "cash crops." Cash crops are grown in large quantities for sale to other people. In the Southern Colonies, crops like tobacco and rice were grown on large farms called *plantations*.

Plantations required many workers. Large landowners who came to the Southern Colonies from England depended on **indentured servants** and African slaves to plant and harvest their crops.

diverse: different from each other

indentured servants: individuals who agreed to work for a period of time in exchange for free passage from Europe

7.3 Massachusetts: New England Colony

As you learned in Chapter 6, the Pilgrims came to Massachusetts aboard the *Mayflower* in 1620. Pilgrims were a type of Puritans who wanted to separate from the English church.

Ten years later, many other Puritans decided to escape mistreatment by the government in England. These Puritans formed the Massachusetts Bay Colony and moved to New England in 1630. They wanted to create a community that was based on their religious beliefs.

The climate and geography of Massachusetts did not discourage the Puritans. The soil was rocky, and winters were very cold. However, there were also vast forests and clean water. In addition, the cold winters helped to kill insects and germs that caused disease. Because of this, colonists in New England often lived longer than people in other regions.

Massachusetts offered many job opportunities. Colonists grew crops and raised animals on small plots of land. They cut lumber in the forests, fished, and built trade ships. Some colonists became skilled whalers. They used whale fat to make oil and candles.

Massachusetts had a more democratic government than either England or other European countries. Nevertheless, only men who were members of the Puritan church could vote in the colony's elections. Once a year, a governor and representatives from different villages were elected to govern the colony. The colony's leaders made strict laws to preserve order.

Puritans came to Massachusetts so that they could practice their religion freely. They found the land to be rocky and the winters cold. Still, there were many jobs available.

Anne Hutchinson is shown here at her Massachusetts trial. Puritan leaders found her guilty of preaching beliefs that were different from those of the Puritan church. She was forced to leave Massachusetts, and she settled in Rhode Island.

7.4 Rhode Island: New England Colony

Rhode Island was founded so that people could freely practice different religions. In 1635, a young minister named Roger Williams ran into trouble for criticizing the government of Massachusetts. Unlike the colony's Puritan leaders, Williams believed that government and religion should be kept separate. Eventually, he was forced to leave Massachusetts.

Williams spent the winter with a group of Native Americans. In 1636, he started a town called Providence. This town became the capital of the New England Colony of Rhode Island.

Two years later, another preacher, Anne Hutchinson, spoke out against Puritan beliefs. She too was forced to leave Massachusetts, and she moved to Rhode Island. In time, the colony became known as a place where people with different religious beliefs were welcome.

Rhode Island's climate and geography allowed colonists to create a strong economy. Narragansett Bay and several rivers provided fish, transportation, and trade. Animals were trapped for their furs. The colony's forests provided timber. The soil in the southern part of the colony was good for farming. Winters were sometimes harsh, but summer rains were enough to grow healthy crops.

Most colonists in Rhode Island were farmers or traders. They raised animals and grew corn, tobacco, and beans on small farms. Ships from Rhode Island carried rum, sugar, wool, and beef to buyers in England and the West Indies (islands in the Caribbean Sea). Some colonists became rich by trading in African slaves, even though few of them owned slaves themselves.

Rhode Island was one of the most democratic colonies. In the early years, all men could vote for the colony's governor and local officials. Later, only men who owned property could vote. But voters did not have to belong to a church.

7.5 New York: Middle Colony

The colony that the British renamed *New York* was originally settled by people from the Netherlands. The Netherlands (often called *Holland*) is a country in Northern Europe. Its people are called *Dutch*. The Dutch came to the colony to set up fur-trading posts. The British, however, wanted this land so that English settlers in New England could move westward. In 1664, the British captured the colony. The king gave the land to his brother, the Duke of York.

New York's geography made it an excellent place for a colony. New York Harbor was ideal for shipping and trade. The valleys of the Hudson and Mohawk Rivers were well suited to farming and trade. Iron, a useful mineral, was available to be mined (dug out of the ground).

Winters in New York were cold, and summers were hot and humid (moist). But long growing seasons in valleys and along the coast made farming easier than in New England.

New York's economy offered good jobs for some people but also used the unpaid work of others. Farmers grew wheat, corn, vegetables, and tobacco. Other New Yorkers became miners, lumbermen, sailors, trappers, merchants, and craftsmen. However, some of these workers were indentured servants or African slaves.

Colonists had little say in New York's government. The colony had a powerful governor who was appointed by British royalty. The governor appointed other officials and enforced the laws.

In 1664, the British took New York, shown below, from the Dutch. After that, British settlers in the New England Colonies could move westward.

William Penn treated the Native Americans fairly and insisted upon paying them for their land. In return, the Native Americans lived peacefully with the Quakers, who came to the colony for religious freedom.

grant: To give to someone something he or she has asked for. For example, the king granted William Penn the land called *Pennsylvania.*

Assembly: a group of government officials who meet to make laws

7.6 Pennsylvania: Middle Colony

The Middle Colony of Pennsylvania was **granted** to an English Quaker named William Penn in 1681. Quakers disagreed with the beliefs and ceremonies of other churches. They had no priests or ministers, and they refused to fight in wars. Before coming to America, Penn was put in jail several times for his beliefs. He wanted to start a colony where Quakers could live safely.

As a result of Penn's ideas, Pennsylvania attracted people from a number of countries and religions. Penn treated Native Americans as friends, and they lived in peace with the colonists. Sadly, African slaves were brought to the colony as well, even though many Quakers were opposed to slavery.

Pennsylvania's geography created many opportunities for colonists. Forests provided plenty of timber. The Delaware River Valley had rich soil for farming. Minerals, such as iron and coal, were plentiful. Rivers provided easy transportation. Winters were cold and snowy, but that did not discourage colonists.

Pennsylvania developed a very successful economy with many available jobs. Farmers raised dairy cattle and grew vegetables, corn, and wheat. Other colonists became miners, lumbermen, merchants, and craftsmen. Pennsylvania became known as the best "poor man's" country, because taxes were lower and there were no special church taxes. At the same time, many Quaker merchants and farmers became quite wealthy.

Pennsylvania's government included a governor and a Provincial Council that made the laws. A General **Assembly** met to pass or to reject these laws. All male property owners could vote for members of the assembly. Penn appointed the governor with the approval of the king.

7.7 Maryland: Southern Colony

Cecilius Calvert started the Southern Colony of Maryland in 1634 for two reasons. First, Calvert hoped to make money. Second, he wanted to provide a safe place for Catholics to practice their religion. In England and in some colonies, Catholics like Calvert were harshly treated by non-Catholics and the British government.

Maryland's geography and climate were perfectly suited for growing and selling tobacco. Tobacco plants grew well in the hot, steamy summers. Chesapeake Bay split the colony in half and provided a route to the sea. Tobacco farmers near the bay could easily ship their crops to Britian and other places. Unfortunately, the climate also encouraged mosquitoes that spread disease.

There were many job opportunities in Maryland. Most colonists there worked small farms. They grew tobacco, corn, wheat, and fruit trees. Other colonists were involved in lumbering, shipping, fishing, and raising cattle for beef and milk. Some bought and sold slaves.

This painting, *The Founding of Maryland* by Emannuel Leutze, shows the importance of religion to the Catholics who settled Maryland.

Families who grew tobacco on large plantations became rich. However, most of the work on plantations was done by African slaves and indentured servants.

Participation in Maryland's government was limited. At first, Calvert himself was in charge of Maryland's government. In 1638, Calvert permitted the colony to have an assembly. Generally, white men with property could vote for members of the assembly. As more non-Catholics moved to the colony, Calvert convinced the assembly to pass a law that protected Catholics' right to vote and to serve in the government.

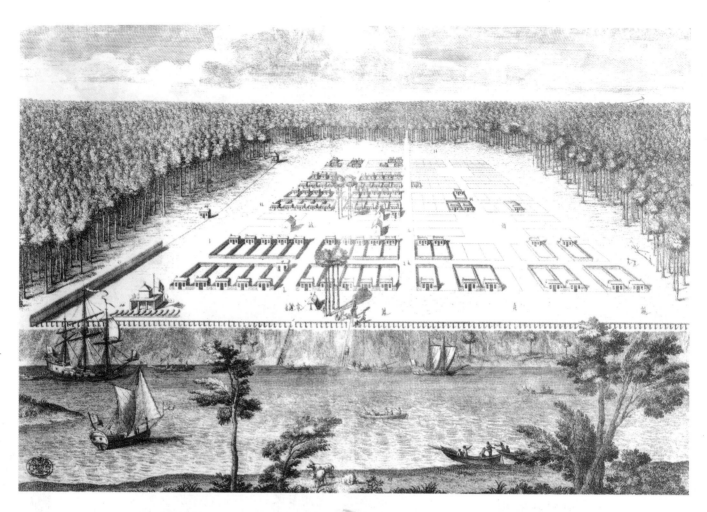

Pierre Fourdrinier made this engraving to encourage people to come to Georgia. The founders hoped to provide a place where poor people could avoid falling into debt.

7.8 Georgia: Southern Colony

The Southern Colony of Georgia was started in 1732 for two main reasons. First, the British government wanted to keep the Spanish from moving north. The Spanish were already in Florida, to the south.

Second, some wealthy Englishmen wanted to help poor people escape debtor's prison. Debtors are people who owe money (debts). At that time, debtors in England went to jail if they could not pay their bills. A colony in America could provide opportunities for poor people to support themselves.

The climate and geography of Georgia were ideal for growing certain crops. Winters were mild. Summers were hot and humid. The southern part of the colony had swampland (low, wet areas). Swampland was good for growing rice and indigo, a plant used to make blue dye (coloring). In the north, forests provided lumber for homes. After trees were cut down, the cleared fields were suitable for farming.

Farming was the most important job in Georgia, but there were other occupations. Besides rice and indigo, farmers grew cotton and tobacco. Other colonists traded goods with Native Americans. Still others were craftsmen such as shoemakers, bricklayers, blacksmiths, and potters. At first, the colony did not permit slavery, but later it was allowed and used widely.

When Georgia began, only the rich men who had started the colony ran the government. They passed laws that they thought were best for the colony. In 1752, however, these men turned control of the colony over to the British king. The king allowed white men to elect an assembly. However, the king could stop any law the assembly passed.

7.9 Chapter Summary

In this chapter, you learned about the British colonies in the future United States. You used a map of colonial regions to study the New England, Middle, and Southern Colonies.

Different opportunities and ways of life developed in the three colonial regions. One cause of these differences was the variety in climate and geography. Another was that colonies were started for different reasons.

Even colonies within the same region differed in their governments and laws. Still, many colonists experienced more democratic government than they had known in England and in other European countries.

Some colonists came to America in search of religious freedom. Others came hoping to become rich or simply to escape from debt. One group, however, did not come to America by choice at all: African slaves. Who were these enslaved people? How did they become enslaved? Why were they put in chains and taken to a new country far from home? You will find out in the next chapter.

Colonial settlers established towns with churches, schools, and government buildings.

What is happening to this young girl?

What might this mother be thinking?

Why is this man being whipped?

Facing Slavery

8.1 Introduction

In Chapter 7, you read about how the British colonies in North America were similar and different. One difference was that southern colonies, such as Georgia and Virginia, depended on the labor of **enslaved Africans**. In this chapter, you will learn about slavery from the point of view of West Africans.

Enslaved Africans responded to many **dilemmas**. A dilemma arises when you are forced to make a decision even though you do not like any of the choices. For hundreds of years, the slave trade forced West Africans to face dilemmas that changed their lives forever.

Beginning in the late 1400s, kingdoms and villages in West Africa had to decide whether to trade enslaved people for European guns and other goods. You will read about how difficult this decision was. Once they were enslaved, Africans had to find a way to survive in gruesome ships that took them across the Atlantic Ocean. This voyage was known as the **Middle Passage**. Finally, when Africans arrived in North America, they had to respond to their new life as slaves.

Look at the illustration below. As you learn about each dilemma that Africans faced during the slave trade, think about how each stage along the voyage took enslaved people farther and farther from their homes.

Three Dilemmas Faced by Enslaved Africans

1. European Slave Trade in West Africa
2. The Middle Passage
3. Arrival in America

8.2 West Africa in the 1500s

The region known as West Africa lies on the continent of Africa, just above the equator. To the north is the Sahara Desert. To the west and the south is the Atlantic Ocean. Most of West Africa is covered by grassland or rain forest.

Here is an illustration showing daily life in a West African village. A couple cook over a fire while other people relax or do other tasks.

In the 1500s, people of many cultures lived in West Africa. In many ways the West Africans were alike. Most people farmed. Some were also miners, craftspeople, or traders. Caravans of camels carried gold and ivory from West Africa to countries north of the Sahara Desert. In return, West Africans received salt, cloth, and other goods.

Throughout West Africa, society was based on the family. Parents, grandparents, and cousins all lived in the same village. They owned the land together and shared their crops. They also worshipped the spirits of their ancestors, singing chants and dancing to ask the spirits to protect them. Another common tradition was storytelling. Fables, legends, and myths helped people learn about their culture and history.

West Africans were also different in many ways. Some lived in small villages, while others lived in large cities, such as Timbuktu. Some villages and cities were part of big empires. The people of West Africa spoke many languages. Often people from different villages could not understand one another.

Most West Africans in the 1500s lived in freedom. But that was about to change as more and more slave traders from Europe arrived during that century.

8.3 Dilemma: The European Slave Trade in West Africa

When the European traders arrived, they saw that some people in West Africa were not as free as others. These people were servants or workers. Some of them had been captured during wars. Some had been found guilty of crimes. Some were even sold as slaves by other West Africans to Arab traders.

The Europeans called all these people "slaves." But their lives were very different from the lives that slaves would have in North America. Many of them became part of the larger family in the village. They did not have all the rights that other people in the village had, but they could own land and farm. They could become skilled workers and earn money. Most of them could gain their freedom one day through work or marriage.

Some West Africans, like those standing in the canoe, captured slaves. Then Europeans traded cloth, rum, guns, and other goods for the slaves.

The European traders introduced a new kind of slavery. Europeans had started huge sugar and tobacco **plantations** in the **Americas**. They needed large numbers of workers on these plantations, and one way to get them was to have slaves. So traders came to West Africa offering cloth, rum, tobacco, and other goods in exchange for slaves. Many Africans became wealthy by trading slaves for goods like these.

The Europeans also offered to trade guns for slaves. This kind of trade changed life in West Africa. A group that traded slaves for guns could begin to threaten its neighbors. Then the neighbors wanted their own guns, so they traded slaves for guns, too. Soon groups all over West Africa were exchanging slaves for guns.

plantation: a usually large area of privately owned land where crops were grown with the labor of workers or slaves who lived on the land

Americas: the continents of North and South America (connected by Central America), along with nearby islands, like those in the Caribbean Sea

A group of captured West Africans are marched away from their village.

8.4 The European Slave Trade in West Africa: What Happened?

West Africans responded to the demand for slaves in different ways.

A few West Africans refused to take part in the slave trade. But it was hard to resist the Europeans. One West African king said that he would not even let slaves be marched through his country. The Europeans tried to bribe him, but he still refused. Then the Europeans got another group of West Africans to go to war against the king. Many of his people were captured and sold as slaves.

Other West Africans tried to find slaves outside their own community. For example, the king of the Congo made war against his neighbors and sold the people he captured to the slave traders. More often, a group from one West African village raided another village. Armed with guns, the raiders captured men, women, and children. Sometimes children were kidnapped while the adults were out farming.

Some West African groups did not raid other villages. Instead, they traded people who were already slaves, such as prisoners they had captured during wars. These groups did not want to be part of the slave trade, but they had little choice. Their neighbors who did trade slaves were becoming richer and more powerful, and they might try to capture them and sell them as slaves.

8.5 Dilemma: The Middle Passage

Millions of West Africans were taken into slavery. These enslaved Africans faced a long and terrible journey. First they were put in chains and marched hundreds of miles to the coast. Many died along the way. Others suffered injuries and died after reaching the coast. The survivors were marked with hot branding irons and loaded on slave ships for the voyage to America.

Europeans called this voyage the *Middle Passage* because it was the second stage of slave trade. The first stage was the capture and movement of slaves to the African coast. The third stage was the movement of slaves from American ports to the plantations. The Middle Passage took from 5 to 12 weeks, and sometimes longer.

This diagram shows the inhumane, crowded conditions on slave ships.

For the slaves, the trip was a nightmare. They were allowed little exercise. Pairs of men were chained together at the ankle and wrist. There was too little space between the ship's decks to sit up or to stand. Often men, women, and children were packed so closely together that they could barely move. Many were covered with sores from lying on the rough floorboards.

The smell and the heat inside the ships were unbearable, and the ships were crawling with lice, fleas, and rats. So many people got sick that the decks were covered with blood and mucus (liquid from the noses of sick people). Sharks followed the ships, feeding on the dead who were thrown overboard.

No one knows how many West Africans made the Middle Passage, but the number was probably at least 10 to 15 million. Between 10 and 20 percent of them died during the voyage. Many others wished that they could die rather than suffer the horror of the voyage and the unknown life ahead.

8.6 The Middle Passage: What Happened?

Many of the Africans on the slave ships had never seen white skin before. Some thought that the white men would boil and eat them. None of them knew where they were going or what would happen to them. They reacted in different ways to their terrifying situation.

Some slaves tried to kill themselves by refusing to eat or by jumping off the ship. But losing slaves meant losing money, so the ships' captains tried to keep them alive. They whipped slaves who refused to eat and forced their jaws open or burned their lips with hot coals. When slaves jumped overboard, the ship's crew went after them in rowboats. Those who were caught were brought back and whipped.

Enslaved Africans sometimes rebelled on slave ships. Here, crew members are stopping a rebellion.

Some slaves tried to revolt, attacking the crew with knives or pieces of iron and wood they tore off the ship. But the white men had guns, and sometimes other slave ships came to help. Once in a while the slaves did win. A slave named Joseph Cinque led a revolt on the ship *Amistad* in 1839. The slaves killed the captain and took over the ship. But most slaves who rebelled were forced to give up.

Many slaves tried to save their energy and just survive the journey. Some were too sick to resist. Others chose not to. One slave told how he found out that he was going to the Americas to work. He wrote that he felt relieved, and thought that his situation was not so terrible if he would only be forced to work. But for many West Africans, life in the Americas was even worse than the Middle Passage.

8.7 Dilemma: Arrival in America

When a slave ship arrived in the American colonies, the West Africans were sold to white plantation owners. Sometimes slaves were sold at "scrambles," where the price was the same for each slave. All the slaves were herded into a large yard. When the gate was opened, buyers rushed in and grabbed the slaves they wanted.

In other cases, slaves were sold at **slave auctions**. The slaves stood on a stand called an *auction block* while buyers bid against each other. One by one the slaves were sold. Parents were sold separately from children, husbands from wives, and brothers from sisters. Often they never saw each other again.

The first year on the plantation was called the "breaking in" or "seasoning" period. The slaves were given new names and were shouted at by an **overseer** in a language they didn't understand. The overseer gave them tools that they had never seen before. When the slaves did not understand what they were supposed to do, or when they resisted, they were whipped, burned, or even killed.

Most slaves worked in the fields. They often worked 16 hours a day planting and picking crops. Sometimes they had to walk for an hour just to get to the fields. There was a short meal break at noon and another in the evening. Then the slaves walked back to their cabins. Often eight or more people lived in one small cabin with a dirt floor. Sometimes all they had for a bed was a bundle of straw with some rags for a blanket.

Slaves worked long hours in the field planting and picking crops. Here, slaves work in a cotton field. Notice the overseer on the horse at left.

slave auction: A sale in which slaves were sold to buyers who bid (offered prices) for them. Usually a slave was sold to the person making the highest bid.

overseer: A person who was put in charge of the work of slaves. The overseer had great power over the slaves and could punish them for disobeying him.

Most slaves lived in cabins like these. Often seven or eight slaves lived in a single small cabin.

8.8 Arrival in America: What Happened?

Slaves reacted to their new life on the plantation in a number of ways.

Sometimes slaves tried to run away. Runaways usually hid in nearby woods and tried to make their way to freedom. Sometimes they banded together. In 1739, a group of about 80 runaway slaves in South Carolina seized guns from a warehouse and started on a march to freedom. But white owners with guns caught up with them, and, in the battle that followed, 44 of the runaways were killed. Most slaves who ran away were caught and punished. One man who hid from his owner was tied to a ladder by his wrists until he died.

Slaves resisted in other ways, too. One way was to "play dumb" and pretend not to understand what they were asked to do. Another way was to pretend to be too sick or hurt to work. Slaves sometimes broke tools or set buildings on fire. A few slaves hanged themselves. They believed that when they died they would return home to West Africa.

Many slaves worked hard and did what they were told. They hoped that their masters would make them house servants or skilled workers. In the "big house," where the master's family lived, slaves worked as cooks, gardeners, coachmen, and personal servants. They ate the leftovers from the master's table and wore the family's old clothing. Some slaves were taught to be carpenters or weavers. Sometimes they were even paid for extra work on Sundays and holidays. They hoped to earn enough money to buy their freedom, but very few slaves became free in this way.

8.9 Chapter Summary

In this chapter, you read about slavery from the point of view of West Africans. You used a map of the slave trade to learn about the dilemmas that West Africans faced. On the map, you tracked how slave traders moved Africans west toward slavery in North America.

In the first part of the slave journey, West Africans were captured and sent to the coast of Africa. In the second part, they struggled to survive the horrible journey across the Atlantic Ocean. That voyage was known as the Middle Passage. Finally, the newly arrived Africans responded in different ways to their lives as slaves in America.

In the next chapter, you will "tour" the city of Williamsburg to learn about what daily life was like for African American and white colonists. How was colonial life like your life today? How was it different? Read on to find out.

Slaves reacted to life on the plantation in different ways. Some tried to run away. Some resisted by breaking tools or working slowly. Many, like those shown here, worked hard in hopes of getting special treatment.

Find these people in the photograph above. What do you think each one is doing?

Life in Colonial Williamsburg

9.1 Introduction

In Chapter 8, you learned how West Africans were enslaved and brought to the American colonies. In this chapter, you will take a walking tour of the colonial town of **Williamsburg**. You will learn what life was like in the colonies for both white colonists and African American slaves.

Williamsburg was the capital of the colony of Virginia. A capital is the town or city where the leaders of **government** meet. As you visit Williamsburg, you will learn about Virginia's government. You will also learn about colonial culture. **Culture** refers to people's beliefs and ways of life. You will see what it was like for colonists to go to church, to school, and to work. You will find out what colonists did to relax and have fun. And you will see how enslaved African Americans lived and worked.

Look at the map of Williamsburg below. As you travel through the town on your walking tour, refer to the map to identify the places you visit.

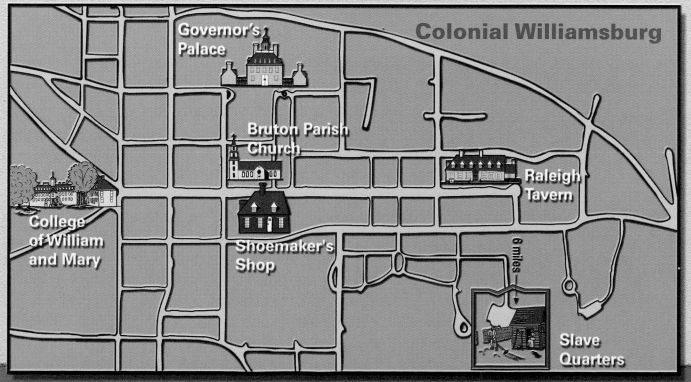

Colonial Williamsburg

Governor's Palace

Bruton Parish Church

Raleigh Tavern

College of William and Mary

Shoemaker's Shop

6 miles

Slave Quarters

This man's clothing suggests that he might have been a lawyer or a government official in Williamsburg. Colonists dressed very differently than we do today.

capital: the town or city where government leaders do their work

capitol: the main government building, where lawmakers meet

9.2 Colonial Williamsburg

From 1699 to 1780, Williamsburg was the **capital** of Virginia, the largest American colony. The town was named in honor of King William III of England.

Williamsburg was the center of government, education, and culture in colonial Virginia. The town was built around four main buildings. The **capitol** was at one end of the main street. At the other end was a college. The Governor's Palace (official home) was to the north of the capitol. In the center of the town was a church.

By 1770, about 2,000 people lived in Williamsburg. Some of them were government workers and lawyers. Many people, such as carpenters and cabinetmakers, worked at crafts. Others worked in shops and taverns (places where drink and food were served).

Like most Virginians, the people of Williamsburg married in their 20s. They stayed married for life, because divorce was against the law.

About half of Williamsburg's people were African Americans. Most of them were slaves who worked in town or on nearby farms and plantations.

On most days, there were also many visitors in Williamsburg. Most Virginians lived in the countryside, far from the capital city. But many of them came to Williamsburg to shop, attend church, and visit government offices.

As you learn about Williamsburg, imagine living there during colonial times. Listen to the bells ringing at the college, church, and capitol building. Imagine people working and shopping, and speaking with British accents. Listen to the tribal languages of Native Americans who visit the city to trade handmade bowls and pots for other goods. See the chickens and sheep wandering through the streets. Hear the stomping of horses' hooves and the rattle of oxcarts and wagons. Imagine walking down the main street to the College of William and Mary.

9.3 Education: The College of William and Mary and Dame Schools

At one end of Williamsburg's main street was the College of William and Mary. The college was named after King William III and Queen Mary II of England, who gave the order to start the school in 1693.

The College of William and Mary was a school for boys. It included a grammar school where boys ages 12 to 15 learned reading, writing, and arithmetic. Older boys could study to become priests in the Church of England (Anglican Church).

In the 1700s, about 100 boys attended William and Mary every year. Many famous people also studied there. In fact, four U.S. presidents—George Washington, Thomas Jefferson, James Monroe, and John Tyler—attended the college.

Boys attending the College of William and Mary were taught in classrooms like this one. This classroom is in the Wren Building, the oldest college building in the United States.

Some girls in Williamsburg attended "dame schools." Dame schools were run by women in their homes. Two young girls, shown here, listen as their teacher reads to them.

Children in the colonies received different amounts of education. In large towns like Williamsburg, boys usually went to school. In the countryside, families with enough money sometimes sent boys to study with a local minister or priest. Or, they might hire a tutor (private teacher) to come to their homes.

In the colonies, women were usually expected to take care of the important jobs at home. As a result, most girls didn't go to school. Instead, they stayed home and learned cooking, sewing, and other skills from their mothers and older sisters.

Some girls attended "dame schools." (*Dame* means "woman" or "lady.") Dame schools were run by women in their homes. Parents hired these women to teach small groups of girls. The girls learned prayers, the alphabet, knitting, and sewing. Education for both girls and boys included strict lessons in "civility" (manners).

Few African American children received a formal, or organized, education. Some slave children were taught to read and write by parents who had learned these skills. Williamsburg did have two very small schools for nonwhite children. One was for African Americans. The other was for Native Americans. Both schools prepared boys to be priests in the Anglican Church. Very few boys attended these schools.

Rules Learned by Colonial Children

Boys and girls in the colonies learned strict rules about correct behavior. They closely studied and followed a book titled *Rules of Civility and Decent Behaviour in Company and Conversation: A Book of Etiquette,* written by George Washington. Washington originally transcribed this document at the age of 16 and called it "The Exercise of a Schoolboy." Here are some examples of the rules (there are 110 rules in the book):

1st Every Action done in Company, ought to be with Some Sign of Respect, to those that are Present.

2nd When in Company, put not your Hands to any Part of the body, not usually Discovered [seen].

3rd Shew [show] Nothing to your Friend that may affright [frighten] him.

4th In the Presence of Others Sing not to yourself with a humming Noise, nor Drum with your Fingers or Feet.

Girls who attended dame schools learned prayers, the alphabet, knitting, and sewing. This is a traditional "alphabet sampler," that has been sewn with fancy stitches.

9.4 Trades: The Shoemaker's Shop

If you walked along the streets of Williamsburg, you would see a number of shops where craftsmen worked at their trades (skilled jobs). These shops were called *trade shops*.

Craftsmen in the colonies made many kinds of items that colonists needed for their homes and farms. Blacksmiths made objects out of iron, like horseshoes and plows. Coopers made barrels and other containers. Millers ground grains into flour. Gunsmiths made muskets. There were also carpenters, cabinet-makers, candle makers, and many other craftsmen.

Three types of craftsmen worked in trade shops. Master craftsmen owned their shops. They were very experienced and

Here we see a shoemaker at work. Notice the different tools and materials he uses to make footwear.

did the most difficult parts of the work. Often they hired one or two journeymen. Journeymen were skilled workers who did not own their own shops. In addition, master craftsmen used apprentices (workers who were learning their craft). Apprentices usually did simpler jobs and watched the other workers do the more difficult ones. Apprentices weren't paid, but they were given food, a place to stay, and a chance to learn their craft. Apprentices worked for seven years, or until they reached the age of 21, before becoming journeymen.

Sometimes, enslaved African Americans were trained in a craft. Some slave owners allowed slaves to earn money by working for other people on Sundays or holidays. A very few

slaves were able to save enough money to buy their freedom.

One of the most common crafts in Williamsburg was shoemaking. Shoemakers specialized in making either men's or women's shoes and boots. At any one time, 9 to 12 shoemakers competed with one another for business in Williamsburg. All of them also competed with merchants (people who bought and sold goods). Merchants' shops sold shoes that were made in other places, including Britain.

Shopping for shoes in Williamsburg was not very different from buying shoes today. Customers could choose to buy ready-made shoes in standard sizes. Or, they might need an unusual size or something else that was special. In that case, the shoemaker measured their feet and created a special, custom-made pair just for them.

9.5 Social Life: Raleigh Tavern

People in colonial times worked hard. But they also enjoyed visiting with one another, sharing news, and relaxing after a hard day's work.

A favorite gathering place for colonists (usually men) was a local tavern. Taverns were restaurant-like places that served food and drink. Many taverns also offered bedrooms for travelers to rent.

Dinners at a Williamsburg tavern might start with peanut soup. This tasty soup was made with peanut butter, celery, and cream. A popular main course was shepherd's pie, a lamb stew with a potato-and-egg topping.

After dinner, guests often drank ale (beer) or wine and sang songs. Some taverns hosted balls (dances). Others had game rooms, where men played board games and dice. A favorite board game in the colonies was "The Royall and Most Pleasant Game of the Goose."

Men went to different taverns depending on their wealth and position in the community. Wealthy planters and lawyers usually met at different taverns from those visited by craftsmen like shoemakers and blacksmiths.

One of the most famous colonial taverns was Raleigh Tavern in Williamsburg. When leading Virginians came to town, they usually went to the Raleigh. They ate meals in the dining room and danced at fancy balls. In addition, wealthy and powerful men met there to discuss politics (government affairs). They included George Washington, Thomas Jefferson, and plantation owners who were also active in politics.

Raleigh Tavern in Williamsburg was one of the most famous colonial taverns. Important Virginians often met there to eat, discuss politics, and attend fancy balls. It was named after Sir Walter Raleigh, who had tried to start the first colony in Virginia in 1585.

"The Royall and Most Pleasant Game of the Goose" was popular throughout the colonies in the 1700s. It might seem like a children's game, but adults in the colonies enjoyed playing it.

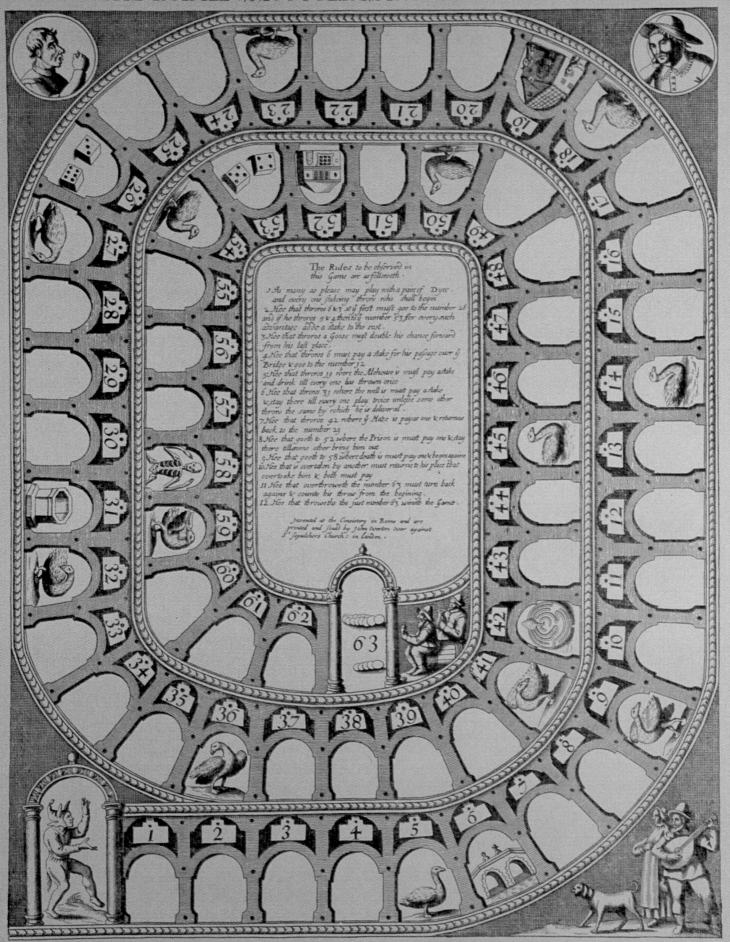

THE ROYALL & MOST PLEASANT GAME OF Y GOOSE.

9.6 Government: The Governor's Palace

As Virginia's capital, Williamsburg was the place where government leaders met to make decisions. Both the royal governor and the colony's lawmakers worked in Williamsburg.

Lawmakers worked in the capitol building in a group called the *Assembly*. Members of the Assembly created and voted on bills (ideas for laws). When they voted in favor of a bill, it was sent to the royal governor. If the governor approved and signed the bill, it became a law.

Virginians could be chosen for the Assembly in one of two ways. Some were elected, while others were appointed by the governor. But most people in Virginia were not allowed to vote in elections or to serve in the Assembly. The Assembly included only white men who owned property. In addition, all Assembly members had to belong to the Anglican Church.

The royal governor of Virginia lived in the Governor's Palace, shown here. It was designed to impress visitors and to remind them of the king's power. The governor worked here and also hosted fancy balls.

The royal governor was appointed by the British king. He was the king's representative in the colony. The governor lived in a large house called the *Governor's Palace*.

The Governor's Palace was designed to impress visitors and to remind them of the king's power. It was three stories high. It had 25 servants and slaves to care for it. Outside, there were large gardens and orchards. Visitors could admire the flowers and trees while floating down a canal (a man-made waterway) in a boat.

Inside the palace, the governor did his official work. One important duty was to read the bills that the Assembly sent him. The governor had great power over which bills became laws. If he disliked a proposed law, he simply refused to sign the bill.

The palace was also the scene of official celebrations. On important occasions like the king's birthday, the governor invited colonial leaders to attend fancy balls.

Bills and Requests for Virginia's Royal Governor

Colonial governors had to make many decisions about bills and other requests. Here are examples of decisions made by the royal governor of Virginia.

A Lighthouse at Cape Henry

In the 1700s, there were many shipwrecks near a place called *Cape Henry* in Chesapeake Bay. Virginia's royal governor worked with the governor of Maryland to get a lighthouse built at Cape Henry. The governors hoped to make it safer for trade ships to sail between their colonies. Virginia's Assembly passed the lighthouse bill. The governor signed it in 1772.

Voting in the Colony of Virginia

A variety of laws and traditions determined who could vote in colonial Virginia. Voters had to be white men who owned property. Women, African Americans, Native Americans, and white men without property could not vote. In addition, voters had to belong to the Anglican Church.

A Pardon for a Teenaged Pirate

Lawbreaking was often punished harshly in Virginia. For a minor crime, such as not attending church, people might be fined or lashed with a whip. For a major crime, such as stealing, they could be put to death. But lawbreakers could ask for a pardon, or a release from punishment. For example, in 1727, a teenager named John Vidal was found guilty of piracy. Piracy is the robbing of ships at sea. Vidal begged for mercy. He pleaded that he "never intended to go a-pirating." The governor pardoned the young man.

Slaves lived in houses and cabins called *slave quarters,* like these shown here, at Carter's Grove Plantation, just outside Williamsburg. The cabins had little furniture, and slaves often slept on piles of straw.

9.7 Slavery: The Slave Quarters at Carter's Grove Plantation

About half the people in Williamsburg were enslaved African Americans. Some worked in town. Most lived and worked on farms and plantations outside of town.

There were different types of slaves in the colonies. Some were house slaves. These were servants who did chores in their master's house. Some were town slaves who worked in places like Williamsburg as gardeners or coachmen. Town and house slaves often worked seven days a week. A few town slaves learned a skilled craft, such as shoemaking or blacksmithing.

Most slaves worked in the fields on plantations and farms. These slaves usually worked six days a week, from sunrise until after sunset.

Slaves lived in houses and cabins called *slave quarters* (housing). Imagine visiting the slave quarters at Carter's Grove, a tobacco plantation located just outside Williamsburg. Inside, you see piles of straw that are used for beds. Against the wall are tools for work in the fields, such as rakes, hoes, and shovels. You might find some musical instruments, such as drums and fiddles. Since some slaves could read, you might see a copy of the local newspaper, the *Virginia Gazette.*

Enslaved people had difficult and painful lives. They worked long, hard days. They had to do whatever they were told. Frequently they were beaten or whipped. If they fought back, they could be killed. They could also be sold away from friends and family at any time.

African Americans survived these terrible conditions by relying on one another. They looked after family members and tried to create strong family ties. In their houses, away from the slave owner, they had their own Christian preachers. The preachers' sermons (lessons) spoke of freedom and justice. As in West Africa, music was an important part of their religious services.

Like West Africans, slaves in the colonies used songs to express themselves. A common type of song was called *call and response*. In these songs, the leader sings a line (call) and everyone repeats it (response). The slaves' songs expressed their anger and pain. They also expressed their hopes for freedom.

"Juba": A Call-and-Response Song

The word *juba* means "leftover food," such as the husks (outer leaves) of corn and the skin from cooked meat. House slaves were often given such leftovers to eat. "Juba" is a song about this.

One African American woman remembered her father talking about the song. He described the way his mother added milk to leftovers to make the family's meal. When his mother and sisters prepared food for the slave master, the mother sang a song. The song tells how she wishes she could give her family good, hot food, like the food she makes for the slave master. Instead, she is only able to give them "juba."

Call:	*Juba this and Juba that*
Response:	*Juba this and Juba that*
Call:	*And Juba killed a yellow cat*
Response:	*And Juba killed a yellow cat*
Call:	*And get over double trouble, Juba*
Response:	*And get over double trouble, Juba*
Call:	*Ah, ah, Juba*
Response:	*Ah, ah, Juba*
Call:	*You sift-a the meal*
Response:	*You sift-a the meal*
Call:	*And you give me the husk*
Response:	*And you give me the husk*
Call:	*You cook-a the bread*
Response:	*You cook-a the bread*
Call:	*You give me the crust*
Response:	*You give me the crust*
Call:	*We fry the meat*
Response:	*We fry the meat*
Call:	*You give me the skin*
Response:	*You give me the skin*
Call:	*Juba this and Juba that*
Response:	*Juba this and Juba that*
Call:	*Juba killed a yellow cat*
Response:	*Juba killed a yellow cat*

9.8 Religion: Bruton Parish Church

In Virginia, the Church of England (Anglican Church) was the official church. Bruton Parish Church, shown here, was the Anglican Church building in Williamsburg. It was located in the center of town.

In some colonies, people demanded freedom to belong to different churches. In other colonies, people attended only the official churches that were supported by the government.

In Virginia, the Church of England (Anglican Church) was the official church. At first, the church leaders tried to discourage people from practicing other religions. Eventually, however, some people demanded freedom to belong to different churches, and the Anglican Church allowed other Protestant groups.

The Anglican Church building in Williamsburg was the Bruton Parish Church. It was given an important setting in the center of town.

In Virginia, as in England, religion and government were not separated. The head of the Church of England was the king. In a similar way, the royal governor was the head of Virginia's Anglican Church. Only Anglicans could vote or hold government positions in Virginia. In addition, the law required all white colonists to attend church. Virginians also had to pay taxes to support the Anglican Church. Throughout the 1700s, Virginia gradually allowed more freedom of religion.

As in most colonial towns, the local church was the center of religious activity in Williamsburg. Many famous Virginians, such as Thomas Jefferson and George Washington, attended services at Bruton Parish Church.

On Sundays, people often arrived at church early to meet and talk. Many of them would have been visiting the town for the first time in weeks. Outside the church, people gossiped and discussed the latest news. They also read and posted important announcements. At times, these gatherings were as lively as town fairs.

Inside the church, people sat in different places, depending on their position in the community. The most important people sat close to the pulpit (the platform or raised desk used by the minister). Less important people sat farther away.

In Bruton Parish Church, the governor's family sat directly across from the pulpit. In the early years of the church, men sat on one side and women on the other. Wealthy plantation owners sat in the front rows. Their slaves were allowed to sit with them. Students from the College of William and Mary sat in the balcony, farthest from the pulpit. Most African Americans stood in the back or looked in through the windows.

When the services ended, the most important people left the church first. Women and poorer men waited for the wealthy plantation owners to leave before going outside.

9.9 Chapter Summary

In this chapter, you learned about life in the colonial town of Williamsburg. You used a map of the town to learn about different places and the activities that went on there.

At schools like William and Mary, town boys learned to read and write. Girls learned skills at home or in dame schools. In trade shops, skilled craftsmen made items to sell. In taverns, men gathered to relax and discuss current events. At the capitol and the Governor's Palace, laws were made for the colony. Meanwhile, enslaved African Americans lived in slave quarters and worked long hours as house servants, or outdoors in the fields.

The parish church was the center of religious activity. It was also a place where colonists gathered to share news.

For many years, white colonists felt that they were a part of Britain. Yet, by the 1760s, trouble developed between the colonies and Britain. Some colonists even began breaking British laws and fighting with the king's soldiers.

What happened to make the colonists so angry? You will find out in the next chapter.

THE FOLLY OF ENGLAND AND THE RUIN OF AMERICA

How is each picture an example of protest against the British?

Growing Tensions Between the Colonies and Britain

10.1 Introduction

In Chapter 9, you read about daily life in the American colonies in the early 1700s. At the time, the colonists were happy to be part of Britain, and they supported the British king. In this chapter, you will learn about events that changed how the colonists felt.

During the 1750s and 1760s, Britain and the colonists fought against the French in the French and Indian War. The war left Britain with huge **debts** and a large amount of new territory to protect. To solve its problems, the British government passed a number of laws, called **acts**. Some of these laws ordered the colonists to pay new taxes. The colonists became angry because they had no representatives in the British government to vote on these laws. They said that **taxation without representation** was unfair. Many colonists began to **protest** against British rule.

Look at the drawing of the parent and child at the right. Some people have compared Britain and the colonies to a parent and a child. Britain was like a parent because it created the colonies and expected them to respect its authority. The colonies were like a child who sometimes refused to obey the parent. This kind of comparison is called a *metaphor*.

As you read through this chapter, think about this metaphor of the relationship between a parent and a child. What can a parent do when a child disobeys? What happens to their relationship when the parent makes new rules or punishes the child?

Britain and the Colonies: A Strained Relationship

Britain   Colonies

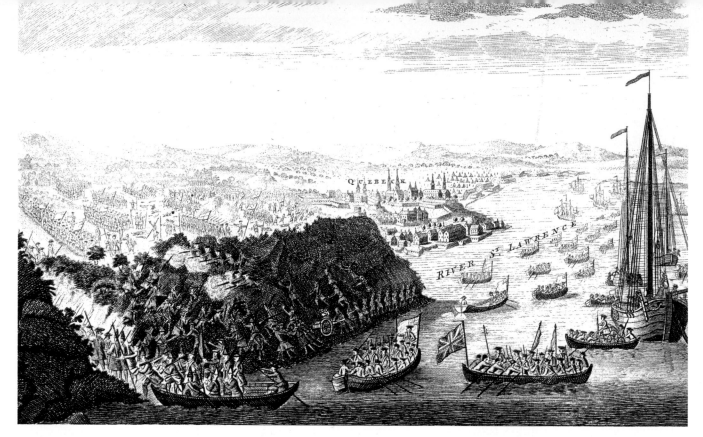

Here we see British troops capturing the city of Quebec in Canada in 1759. This was a key event in helping the British win the French and Indian War.

10.2 The French and Indian War

By the late 1600s, Britain, France, and Spain often fought one another to gain more territory around the world. They fought in Europe, Asia, and the Americas.

In North America, Britain and France both claimed the Ohio River Valley. British settlers wanted to farm the rich soil there. The French wanted to trap beavers so that they could trade their furs.

In 1754, the argument over the Ohio Valley turned into a war. The war lasted almost 10 years. Thousands of British soldiers fought along with many colonists against the French. Most Native Americans were friendly with the French, and they fought on their side. Some Native Americans fought on the British side. Europeans called Native Americans "Indians," so the British colonists called the conflict the French and Indian War.

At first, Britain lost many battles. The bright red uniforms of the British soldiers made them easy targets. But things changed in 1759 when British troops captured the city of Quebec in Canada. By 1760, the French had lost Canada, and in 1762, they asked for peace. In 1763, a peace treaty gave Britain control of Canada. Britain also won the land between the Mississippi River and the Appalachian Mountains.

The war gave Britain more land, but it also created huge problems. Most important, it left Britain with unpaid bills, called *debts*. By 1763, Britain's debts added to an amount that would be equal to more than 30 billion dollars today.

10.3 The Proclamation of 1763

After the French and Indian War, many British moved west into the land that Britain had won from the French. Native Americans were afraid that this movement of settlers would destroy their way of life. Some of them tried to drive the settlers away by attacking their forts and houses. In 1763, nearly 2,000 settlers died because of the fighting.

To stop the fighting and to protect the colonists, Britain announced a law called the Proclamation of 1763. The law said that Native Americans could have all the land west of the Appalachian Mountains and that settlers could not move there.

The colonists disliked this law. Many of them simply ignored it and continued to move west. Even more of them didn't like the way that Britain was trying to control the colonies.

The Proclamation of 1763 prevented the colonists from moving west of the Appalachian Mountains. This was the first of many British actions that angered the colonists.

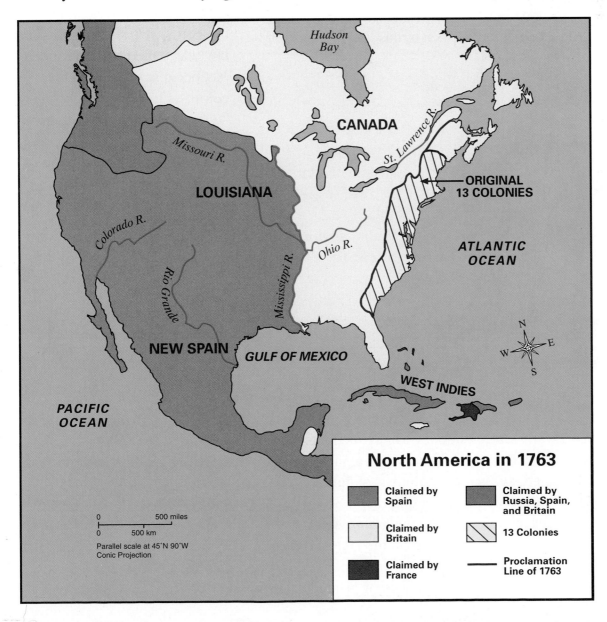

Hudson Bay

CANADA

St. Lawrence R.

Missouri R.

LOUISIANA

ORIGINAL 13 COLONIES

Colorado R.

Ohio R.

ATLANTIC OCEAN

Rio Grande

Mississippi R.

NEW SPAIN

GULF OF MEXICO

N
W   E
S

WEST INDIES

PACIFIC OCEAN

0   500 miles
0   500 km
Parallel scale at 45˚N 90˚W
Conic Projection

North America in 1763

Claimed by Spain

Claimed by Russia, Spain, and Britain

Claimed by Britain

13 Colonies

Claimed by France

Proclamation Line of 1763

The Quartering Act ordered colonists to provide "quarters" for British soldiers, like the one shown here. This meant that colonists had to allow soldiers to stay in their homes and provide them with food and other supplies. Colonists were upset by this law.

10.4 The Quartering Act

The British government left thousands of soldiers in the colonies to protect the colonists after the French and Indian War. The British were afraid that Native Americans or Spanish settlers in Florida might attack the colonies.

Britain thought that the colonists should help to pay for this army. As a result, in 1765, a new law called the *Quartering* Act was passed by the British **Parliament**. The law was called the Quartering Act because it ordered the colonists to provide "quarters" (places to live) for British soldiers. It also ordered them to supply the soldiers with food, fuel, and candles, and to provide them with transportation.

The colonists were angry about the Quartering Act. They didn't want to pay for British troops staying in the colonies. Many colonists treated the soldiers badly.

10.5 The Stamp Act

After fighting the French and Indian War, Britain needed money to pay its debts. Britain also needed to pay for the soldiers who remained in America. British leaders thought that the colonists should help pay for the troops who were protecting them. So, in 1765, Parliament passed a new tax law called the *Stamp Act*.

The Stamp Act said that the colonists would have to pay a tax on printed papers. To prove that the tax was paid, almost every piece of printed paper would have to show a large blue stamp. Newspapers, pamphlets, marriage licenses, and playing cards were taxed.

News of this new tax made the colonists furious. They didn't want to pay more money for things they used every day, especially since the money went to the British government. But they were even angrier because they had no say in making the law.

Colonists showed their anger in many ways. Some of them refused to buy the stamps. Some protested in the streets and town squares. And some tried to scare off the tax collectors, at times even attacking them and their homes.

Groups from different colonies also joined together to protest the stamp tax. In several colonies, merchants

The Stamp Act required colonists to pay a tax on printed papers. Here, we see a stamp that was put on printed papers to prove that the tax had been paid. The Stamp Act made colonists furious. Later, it was canceled.

(shopkeepers and other businesspeople) agreed not to buy British goods. Many women, such as the Daughters of Liberty in Boston, refused to buy British cloth and wove their own cloth instead.

In October 1765, nine of the colonies sent delegates to a special meeting in New York called the *Stamp Act Congress*. The delegates believed that all British subjects had a right to vote on taxes through their representatives. Since the colonies had no representatives in Parliament, the delegates said that it was unfair for Parliament to pass laws like the Stamp Act. They said that passing such laws was "taxation without representation."

The colonists' angry protests surprised the king and the rest of the British government. However, British leaders realized that they had no way to force the colonists to obey the Stamp Act. In March 1766, Parliament **repealed** the law. But Parliament let the colonies know that it still believed in its right to tax them.

repeal: to take back, or to cancel, a law

10.6   The Boston Massacre

In 1770, the colonists were still angry that British soldiers were living in their towns and cities. They thought the soldiers were rowdy and rude. Also, they were upset when soldiers took jobs away from them by working for low pay in their spare time.

The soldiers weren't happy, either. They were far from their homes. Not getting along with the colonists only made their job more difficult.

As time went on, the relationship between the soldiers and colonists became worse. Things were especially tense in the city of Boston. The colonists showed their hatred for the soldiers by making fun of their red coats. They called them

Here, we see Paul Revere's famous engraving of the Boston Massacre. The engraving shows soldiers firing at a peaceful crowd, though that isn't exactly what happened.

names like "lobsterback."
And some soldiers went out
of their way to bother local
citizens. Before long, name-
calling and fist fights in the
streets were common.

On March 5, 1770, the bad
feelings in Boston erupted
into violence. It was a bitterly
cold night, and a soldier was
standing guard in front of the
Customs House (a building
where taxes were collected).
Sometime before nine
o'clock, a crowd began to
gather. People in the crowd
called the soldier names.
Some of them threw stones
and snowballs. Captain
Thomas Preston and seven
other soldiers hurried to the
guard's side. Loading their
muskets (guns similar to
rifles), they stood in front of
the angry crowd.

The crowd taunted
(insulted) the soldiers. More
snowballs and chunks of ice were thrown. No one is sure
exactly what happened next. Afterward, some said that Captain
Preston told his soldiers not to fire their guns. But one soldier
said that he heard the command, "Fire!" and so shot his gun
into the crowd. When the crowd moved toward them, the
soldiers panicked and fired. Within moments, five people lay
dead or dying. Six more were wounded.

The colonists called this tragic event the *Boston Massacre*.
(A *massacre* is the murder of people who cannot defend
themselves.) A silversmith named Paul Revere pictured the
event in an engraving (an image etched into copper). The
engraving shows soldiers firing at a peaceful crowd, though
that isn't exactly what happened. Samuel Adams, a leader
of protests against the British, made sure that news of the
massacre spread throughout the colonies.

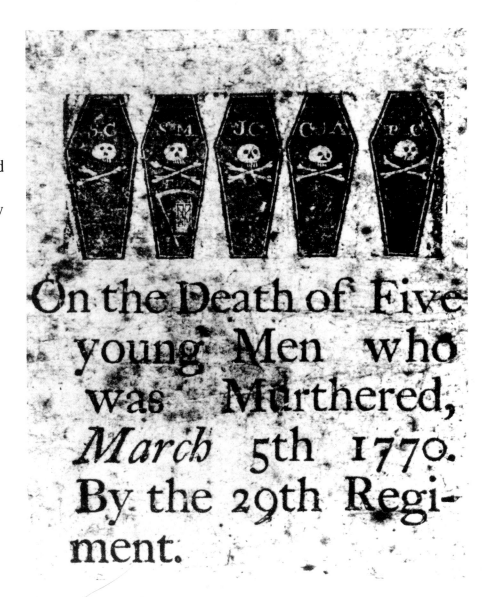

This illustration was created by
Paul Revere to remind colonists
of the tragedy of the Boston
Massacre.

10.7   The Boston Tea Party

After the Boston Massacre, the British government repealed all of the unpopular taxes on the colonists, except the tax on tea. The colonists loved tea, but many of them refused to buy it from Britain. As a result, the largest British tea company, the British East India Company, was losing a great deal of money.

To save the company, Parliament passed the Tea Act in 1773. The act said that the British East India Company was the only company that could sell tea to the colonies. The British thought that this law would force the colonists to give in and buy British tea again.

The Tea Act also lowered the cost of tea, but it still made the colonists very angry. To them, it was another unfair law that was passed without their approval. And they didn't like the fact that the law tried to force them to buy tea from just one company. What if the British government decided to let other companies have total control over items other than tea?

Once again, the colonists protested. Many spoke out against the law and refused to buy tea. In Boston, local citizens went even further. On December 16, 1773, a group of men dressed up as Native Americans and climbed aboard the tea ships in Boston Harbor. There, they split open hundreds of boxes and dumped 90,000 pounds of loose tea into the water. The protesters were careful not to damage anything besides the tea. According to one newspaper, they even sent a ship captain a new padlock to replace one that they had broken.

Afterward, the colonists called this incident the *Boston Tea Party*. Soon people were singing a song about it throughout the colonies. "Rally, Mohawks [Native Americans]," they sang. "Bring out your axes / And tell King George we'll pay no taxes/ On his foreign tea." But in England, people were shocked and angry. And King George was furious.

Here, we see colonists dressed as Native Americans throwing tea into Boston Harbor. Colonists did this to protest the Tea Act, which they thought was unfair. The colonists later called this incident the *Boston Tea Party*.

10.8   The Intolerable Acts

After the Boston Tea Party, Parliament decided to punish the colonists by passing several new laws. These laws were so harsh that many colonists said they could not tolerate (accept) them. They called the laws the *Intolerable Acts.*

One law, the Boston Port Act, closed Boston Harbor. Trade ships were forbidden to enter or leave the harbor until the lost tea was paid for. Many workers lost their jobs. Some colonists were afraid that the citizens of Boston would starve.

People throughout the colonies promised to help Boston by sending money, food, and supplies. In September 1774, leaders from 12 colonies gathered in Philadelphia to discuss the problems with Britain. Because this meeting included almost all of the colonies on the North American continent, it was called the *First Continental Congress.* The angry delegates agreed to fight the Boston Port Act and the other Intolerable Acts.

The British viewed colonial protestors, especially after the Boston Tea Party, as lawless troublemakers. This illustration shows a tax collector who had been tarred and feathered by colonists. The colonists force tea down the tax collector's throat. To punish the colonists for actions like these, the British passed the Intolerable Acts.

10.9   Chapter Summary

In this chapter, you read about events that created tensions between the colonies and Britain from 1754 to the end of 1774. You also used the metaphor of a parent and a child to describe the relationship between the colonies and Britain.

For example, the British behaved like concerned parents who protected the colonists. They thought that the colonists should be grateful and respect British authority. But, like a growing child, the colonies wanted to make their own decisions. They did not like Britain's efforts to control them. When Britain ignored their complaints, they protested, sometimes violently. By 1775, people on both sides were very angry.

In the next chapter, you will learn how some colonists wanted to break away from Britain and create a separate country. Other colonists, however, wanted to remain loyal. Why did some people want to make the colonies a separate nation? Read on to find out.

Patriots cheer the soldiers as they pull down a statue of King George III, a symbol of British rule.

A statue of King George III of England in a Massachusetts town square.

Loyalists look on in dismay as the statue of their king is torn down by excited Patriots.

To Declare Independence or Not

11.1 Introduction

In Chapter 10, you read about how tensions grew between Britain and the American colonies from 1754 to 1774. In this chapter, you will learn about colonists who argued for and against **independence** from Britain.

People in favor of independence wanted America to be a separate country that would no longer be ruled by Britain. Colonists who wanted independence were called **Patriots**. Some Patriots gave arguments in favor of independence in speeches and newspaper articles. Others took stronger actions, such as rushing into the streets to join mobs that attacked the homes and businesses of Loyalists.

Colonists who remained loyal to Britain were called **Loyalists**. Some Loyalists gave speeches arguing against independence. Others took even stronger actions, such as attacking Patriots with guns.

Many colonists did not take sides. Instead, they remained **Neutralists,** becoming neither Loyalists nor Patriots.

As you read this chapter, use the T-chart on this page to keep track of how six important colonists felt about independence. The Loyalists on the left side of the T-chart argued against independence. The Patriots on the right side of the T-chart argued in favor of independence. Why did some colonists stay loyal to the king and Britain? Why did others want the colonies to be independent?

Comparing Loyalists and Patriots

Loyalists   Patriots

Britain's King George III enjoyed the support of only about one-fifth of the American colonists. Those colonists became known as Loyalists.

11.2 Who Were the Loyalists and Patriots?

When colonists began arguing over independence, thousands of them chose to become Loyalists. The Loyalists included many kinds of people.

Some Loyalists were rich landowners. They feared that Patriot mobs might take their property.

Some Loyalists were governors who had been appointed to their jobs by King George III. They liked their government, and they felt that it was their duty to make sure that British laws were obeyed in the colonies.

Other Loyalists were religious leaders who believed that the king's power came from God. Many of them were members of the Church of England, Britain's official church. They believed that it was wrong to oppose the king. They told their followers, "You have a duty to be loyal to the church and to the king!"

Loyalists gave many arguments against independence. Still, only about one-fifth of the colonists became Loyalists.

About two-fifths of the colonists became Patriots. Many of them were merchants who lived in and around the city of Boston. They were angry about British taxes on goods such as tea and cloth. The taxes hurt their businesses because many colonists refused to buy the taxed goods.

Some Patriots were lawyers. They fought in the courts against British laws that they thought were unfair. They believed that the colonists should have more say in making laws that directly affected them.

Other Patriots were farmers or people who worked at crafts such as printing, shipbuilding, and making clothes. They agreed with Patriot leaders who said that independence would bring more freedom and riches to the colonies.

In the rest of this chapter, you will learn about three Loyalists and three Patriots. As you read about these people, think about why they felt the way they did. What reasons did each give for being a Loyalist or a Patriot?

11.3 Thomas Hutchinson: A Loyalist Governor

Thomas Hutchinson was a Loyalist who lived in Massachusetts. He was a dedicated official who was named royal governor of Massachusetts in 1771. Over time, Hutchinson became one of the most hated men in the colonies because he always sided with the British against the Patriots.

Hutchinson was a thin, serious man who rarely smiled. He didn't like to show much feeling. Even though he was a successful businessman, he didn't wear fancy clothes. Instead, he liked to wear a simple black coat and hat.

As an official serving the king, Hutchinson believed firmly in enforcing British laws such as the Stamp Act and the law that closed Boston Harbor for a time. Patriots were so angry about the Stamp Act that one night an angry mob burst into Hutchinson's house. The mob stole money and broke furniture. They also destroyed his prized collection of books. From then on, Hutchinson was a bitter enemy of the Patriots.

Thomas Hutchinson was a Loyalist. As governor of Massachusetts, he enforced British laws that were unpopular among the American colonists.

As a Loyalist, Hutchinson argued against independence for several reasons. He said that the colonies needed Britain to help protect them against other countries. He argued that the colonists could not govern themselves without Britain to guide them. And he said that the king knew what was best for the colonists because he was wiser and more experienced.

In 1773, Patriots embarrassed Hutchinson by printing some letters that he had written to the British government. The letters said that Britain should be even more strict with the colonists. When colonists read the letters in the newspaper, nearly everyone turned against him.

11.4 Jonathan Boucher: A Loyalist Religious Leader

Reverend Jonathan Boucher was a British religious leader who used his sermons (speeches in church) to spread his Loyalist beliefs.

Boucher first came to the colonies as a young man in 1759. Later, he went back to Britain and became a priest in the Church of England. After returning to America, he became a well-known religious leader in the colony of Maryland.

Many people liked being around Boucher because he was intelligent and full of charm. He usually dressed simply, in dark suits and a priest's collar. He was balding and usually wore spectacles (glasses).

Even though he dressed plainly, Boucher was full of energy and ambition. He was a forceful man who was comfortable talking in front of large groups. As a minister, he used his talents to argue for the Loyalist cause.

Jonathan Boucher was a British religious leader who lived in Maryland. He used his sermons to spread Loyalist beliefs.

Boucher preached that the king's power came from God. He said that Christians had a special duty to obey British laws because disobeying the king was like disobeying God.

Boucher also argued that colonists should obey the laws for their own good. He said that British laws made life safer and better for most colonists.

Finally, Boucher warned that actions for independence were dangerous because they could lead to a war with Britain. Such a war would hurt thousands of people much more than living with a few bad laws.

Boucher's Loyalist sermons made some Patriots so angry that they threatened to kill him. Realizing that he was in danger, Boucher began keeping loaded pistols nearby when he gave his sermons.

11.5 Lord Dunmore: Loyalist Governor of Virginia

John Murray, known as Lord Dunmore, was one of the fiercest Loyalist leaders. "Lord Dunmore" was his British title as the head of an important family in Britain. In 1771, King George III named Dunmore royal governor of the colony of Virginia.

Dunmore was a proud and rich man. He dressed in fancy clothes that showed off his wealth and importance. He was stubborn, strict, and bad-tempered. And he was very loyal to Britain.

It was Britain, Dunmore said, that created the colonies and continued to protect them. For these reasons Britain had a right to rule the colonies and to make them pay taxes on British goods.

Dunmore also argued that independence was a mistake because Britain knew what was best for the colonies. And he strongly believed that the colonists had a duty to obey British laws. The colonies, he said, were part of Britain. Colonists who would fight against the king were **traitors**.

As governor, Dunmore thought that being tough would frighten the colonists into accepting British rule. Instead, his firm actions only angered many people in Virginia. Worried for his safety, Dunmore moved his family onto a British warship in June 1775. Then he collected a number of boats and began attacking Patriots' homes and plantations along the James River. He even promised to free any slaves who fought with him against the Patriots. At least 800 African Americans answered his call.

In the end, Dunmore's actions only made the Patriots more popular. Because of Dunmore, many neutral colonists began to think that independence might be worth fighting for after all.

John Murray, known as Lord Dunmore, was a fierce Loyalist leader. He launched a naval attack against the homes of Patriots along the James River in Virginia in 1775.

traitor: a person guilty of acting against his or her own country

11.6 Benjamin Franklin: The Thoughtful Patriot

Benjamin Franklin was one of the most respected Patriots in America. Franklin was not in favor of independence right away. Instead, he hoped that Britain would start to treat the colonies more fairly. But when that didn't happen, Franklin sided firmly with the Patriots.

Franklin had many talents. He was a successful writer, printer, inventor, and scientist. As a citizen of Philadelphia, he helped to establish a library, a hospital, and a college.

Although he was an important man in the colonies, Franklin often dressed in plain suits. He sometimes wore spectacles. He was known to wear two caps over his gray hair to keep warm in winter.

People liked and admired Franklin. He was knowledgeable, funny, and wise. He had a talent for staying calm when other people were angry. He was especially good at helping people to understand one another's ideas during arguments.

Benjamin Franklin was one of the most respected Patriots in America. At first he tried to reach agreements with Britain, but, by 1775, he fully supported independence.

From 1757 to 1775, Franklin used his talents as the colonies' representative to the British government in England. Patiently, he tried to persuade Britain to stop making laws that the colonists thought were unfair. He did succeed in helping to get the government to repeal (cancel) the Stamp Act. But Britain continued to pass unfair laws. So, Franklin returned home and became a Patriot leader.

Franklin favored independence for several reasons. He thought that Britain would continue to make unfair laws. He also believed that the colonists should no longer trust England. Finally, Franklin believed that the colonists had the ability to govern themselves. By 1775, he was ready to help them prove that he was right.

11.7 Mercy Otis Warren: Patriot with a Pen

Mercy Otis Warren was a Patriot writer from Massachusetts. She wrote plays and poems supporting independence. She also held lively meetings in her home where Patriots discussed their ideas. Her husband James attended the meetings as well.

Warren was thin and dark-haired. She spoke in a low, firm voice. Her favorite color was blue, and she liked to wear blue dresses and bonnets with lace trimming.

Even as a girl, Warren loved reading, writing, and discussing politics. After she married James, they began reading the newspaper together. They became upset by Britain's harsh treatment of the colonies. They felt that taxes were too high and that workers were paid too little. Warren also believed that women should have the right to vote and to be elected to positions in government.

Mercy Otis Warren was a Patriot writer from Massachusetts. She wrote plays and poems supporting independence.

In her writing and discussions, Warren made several arguments in favor of independence. She said that Britain's laws and taxes were unfair. Families in the colonies had a hard time earning enough money to pay for expensive British goods. She also said that Britain was too far away to understand the colonists' needs and daily lives. For this reason, the colonies would be better off with their own government. And she disliked the fact that Britain did not allow women to take part in politics. She believed that women would have more rights if the colonies were independent.

Warren used her writing talent to express her ideas. Two of her plays cleverly attacked the Loyalists. Her writings helped to encourage many people in Massachusetts to become Patriots.

Samuel Adams was one of the leading Patriots in Massachusetts. In 1765, he organized the Sons of Liberty. The Sons actively encouraged colonists to disobey British laws.

11.8   Samuel Adams: True Patriot

Samuel Adams was one of the leading Patriots in Massachusetts. Adams believed that the British were terrible, unfair rulers. He called on the colonies to break away from Britain and to fight for their independence.

Adams was always interested in politics. As a college student at Harvard University in Massachusetts, he wrote a paper on people's right to fight against unfair government. Other local Patriots saw him as a leader, and by the mid 1760s he was a full-time politician.

Adams spoke in a low, careful voice, often rubbing his chin in thought. Like many other men at that time, he wore a powdered white wig over his brown hair. He believed so much in fighting for independence that he wore a military coat and hat every day. He only took them off when he went to bed!

Adams argued for independence in newspaper articles, speeches, and town meetings. He believed that colonists couldn't afford to pay such high taxes on British goods. He also said it was unfair that the king chose governors for the colonies. The colonists, he argued, should be able to elect their own governors. In addition, Adams believed that the colonists should have the power to change unfair laws. If Britain refused to give them this power, then they should become an independent country.

In 1765, Adams helped to organize a group of Patriots called the *Sons of Liberty*. The Sons encouraged colonists to disobey laws like the Stamp Act. In 1773, Adams and the Sons led the Boston Tea Party to protest British taxes on tea. Before long, Samuel Adams was working day and night to help the colonies win their independence.

11.9 Chapter Summary

In this chapter, you read about six important colonists who had different ideas about independence. You used a T-chart to identify these six colonists as either Loyalists or Patriots.

Loyalists argued that the colonies should remain loyal to Britain and the king. Many kinds of people became Loyalists. Some, like Thomas Hutchinson and Lord Dunmore, were royal governors who believed in Britain's right to make and enforce laws for the colonies. Some, like Jonathan Boucher, were religious leaders who believed that the colonists had a duty to obey the king. Some were rich landowners who were afraid of losing their property.

Patriots wanted the colonies to become independent. Some, like Benjamin Franklin, became Patriots only after giving up hope that Britain would change its actions toward the colonies. Others, like Mercy Otis Warren and Samuel Adams, started out by angrily protesting against British laws and taxes. Before long, Patriots such as these were openly calling for independence.

In 1775, many colonists were not ready to take such a bold step. How did most colonists become convinced to support independence? Read on to find out.

The Sons of Liberty raising a Liberty Pole in 1776.

This plaque honors the men who planned the Continental Army. What was their plan?

This plaque honors the men who selected the leader of the Continental Army. Whom did they choose?

This plaque honors the men who debated independence. What did they decide?

The Declaration of Independence

12.1 Introduction

In Chapter 11, you read how American Loyalists and Patriots argued over whether to declare independence from Britain. In this chapter, you will learn about American independence from the point of view of Patriot leaders, such as Thomas Jefferson. Jefferson wrote one of the most important documents in American history: the Declaration of Independence.

In 1775, the colonies sent delegates to the **Second Continental Congress** in Philadelphia. War was already starting between the colonies and Britain, and the Continental Congress became the government for the American revolutionaries. The delegates had to decide how to fight the war and whether to take the bold step of declaring independence.

By early 1776, more and more colonists favored independence. Many of them were influenced by a booklet written by Thomas Paine called **Common Sense**. Paine argued strongly for independence in simple language that everyone could understand.

In June, Congress asked five of its delegates to write a document telling why the colonies had the right to be a separate nation. Young Thomas Jefferson sat at his portable desk in the room where he was staying and wrote the first draft of the **Declaration of Independence**.

Look at the drawing of Jefferson's desk to the right.

To learn about this important document, imagine Jefferson sitting at his desk. What objects does he see? What might they tell us about the Declaration of Independence?

Thomas Jefferson's Desk

Amos Doolittle's engraving shows a small local militia attacking British soldiers. The Second Continental Congress created a large, organized army to fight the British after this battle.

12.2 The Second Continental Congress

On May 10, 1775, Patriot leaders began meeting in Philadelphia in the Second Continental Congress. People in the streets cheered as George Washington arrived from Virginia in his blue and gold military uniform. John Adams came by carriage from Massachusetts, and wise Benjamin Franklin sailed back from Britain to represent Pennsylvania. All together, 65 delegates took part in the Congress. Soon, these men were acting as the new government for the colonies.

The Congress faced three important tasks. The most urgent task was to organize the colonies for war against the British. Just before the Congress met, British soldiers fought with members of the Patriot **militia** at the towns of Lexington and Concord in Massachusetts. The colonies' small militias were made up of ordinary men who were not full-time soldiers. The Congress decided that the colonies needed a more organized army to fight the British, so it created the Continental Army.

The next task was to decide who should lead the new army. Congress quickly chose an experienced soldier and a strong leader: George Washington.

The third and most difficult task was to decide whether to declare independence from Britain. Some Patriots, such as John Adams, were ready to take this step. But most of the delegates were still loyal to King George. Even as the fighting spread throughout the colonies, they hoped the colonies could eventually make peace with Britain.

militia: a small army made up of ordinary citizens

12.3 Thomas Paine and *Common Sense*

Like the delegates to the Continental Congress, most colonists were not sure that they wanted independence. They wanted Britain to pay attention to their complaints, but they were still loyal British citizens. And many were afraid that the colonies could not win a war against one of the most powerful armies in the world.

Then, in January 1776, Thomas Paine published a booklet called *Common Sense*. Paine had come to America from Britain in 1774. He had been in the colonies only a short while, but he was strongly in favor of independence. He argued that it was only natural for people to rule themselves instead of being ruled by a king. America, he said, had a chance to show the whole world a better form of government.

Common Sense had a powerful effect on the colonists. Paine wrote simply and strongly in words that everyone could understand. Many colonists still thought of Britain as the parent country, but Paine said that parents do not "make war upon their own families." The blood of the Patriots killed in Massachusetts, he wrote, "cried out" that it was time to separate from Britain. And he told the colonists that they were strong enough to defeat the British army.

Within a few months, 120,000 copies of *Common Sense* were printed, more than any other book in America up to that time. People everywhere read it. Soldiers in the Continental Army passed copies of the book among themselves. George Washington wrote that *Common Sense* was changing many people's minds. By the spring of 1776, most people were ready for the Continental Congress to vote for independence.

Thomas Paine's booklet *Common Sense* convinced many colonists to declare independence.

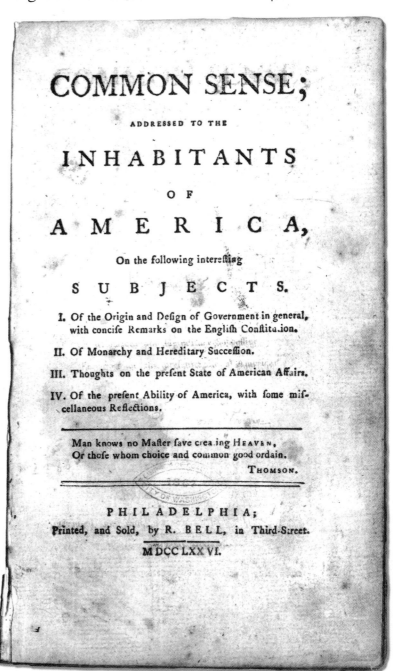

Thomas Jefferson wrote the first draft of the Declaration of Independence.

12.4 Writing the Declaration of Independence

The success of *Common Sense* helped convince the Continental Congress to move toward independence. On June 7, 1776, delegates from Virginia introduced a resolution (a statement for Congress to vote on). The resolution declared that "these United Colonies are, and by right ought to be, free and independent States."

Congress agreed to take a few weeks to think over this dramatic step. In the meantime, it asked a committee to write a document explaining why the colonies were announcing their independence. John Adams and Benjamin Franklin were on the committee. So was a shy, red-headed Virginian named Thomas Jefferson.

Jefferson was only 33 years old, but he was already known as a fine writer and thinker. Adams and Franklin asked him to write the first draft of the colonies' declaration of independence.

Setting up a folding desk in his room in Philadelphia, Jefferson went to work. For almost two weeks, he wrote and rewrote the document, working by candlelight late into the night. After Adams and Franklin made a few changes, the committee presented their document to Congress.

For several days, Congress argued about independence for the last time. Then, on July 2, the delegates voted to separate from Britain.

Congress spent the next two days discussing every word of the declaration and voting on changes. Delegates from two southern colonies, where slaves worked on huge plantations, insisted on taking out Jefferson's statement that slavery was a "cruel war against human nature." Several other delegates agreed. Some of the changes angered Jefferson, but everyone realized that all the colonies had to agree in order for them to become a united country. Finally, on July 4, 1776, Congress voted to approve the Declaration of Independence.

12.5 Signing the Declaration of Independence

After the Continental Congress approved the Declaration of Independence, a handwritten copy was prepared for the delegates to sign. The delegates knew that signing the declaration was an act of **treason** toward the king, and the punishment for treason was death. John Hancock, the president of the Congress, warned the delegates that they must stay united and "all hang together." Benjamin Franklin replied, "Yes, we must indeed all hang together, or most assuredly we shall all hang separately."

John Hancock signed first, writing his name in bold letters. Hancock's signature became so famous that to this day people call their signature a "John Hancock."

After Jefferson and the other delegates signed the declaration, Congress sent copies to the governments of each colony and to the Continental Army. People throughout the colonies celebrated when they heard the news. A crowd in Philadelphia cheered when the declaration was read for the first time in public on July 8. George Washington had the declaration read to his troops the next day. Afterward, soldiers tore down a statue of King George. Later, the statue was melted to make bullets for the Continental

treason: the crime of disloyalty toward a ruler or government

Jefferson and other committee members presented the Declaration of Independence to the Continental Congress.

Yale University Art Gallery, Trumble Collection

Colonists celebrated the news that independence from Britain had been declared.

Army. When news of the declaration reached Boston, troops there fired guns and cannons in celebration.

Everywhere, church bells rang, and there were parades and bonfires. Even today, Americans celebrate in a similar way on the Fourth of July, the anniversary of the signing of the Declaration of Independence.

12.6 The Declaration of Independence

The delegates to the Second Continental Congress wanted to explain why they wished to be a separate nation. The following excerpts from the Declaration of Independence are part of this explanation. The entire Declaration of Independence begins on page 216.

The first excerpt explains why the colonists felt it was necessary to write the document.

> When in the Course of human events it becomes necessary for one people to dissolve the political bonds which have connected them with another… a decent respect to the opinions of mankind requires that they should declare the causes which impel them to the separation.

The second excerpt describes the rights all people should have.

> We hold these truths to be self-evident, that all men are created equal, that they are endowed by their Creator with certain unalienable Rights, that among these are life, liberty and the pursuit of happiness.

The third excerpt explains why governments are established and describes the citizens' rights if the government acts unfairly.

> To secure these rights, Governments are instituted among Men, deriving their just powers from the consent of the governed. That whenever any Form of Government becomes destructive of these ends, it is the Right of the People to alter or to abolish it, and to institute new Government.

The fourth excerpt presents a general complaint against the British king.

> The history of the present King of Great Britain is a history of repeated injuries and usurpations, all having, in direct object, the establishment of an absolute Tyranny over these States. To prove this, let facts be submitted to a candid world."

The fifth excerpt declares the colonies' independence.

> (We) solemnly publish and declare, That these United Colonies are, and of right ought to be Free and Independent States; that they are Absolved from all Allegiance to the British Crown, and that all political connection between them and that State of Great Britain, is and ought to be totally dissolved.

The Declaration of Independence explains why the colonists wanted to be a separate nation.

12.7 Chapter Summary

In this chapter, you read about how the American colonies decided to become a separate nation. You learned how young Thomas Jefferson wrote the first draft of the Declaration of Independence. By examining a drawing showing artifacts on Jefferson's desk, you learned about the events that led up to the signing of the declaration on July 4, 1776. You saw his invitation to attend the Continental Congress. You noticed his copy of the powerful booklet *Common Sense*. You learned how Congress and most of the colonists were finally convinced to turn the fight with Britain into a war for independence.

In the next chapter, you will learn about how the newly united colonies fought the American Revolution. How could the new United States defeat one of the most powerful armies in the world? Read on to find out.

On which side were these men fighting? How can you tell?

On which side were these men fighting? How can you tell?

The Revolutionary War

13.1 Introduction

In Chapter 12, you learned how the American colonies declared their independence from Britain. From 1775 to 1783, the two countries fought in the **Revolutionary War**. In this chapter, you will learn how America won the war.

The two sides used different **strategies,** or war plans. When the war began, Britain seemed sure to win. The British had a large navy and a **professional army**. The colonial army, known as the **Continental Army,** was small and inexperienced. The British won most of the early battles.

The Continentals, though, had some advantages of their own. Continental soldiers had better reasons for fighting. They were defending their homes and their rights. In addition, other countries, called **allies,** sent soldiers and supplies. And unlike the British, the Continentals were fighting in familiar territory that was close to home.

Look at the visual metaphor at the bottom of this page. The Revolutionary War can be compared to a tug-of-war between two unequal teams. The British army was like the team on the right, strong and confident. The Continental Army was like the team on the left, small but very determined.

As you read this chapter, think about how the smaller team might win this tug-of-war. How were the Continentals able to defeat a much larger army?

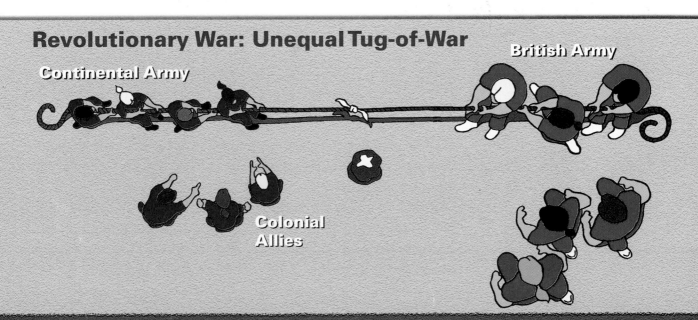

Revolutionary War: Unequal Tug-of-War

Continental Army

British Army

Colonial Allies

Volunteers, such as these Minutemen of Concord, were ready to fight with a "minute's" warning. At the beginning of the Revolutionary War, colonial armies only had such part-time soldiers.

volunteers: people who freely perform a service

13.2 The Continental Army

When the war started, there was no American army. Instead, colonies had their own militias. The militiamen were part-time soldiers, like the farmers and merchants who fought British soldiers at Lexington and Concord.

In 1775, the Continental Congress asked George Washington to lead an army. The Continental Army was made up of **volunteers**. Most volunteers were poor farmers, merchants, and workers. At the start of the war, they volunteered for one year at a time. After that period, they returned home to take care of their families.

About 15,000 men initially volunteered for Washington's army, including many African Americans. Women took part as well. They cooked for soldiers, mended uniforms, and cared for the sick and wounded. Some even fought in battles. One of them was Deborah Sampson. She dressed in men's clothes and fought in several battles. Eventually, she was wounded, and an army doctor discovered her secret.

The Continental Army had a number of problems. Congress had little money to pay the soldiers or buy supplies. As a result, volunteers had to supply their own uniforms and guns. In addition, they knew very little about being soldiers. Often, they had little discipline.

Washington worked hard to train his men. He taught them to obey orders and to fight together. In speeches and written messages, he encouraged them to believe that they could beat the mighty British.

Like the army, the colonial navy was small. Mostly it was made up of trade and fishing ships that carried small cannons.

With its inexperienced army and small navy, the Continentals were like a small man about to do battle with a giant.

13.3 The British Army

At the start of the war, Britain was confident of quickly ending the revolution. Britain had one of the strongest armed forces (military) in the world. The British navy controlled the seas with 270 warships. Britain's shipyards built another 200 warships before the war was over.

Britain's army was large and professional. Professional soldiers are paid. Being in the army is their job. And British soldiers were well trained. Most were experienced fighters. They were also harshly disciplined. A soldier could be whipped just for having a button sewed on wrong.

Unlike the Continental Congress, the British Parliament had money to buy food and equipment for its army. Each soldier had a uniform, a good musket, and a **bayonet**. Soldiers attached their bayonets to the front ends of their muskets to use in close-up fighting.

There were about 45,000 British soldiers in the army. Most of them were poor men who earned low pay. Others were soldiers from other countries. For example, Britain hired about 30,000 Germans to fight in America. These men were mercenaries, soldiers who fight for anyone who will pay them.

Thousands of Native Americans fought for the British as well. They sided with Britain because the British had helped to keep their lands safe from settlers since 1763. Thousands of Loyalists also fought for Britain. In the New York colony, for example, many men were willing to join the British side at the start of the war.

bayonet: a sharp blade, like a sword, attached to the end of a rifle

The British army had professional soldiers. They were well trained and well disciplined. The government provided them with sufficient food and good equipment.

13.4 The British Army: A Long Way from Home

Even though the British army and navy were very strong, the British had a major problem. They were a long way from home. Supplies, military orders, and soldiers had to travel 3,000 miles by sea across the Atlantic Ocean. The trip from Britain to America could take three months.

Even after British supplies made it across the Atlantic Ocean, it was often hard to get them ashore. The Continentals had few ships that could attack the British warships. But they did call on hundreds of "privateers." Privateers were small, fast ships with a few light cannons. Congress gave their captains permission to attack British supply ships. They could also keep most of the goods they captured. Later in the war, French warships also attacked British ships.

Unlike the British, Continentals were fighting in their home country and could get supplies easily. As the war went on, the Continental Army found new ways of gathering equipment and supplies. Often, local citizens sold or gave the army food. Soldiers also captured cannons and muskets from the British.

Continental soldiers also had the support of women. Women ran the farms and businesses while the men were away fighting. They brought supplies to camp, made uniforms, and worked as nurses. They also spied among the British.

In contrast, the British had to fight in a country that they didn't know well. Most colonists refused to help them when they needed food or supplies. Often, the British felt surrounded by people who disliked and even hated them. These feelings made it harder to want to fight.

Although weak, the Continental navy enjoyed a few heroic successes. Here, Continental naval captain John Paul Jones is shown capturing the British warship *Serapis*. When asked to surrender, Jones responded, "I have not yet begun to fight."

During the winter of 1777–1778, the men in Washington's army suffered from freezing cold and starvation — yet they refused to give up.

13.5 The Continental Army's Motivation to Win

Continental soldiers had a special advantage over the British. They had a stronger motivation, or desire, to win.

Continental soldiers believed they were defending their rights described in the Declaration of Independence. They were trying to make a better future for themselves. To many Continentals, these were things worth dying for.

The men in Washington's army showed their strong motivation during the winter of 1777–1778. The army was camped in the snow at a place called *Valley Forge*. The soldiers were tired and starving. They didn't have warm clothing to protect them from the freezing cold. Many didn't even have shoes. More than 2,500 men died that winter from cold and sickness. Yet the army refused to give up.

The British, on the other hand, had less motivation than the Continental soldiers. Most British soldiers were fighting because it was their job, not to defend their homes or their rights. Even the British government had problems other than the war to worry about. The British had colonies to protect in many parts of the world besides North America. They had to worry about possible enemies like France and Spain. And many people in Britain were unhappy about fighting an expensive war in North America.

Of course, not all Americans were motivated to fight the British. Loyalists still believed that independence was unwise. In addition, the British sometimes promised to free slaves who joined their side. As a result, some African Americans fought for the British to gain their freedom. As you know, many Native Americans also fought for the British to protect their lands.

Washington Crossing the Delaware by Emanuel G. Leutze, (97.34) The Metropolitan Museum of Art, Gift of John Stewart Kennedy, 1897. Photograph © 1992 The Metropolitan Museum of Art

The Continental Army relied upon surprise attacks against the British. George Washington crossed the Delaware River on Christmas Eve. He defeated the German mercenaries who were celebrating the holiday.

strategies: overall plans, such as for winning a war

tactics: specific ways of carrying out a plan, such as ways of fighting battles

guerilla tactics: tactics used by fighters outside of a regular army (guerillas), such as shooting at soldiers from hiding places in the woods

13.6   Different War Strategies

The British and the Continentals used different **strategies** to fight the Revolutionary War.

Britain had to fight an offensive war. They had to attack the Continentals and take control of the cities and countryside. In contrast, the Continentals could fight a defensive war. They didn't have to destroy the British army, only hold them off.

At first, the British tried to end the war by stopping the rebellion in Boston. They thought that most Patriots were there. But they soon discovered that thousands of other colonists were willing to fight for independence.

So the British changed strategies. They tried to show power by capturing important cities like New York. After losing New York, Washington moved his men into the countryside. From there, they used "hit and run" **tactics**. They made surprise attacks against small groups of British and then retreated.

Continentals also used **guerilla tactics** to frighten and discourage the British. For example, sharpshooters (riflemen) hid in the woods and shot down British soldiers, one by one.

By 1777, the British strategy was to destroy the Continental Army. They wanted to fight the army face to face, the way armies fought in Europe. They tried to force Washington's army into the open by capturing the important city of Philadelphia.

But Washington had a different strategy. He wanted to keep his army together until the British became discouraged. Rather than risk losing soldiers, he let the British have Philadelphia. Then he took his men to Valley Forge for the winter.

13.7 The Continental Army Gains Allies

Continental Army leaders knew that they needed **allies** to win the war. In 1776, Congress sent Benjamin Franklin to Paris, France, to seek help.

France helped the Patriots by supplying gunpowder (ammunition) and by lending Congress money. Some European soldiers also joined the Continental cause. A 19-year-old Frenchman, the Marquis de Lafayette, become a general in the Continental Army. Friedrich von Steuben, a German soldier, helped to train the Continental Army at Valley Forge.

In mid 1777, close to 9,000 British troops marched down from Canada. About 1,500 Vermont militiamen attacked them. Other Continental troops rushed to help. With his army trapped, the British commander surrendered at Saratoga, New York.

The Battle of Saratoga showed that the colonists could beat a British army. After that, France openly supported the Continental Army. Spain pledged support to France. In 1781, Spain captured a British fort at Pensacola, Florida. Now the Continental Army had powerful allies.

After their defeat at Saratoga, the British again changed strategies. For the next three years, they tried to win the war in the southern colonies. They thought that Loyalists there would help them.

In the summer of 1781, a large British army marched to the Virginia coast. British ships were bringing supplies from New York, but French warships cut them off. Meanwhile, Washington's army and thousands of French soldiers hurried down from the north.

The Continentals and the French trapped the British in the port of Yorktown. For more than a week, they pounded the British with cannon fire. Finally, the British surrendered.

The Battle of Yorktown was the last big battle of the war. With the help of their French allies, the Continentals had won an important victory.

> **allies:** people or countries fighting on the same side against a common enemy

Following their defeat at Yorktown, the British troops surrendered to the Continental Army and their allies. The Battle of Yorktown in October 1781 was the last big battle of the war.

13.8 The Treaty of Paris: American Victory

After the Battle of Yorktown, Britain was ready to end the war. By this time, Britain was fighting Spain and France as well as America. Representatives from all these countries met in Paris to work out peace agreements.

In 1783, the Revolutionary War was ended with the Treaty of Paris. This painting of the American representatives to the peace talks was never finished because British representatives refused to pose.

Meanwhile, the fighting continued. On the seas, the British navy wiped out American shipping. On land, the British still controlled the cities of New York, Charleston, and Savannah. To the west, small but terrible battles were fought in places like Ohio, Kentucky, and western New York. There, Continental soldiers fought against British soldiers, Loyalists, and Native Americans. Villages burned. Women and children on both sides were killed.

In September 1783, the war finally ended with a set of agreements called the *Treaty of Paris*. Britain agreed to recognize the United States as an independent nation. Britain also gave the United States a huge amount of land. It included all the territory that was east of the Mississippi River, south of Canada and the Great Lakes, and north of Florida. (Britain kept Canada, and Florida was returned to Spain.) This vast area included land that the British had promised to Native Americans.

In the treaty, the United States promised to restore the rights and property of Loyalists. Unfortunately for the Loyalists, Americans did not keep this part of the agreement. Instead, thousands of Loyalists left the United States to live in Britain, Canada, and other places. African Americans who had fought for the British also escaped to other countries.

The Patriots had won the war. From now on, the former colonists would be known simply as Americans.

13.9 Chapter Summary

In this chapter, you learned how Americans won the Revolutionary War. You compared the war with a game of tug-of-war between two unequal teams. As in the game, the smaller side won because of some special advantages.

The Continental Army and Navy were far weaker than those of the British. But unlike the British, Continentals were fighting close to home. They also had a stronger motivation to win. In addition, they could fight a defensive war. In contrast, the British had to try to control large amounts of territory and destroy the Continental Army.

When the Continentals won the Battle of Saratoga, powerful allies joined the American side. In the decisive Battle of Yorktown, French soldiers helped the Continentals defeat the British. The Treaty of Paris recognized American independence and gave a huge amount of land to the United States.

America had won its independence. But what kind of government would the new country have? Who would replace the king and Parliament? You will find out in the next chapter.

George Washington

James Madison

Benjamin Franklin

What did each of these
delegates do at the
Constitutional Convention?

chapter 14

The Constitution

14.1 Introduction

In Chapter 13, you learned how Americans won their independence in the Revolutionary War. Now they needed their own government to protect their freedoms and maintain order. In this chapter, you will learn how a national government was created by the Constitution.

Americans first tried to set up a national government in a document called the **Articles of Confederation**. But this government had very limited powers, and it was too weak to keep order. So, in 1787 the states called a meeting to improve the Articles of Confederation. This meeting was called the **Constitutional Convention**.

Instead of revising the Articles, the convention delegates decided to describe a new government in a document called the **Constitution**. The Constitution created a strong national government. It also divided the U. S. government into three parts, or **branches,** each with its own powers and responsibilities. To keep any one branch from becoming too powerful, the Constitution included a system of **checks and balances**. Under this system, each branch limited the powers of the others.

Some say the Articles of Confederation were as weak and unsteady as a one-legged stool. Look at the drawing of the stool on the right. As you read this chapter, think about how this stool can be compared to the Constitution. How is the Constitution like a three-legged stool?

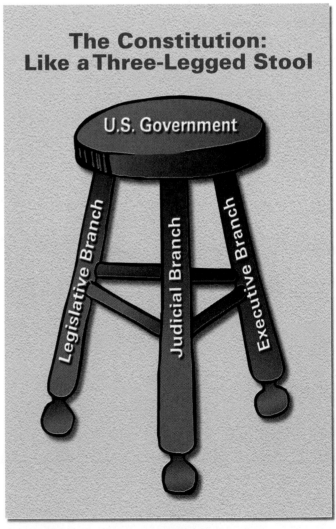

The Constitution: Like a Three-Legged Stool

U.S. Government

Legislative Branch

Judicial Branch

Executive Branch

14.2 The First American Government: The Articles of Confederation

After declaring their independence, the 13 American states (the former colonies) created a government to fight the war against Britain and to solve common problems. They described this government in a document called the *Articles of Confederation.*

The government created by the Articles was very weak. It had a Congress that could make war and pass other laws. But making laws was difficult, because every law had to be approved by 9 of the 13 states. In addition, the government did not have a president, and it did not have a court that could settle disagreements between states.

The Confederation Congress succeeded in directing the Revolutionary War. But once the war was over, Congress had a difficult time solving the new country's problems. For one thing, it had no power to collect taxes or to force the states to give it money. It could not even pay the soldiers who had fought in the Continental Army.

Imagine losing your home because you can't pay your bills. That is what happened to many former soldiers and poor farmers. Some of them were even put in jail. One farmer complained, "The great [rich] men are going to get all we have, and I think it is time for us to rise and put a stop to it."

In Massachusetts, a former soldier named Daniel Shays tried to do just that. Shays and hundreds of other men took up their guns and tried to stop the courts from taking people's property. Their fight against the government became known as *Shays's Rebellion.*

Shays's Rebellion frightened many leaders. More and more, they wanted a strong government that could pay the nation's bills, settle arguments between states, and maintain order.

A farmer attacks a government official as others cheer him in this scene from Shays's Rebellion. Shays's Rebellion frightened many leaders. They saw the rebellion as a sign that the Articles of Confederation were not working.

14.3 Inventing a New Government: The Constitutional Convention

In May 1787, delegates from 12 of the 13 states met in Philadelphia. Their task was to improve the Articles of Confederation, but they ended up writing an entirely new document. Today, their meeting is known as the *Constitutional Convention*.

The 55 delegates included some of the best-known leaders in America. As a group, they were well educated and richer than most Americans. All were white men. Many were lawyers, but the group also included doctors, merchants, farmers, and soldiers.

Several delegates were especially important at the convention. As president of the convention, George Washington kept the debates respectful. Eighty-one-year-old Benjamin Franklin wisely stepped in when tempers flared. James Madison of Virginia brought his plan for a powerful national government with him and argued strongly for it. Gouverneur (his first name) Morris of Pennsylvania wrote much of the final draft of the Constitution.

All through the hot, sticky summer, the delegates worked behind closed doors. Some, like Madison, favored a strong, united government. Others were afraid of losing freedoms if the national government was too strong.

In the end, the delegates agreed to have both state governments and a strong national government. They also agreed to divide the national government into three parts, or branches. The **legislative branch** would make the laws. The **executive branch** would carry out the laws. The **judicial branch** would settle disagreements over the meaning of the laws.

One of the convention's fiercest debates concerned the number of representatives in the legislative branch. Larger states wanted the number to be decided by the number of people living in a particular state. Smaller states were afraid of losing power in such a plan. They wanted every state to have the same number of votes in the legislative branch.

This disagreement was so intense that at times it seemed the convention would fall apart. Eventually, the two sides reached a

Independence Hall in Philadelphia, shown here, was the site of the Constitutional Convention.

legislative branch: the branch of government that makes laws (Another word for "make laws" is *legislate*.)

executive branch: the branch of government that carries out ("executes") laws

judicial branch: the branch of government that interprets laws and settles disagreements about them ("Judicial" is related to the word *judge*.)

compromise (an agreement in which each side gave up some of what it wanted). They created a legislative branch with two parts, called *houses,* one for each idea.

The delegates made many such compromises during four months of hard work. Finally, on September 17, 1787, they signed the final Constitution. By June 1788, 9 of the 13 states had approved it. The United States had a new government.

14.4 Making the Laws: The Legislative Branch

The main text of the Constitution is organized into parts called *articles.* Article I of the Constitution describes the legislative branch. The legislative branch, or Congress, has the responsibility of making laws.

Congress is made up of two houses, the Senate and the House of Representatives. Every state elects two members, called *senators,* to the Senate. But in the House, the number of representatives depends on the number of people who live in a state. States with more people have more representatives in the House.

To make laws, members of Congress write bills. A bill is an idea for a new law. If a majority in both houses of Congress votes to pass (approve) a bill, it is sent to the head of the executive branch, the president. If the president signs the bill, it becomes a law.

If the president refuses to sign a bill, Congress has the power to overrule the president's decision. But a two-thirds majority of both houses must vote in favor of overruling the president. Otherwise, the bill does not become a law.

In addition to making laws, the legislative branch has many other powers. The Senate has the power to approve or reject important appointments made by the president. For example, the Senate must approve the president's choice of ambassadors (representatives of the United States in foreign countries). The Senate must approve the president's choice of federal (national) judges. It also approves members of the president's **cabinet**.

Congress has some special powers in foreign affairs (matters between the United States and other countries). Two-thirds of the Senate must approve any **treaty** between the United States and another country. And the United States can declare war on another country only with the approval of both houses of Congress.

cabinet: a group of advisOrs to the president, including the heads of important departments in the executive branch

treaty: a formal agreement between two or more nations

The Constitution also gives Congress the ability to control officials in the executive and judicial branches who abuse their powers. The House of Representatives has the power to accuse the president, judges, and other officials of serious crimes. This action is called **impeachment**. The Senate has the power to put an impeached official on trial. If the Senate finds the official guilty, the official must give up his or her job in the government.

Article I also lists other specific powers of Congress, including the powers to collect taxes and to create a national currency (system of money). Congress's powers make the national government much stronger than it was under the Articles of Confederation.

impeachment: the act of accusing a government official of serious crimes, as defined by the Constitution

Congress meets in the U.S. Capitol building, shown here.

The president, who is the head of the executive branch, lives in the White House, at center. Behind the White House are many office buildings, some of which are used by government officials.

veto: To reject a bill and prevent it from becoming a law. Only the president has the power to veto bills.

14.5 Carrying Out the Laws: The Executive Branch

Article II of the Constitution describes the powers of the executive branch. The executive branch is responsible for carrying out ("executing") the laws of the country.

The head of the executive branch is the president. The president is often called the *chief executive*. Working under the president are the people and organizations that are needed to carry out the laws passed by Congress.

The men who wrote the Constitution did not want the United States to have its own kind of king. So they tried to limit the president's power. For example, the Constitution gives the president the power to either sign (approve) or **veto** (reject) the bills passed by Congress. At the same time, the Constitution gives Congress the power to override (overrule) the president's veto by a two-thirds vote.

Presidents cannot make laws, but they can try to lead the country by making proposals to Congress. One way that presidents make such proposals is by giving a State of the Union speech every year. Presidents use these speeches to suggest ideas for new laws.

The president has the power to call Congress together for a special session (meeting). This power is especially useful when a president believes that there is a national emergency.

The president shares power over foreign affairs with Congress. The president can sign treaties with other nations, but two-thirds of the Senate must approve them. As commander in chief, the president is in charge of the nation's armed forces (such as the army and navy), but only Congress can declare war.

As chief executive, the president has the power to nominate (suggest) people for important jobs in the government. For example, the president nominates Cabinet members, ambassadors, and federal judges. However, the Senate has the power to accept or reject the president's choices.

The president has the special power to grant pardons to people who have been found guilty of crimes against the United States. A pardon is a release from punishment. But the president cannot give pardons in cases of impeachment.

Even though the president is only the head of the executive branch and not a king, most people see the president as the leader of the country. In many ways, especially in relations with other countries, the president represents the United States.

14.6 Interpreting the Laws: The Judicial Branch

Article III of the Constitution describes the judicial branch. The judicial branch has the responsibility for interpreting the nation's laws, settling disagreements between states, and protecting the Constitution.

The judicial branch is headed by the Supreme Court. The Supreme Court is made up of nine judges. The Court's leader is called the *chief justice*. Justices are appointed by the president and approved by the Senate. Justices serve on the Court for life. Congress has the power to create other federal courts under the Supreme Court.

Over time, the judicial branch has gained some important powers. An especially important one is the power to decide whether a national or state law conflicts with the Constitution. Such a law is called **unconstitutional**. Because the Constitution is the most basic law of the country, the judicial branch can throw out laws that are unconstitutional.

The Constitution gives the judicial branch a similar power concerning treaties with other countries. If the courts find that a treaty violates the Constitution, it does not go into effect.

Importantly, the judicial branch also has the power to interpret the law. That is, the courts have the power to settle disagreements about what a law means or how it applies to a particular situation.

The judicial branch also has power during impeachment trials. Most notably, the chief justice acts as the presiding judge in such trials.

By using these powers, the judicial branch protects the Constitution and the rights of Americans. If the actions of the other branches conflict with the Constitution, the judicial branch tries to make sure that the Constitution always "wins."

unconstitutional: In conflict with the Constitution. Laws that do not conflict with the Constitution are called *constitutional.*

Here, we see the Supreme Court building, where the nine Supreme Court justices make many important decisions.

Checks and Balances in the Constitution

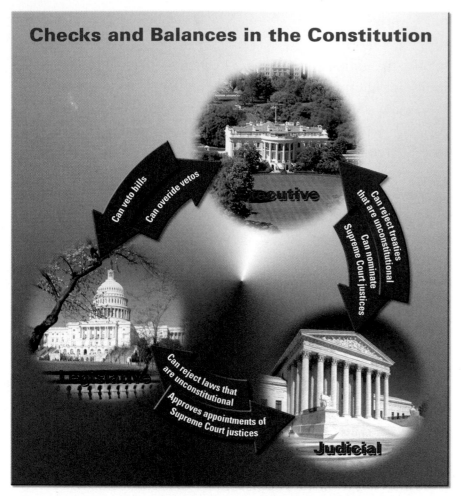

Can veto bills
Can override vetos

Can reject treaties that are unconstitutional
Can nominate Supreme Court justices

Can reject laws that are unconstitutional
Approves appointments of Supreme Court justices

Executive

Legislative

Judicial

The Constitution gives each branch of the government the power to check, or stop, certain actions of the other branches. The men who wrote the Constitution wanted a balance of power among the branches. They didn't want any one branch to become too powerful.

14.7 Limiting Power: Checks and Balances

The men who wrote the Constitution wanted a strong and lasting government. One way that they tried to achieve this goal was by designing a system of "checks and balances." The Constitution gives each branch of government the power to "check" (stop) certain actions of the other branches. It also balances each branch's powers with the powers of the other branches.

Checks and balances help to make sure that no one branch becomes too powerful. For example, Congress can pass laws, but the president approves or vetoes them. The president's power is a check on the power of Congress.

What if Congress and the president agree on a law that disagrees with the Constitution? If the law is challenged in court, the judicial branch has the power to decide whether it is unconstitutional. The court's power is a check on the power of the other two branches.

How are the powers of the different branches balanced? Suppose the president wants one thing and Congress wants another. Congress cannot make laws without the president's signature, and the president needs Congress to pass the laws he wants. Their powers balance each other. And even though the courts can declare laws unconstitutional, federal judges are appointed by the president with the approval of the Senate.

Another example of checks and balances is impeachment. Suppose members of the executive or judicial branch try to abuse their power. Congress can impeach them and remove them from office. In these ways, the Constitution tries to make sure that no one branch of the government becomes too powerful.

14.8 Chapter Summary

In this chapter, you read about how the Constitution gave the United States a new government. You used a metaphor of two stools to compare the government described by the Constitution with the government that was described by the Articles of Confederation.

You learned that the Articles of Confederation were Americans' first attempt to set up a national government. But Shays' Rebellion and other events showed that America needed a stronger government. After much debate and compromise, delegates attending the Constitutional Convention agreed on a new Constitution for the United States.

The writers of the Constitution divided the government's powers among three branches. They used a system of checks and balances to make sure that no one branch became too powerful. In this way, they tried to create a strong and lasting government that would respect Americans' rights and freedoms.

In the next chapter, you will learn about how the Bill of Rights was added to the Constitution to protect citizens' rights. What rights does this document protect? Read on to find out.

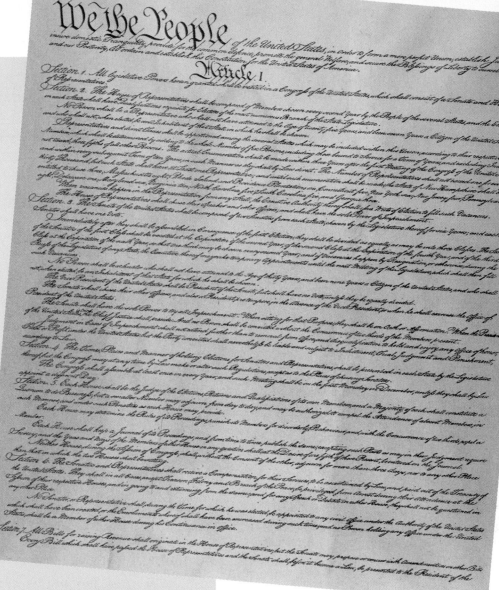

Here, we see the first page of the Constitution.

Why did Americans feel they needed to protect their rights?

Congress of *the* United States
begun and held at the City of New-York, on
Wednesday the fourth of March, one thousand seven hundred and eighty nine

chapter 15

The Bill of Rights

15.1 Introduction

In Chapter 14, you learned how the Constitution created a strong government for the United States. In this chapter, you will read about the first 10 **amendments,** or changes, to the Constitution. These amendments protect the rights and **liberties** of American citizens. Together, they are called the **Bill of Rights**.

The Constitution described how America's new government would work. But it did not say how citizens would be protected from this powerful government. Many Americans wanted the Constitution to include a bill, or list, of rights that the government would always have to respect.

The Bill of Rights is like a shield that protects all citizens. For example, it describes the **rights of the accused** (persons accused of a crime). Among these rights are the right to a lawyer and the right to a trial by a jury.

Look at the drawing to the right. As you learn about the Bill of Rights, think of it as a shield. Why did Americans in 1789 want a shield to protect them from a strong government? What rights and liberties are protected by the Bill of Rights?

The Bill of Rights: A Protective Shield

15.2 The Need for a Bill of Rights

When the Constitution was completed in 1787, it still had to be **ratified** by at least nine states. Americans fiercely debated whether to approve the Constitution. Many people were afraid that it gave the national government too much power. Americans had just fought the Revolutionary War to protect their rights against the British government. They wanted to be sure that their new government would respect their rights.

In several states, the vote on the Constitution was very close. Supporters of the Constitution gained votes by promising to add a bill of rights. A bill of rights is a document that lists the rights and liberties that the government cannot take away.

This promise helped to win approval for the Constitution. By July 1788, 11 states had ratified it. The following April, the new national government gathered for the first time in New York City.

The First Congress faced the important task of considering changes to the Constitution. The states had sent Congress a number of ideas for amendments. Many of them concerned a bill of rights. James Madison of Virginia sorted through the various ideas. Then, he proposed a set of amendments to Congress.

At first, James Madison wasn't sure if adding a bill of rights to the Constitution was necessary. But after he talked to many leaders and sorted through different ideas, he changed his mind. He then proposed the set of amendments to Congress that were later known as the Bill of Rights.

On September 25, 1789, Congress voted to approve the 10 amendments known as the Bill of Rights. The amendments were then sent to the states for ratification (approval). When the state of Virginia approved them on December 15, 1791, they became part of the Constitution.

Over time, the courts have interpreted how the Constitution applies to various situations. In this way, the meaning of the Bill of Rights has grown in the years since 1791.

15.3 The First Amendment

The First Amendment prevents Congress from making laws that take away certain basic freedoms. Among these are freedom of religion, freedom of speech, and freedom of the press.

Freedom of religion was very important to many early Americans. For example, the Pilgrims left England because people there were forced to join the Church of England. Some American colonies also required people to belong to only one church.

The First Amendment protects Americans' freedom to choose their religious beliefs and practices. For example, not everyone prays to the same God. Some people don't pray to any God. For these reasons, courts have said that public schools cannot require students to say prayers.

Freedom of speech is the freedom to express opinions and beliefs. Because of the First Amendment, Americans are free to criticize the government and to express unpopular ideas.

Americans wanted this freedom because many colonists had been arrested for criticizing British laws. In modern times, leaders like Martin Luther King, Jr. have demanded laws to protect the rights of all people. Without the First Amendment, King could have been put in jail just for saying what he believed in public.

Freedom of speech does have limits. People cannot use this freedom to harm others or to break the law. An example is yelling "Fire!" in a crowded theater just for fun. People don't have this freedom because someone might get hurt in the rush to escape the theater.

Freedom of the press means the freedom to report news and express opinions in newspapers and in other ways. In the colonies, British officials had closed down newspapers and smashed printing presses. Like freedom of speech, freedom of the press has limits. For example, it does not include the freedom to spread lies about other people.

The First Amendment also protects people's right to assemble (gather in groups) and their right to petition (ask the government to correct injustices).

The First Amendment protects citizens' rights to speak out against the government. Antiwar demonstrators, shown here, exercise their right of freedom of speech. These citizens disagreed with U.S. actions in the Persian Gulf conflict in 1991.

Minutemen, like the one shown here, were called to battle at the beginning of the Revolutionary War. Americans in 1789 wanted to be sure citizens could defend themselves, especially since there were no police. So, the Second Amendment was included in the Bill of Rights to protect people's right to "keep and bear arms."

15.4   The Second Amendment

The Second Amendment describes the need of states to have a militia, or volunteer army. For this reason, it says that the government cannot take away people's right to "keep and bear (carry) arms," or weapons.

Americans in 1789 wanted to be able to defend themselves. The Revolutionary War had started when militiamen grabbed their muskets to resist British soldiers. Americans remembered how "citizen soldiers" fought the British army to protect their rights. They also wanted to be able to hunt for food and to defend their families. In 1789, there were no police to protect people. In addition, many Americans lived in the countryside and feared attacks by Native Americans and outlaws.

Today, the Second Amendment protects the right to own hunting rifles and certain other kinds of guns. However, people argue whether every citizen has the right to own any type of gun. Many people say no. They are disturbed by violent crimes, accidental shootings, and other events involving firearms. They think that there should be laws controlling who can own and carry guns. Others argue that such laws are forbidden by the Second Amendment. They do not think that citizens should lose the right to carry guns just because some people misuse them.

15.5 The Fourth Amendment

The Fourth Amendment forbids "unreasonable searches and seizures" by police and other officials. *Seizure* means taking away property by force. The Fourth Amendment says that searches and seizures cannot be performed without a good reason.

In 1789, Americans wanted to protect their right to safety and privacy. British officials could go into colonists' homes, shops, and barns without warning. They didn't need a good reason to suspect that a crime had been committed. They could seize anything they liked and use it as evidence in court.

The Fourth Amendment limits the power of police to search people or to invade their homes and businesses. Most searches require a warrant (an order from a judge). The Amendment says that officials must show "probable cause" (good reason) to obtain a warrant. This means convincing the judge that the search is likely to uncover evidence of a crime. In addition, police can search only for the specific items that are listed in the warrant.

The Fourth Amendment protects citizens from the power of the police and other officials who enforce laws. If a search or seizure violates the Fourth Amendment, the evidence cannot be used in court.

Over the years, courts have said that some "reasonable searches" do not require a warrant. For example, to protect public safety, airport officials can search people's carry-on luggage for weapons. Police can search cars for drugs and stolen goods. But they must have good reason to believe that the car is involved in a crime.

In 1789, Americans wanted to protect their right to safety and privacy. Before the Revolutionary War, British officials, like those pictured here, could go into colonists' homes or shops without warning. They could search their possessions and take anything they wanted to use as evidence in court.

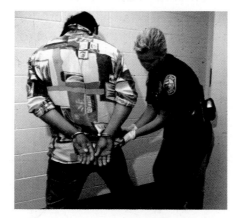

The Fourth Amendment limits the power of police to search people. The officer shown here must either have a search warrant or "probable cause" to conduct this search.

The Bill of Rights 155

A person accused of a crime is protected by the Fifth Amendment from having to give evidence against himself or herself in court. The expression "I take the Fifth" means "I choose to remain silent."

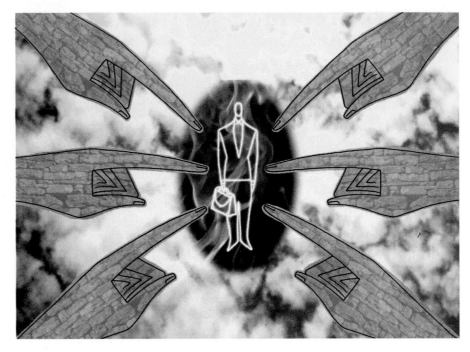

15.6   The Fifth Amendment

The Fifth Amendment protects the rights of Americans who are suspected of a crime. British law had similar protections, but courts in the colonies did not always respect them. Americans wanted to make sure that police and courts treated them fairly.

The Fifth Amendment protects citizens against "double jeopardy." *Jeopardy* means danger, such as the danger of losing freedom by being put in jail. This protection means that people cannot be put on trial or punished twice for the same crime. When a **jury** finds a person "not guilty," he or she goes free. The government cannot try the person again with a different jury. The government can ask for another trial only if a jury cannot come to a decision.

The Fifth Amendment also says that people cannot be forced to be witnesses against themselves. Witnesses are people who give evidence. The amendment protects people from being forced to say things that can be used against them. In some countries, even innocent people have been tortured until they confessed (admitted) to crimes. In the United States, confessions must be given freely. People accused of a crime have the right to say nothing at all. In addition, when making arrests, police must tell citizens that they have this right.

The Fifth Amendment also says that people cannot be punished or lose their property without "due process of law." *Due process* means proper legal procedures, such as a fair trial.

jury: a group of citizens who decide the outcome of a trial

15.7 The Sixth Amendment

The Sixth Amendment describes additional rights of people who are accused of crimes. It guarantees the right to a fair trial. It also guarantees the right to have a lawyer.

Both British law and the Constitution included the right to a trial by jury. Americans wanted to make sure that a jury trial was also a fair trial.

The Sixth Amendment says that trials must be speedy and public. *Speedy* means that people cannot be kept in jail for a long time without a trial. *Public* means that trials cannot be held in secret. Accused persons also have the right to present witnesses and to question witnesses who testify against them.

The amendment also says that juries must be "impartial." This means that jury members must not be **prejudiced** against the accused person. Courts have applied this rule in a number of ways. For example, an all-white jury in Mississippi found a black man guilty of killing a white man. The Supreme Court threw out the jury's decision. It said that the jury was not impartial because only white people were on the jury.

Finally, the Sixth Amendment protects the right of accused people to have a lawyer. Courts have extended this protection to people who cannot afford to hire a lawyer. If an accused person is too poor to pay a lawyer, the government must provide one.

prejudiced: having a negative judgment or opinion without knowledge of the facts

The Sixth Amendment guarantees the rights of people who are accused of a crime. Among those rights are the right to a fair, speedy public trial and the right to a lawyer. Here, a lawyer talks to the jury.

15.8 The Eighth Amendment

The Eighth Amendment protects citizens' rights to fair and reasonable punishment when they break the law. Courts can sentence criminals to time in jail, like the one pictured here. But the Eighth Amendment forbids "cruel and unusual" punishments, like cutting off a thief's hand.

The Eighth Amendment protects citizens' rights to fair and reasonable punishment when they break the law. It says that punishments cannot be so harsh that they are unfair.

Courts can make people pay fines (money penalties) for breaking the law. The amendment says that fines cannot be "excessive," or unreasonable. For example, making someone pay $1,000 for a parking ticket would be excessive.

The Eighth Amendment also forbids excessive bail. Bail is the money someone pays to get out of jail while waiting for a trial. But the amendment doesn't force courts to allow bail in all cases. For instance, a judge can deny bail to someone accused of murder.

Most important, the Eighth Amendment forbids "cruel and unusual" punishments. Americans wanted this protection because punishments for crimes in the 1700s were often very harsh. For example, a thief could have a hand cut off. People who owed money could be put in jail with little chance of ever getting out.

Over the years, courts have applied this protection to people in prison, as well. For instance, not giving prisoners enough food is cruel and unusual punishment.

Americans often find it hard to decide whether a punishment is "cruel and unusual." For example, they disagree about the death penalty, also called *capital punishment.* Many people think that the death penalty is fair for murder and certain other very serious crimes. Others argue that taking someone's life is always too harsh a punishment.

Courts have ruled that the Eighth Amendment does not forbid the death penalty. Even so, some states do not allow capital punishment.

15.9 Other Rights Protected by the Bill of Rights

The Bill of Rights protects several other rights and liberties as well.

The Third Amendment says that Americans cannot be forced to let soldiers stay in their homes. The Seventh Amendment protects people's right to settle disputes with a trial by jury. For example, someone injured in a car accident might want the driver to pay for hospital expenses. The amendment states that people can demand a jury trial to settle arguments over things of value.

The Ninth Amendment says that the Constitution's list of rights is not meant to be complete. Other rights that Americans have include the freedom to choose where to live and what kind of work to do.

The Tenth Amendment limits the power of the national government. It says that the government has only those powers that are listed in the Constitution. All other powers belong to the states or to the people.

15.10 Chapter Summary

In this chapter, you learned how Americans wanted a bill of rights in the Constitution. You compared the Bill of Rights to a shield that protects citizens from the power of the government.

The 10 amendments in the Bill of Rights protect several important rights and liberties. For example, Americans are free to choose their religion. They can speak and publish their opinions. They can own guns. They have protection against unreasonable actions by police and courts.

Many Americans take the Bill of Rights for granted. But in 1789, few people in the world had these rights and freedoms. Even today, many governments around the world do not respect them.

When the Bill of Rights was written, the United States was still a small country. Sixty years later, it stretched all the way to the Pacific Ocean. How did this great expansion happen? And what happened to the people who were already living in the vast areas to the west? Read on to find out.

What changes did settlers bring to the West in the early 1800s?

What might these people already living in the West be thinking of all the changes?

Manifest Destiny and Settling the West

16.1 Introduction

In Chapter 15, you learned how the Bill of Rights was added to the Constitution to protect the rights and freedoms of Americans. At that time, the United States stretched from the Atlantic Ocean to the Mississippi River. In this chapter, you will read about how the United States spread across North America by taking control of **territories,** or large regions of land.

In the 1800s, the lands west of the Mississippi River were claimed by several other nations. Many Americans wanted to move into these lands. Some believed that it was natural and right for the United States to take over these territories. They said that expanding westward was America's **Manifest Destiny,** or obvious fate.

American leaders used a variety of methods to **annex,** or add, territory to the United States. Sometimes they bought territory. Sometimes they made agreements with leaders of other countries. Once, the United States added territory after fighting a war.

Many Americans thought that expanding the United States was good for the country. But as you will see, it definitely was not good for everyone.

Look at the map to the right. The map shows the various territories that were added to the United States between 1783 and 1853. As you read through this chapter, look back at this map. How did the United States gain control of each territory? What happened to the people who already lived there?

Territorial Acquisitions Made by the United States Between 1803 and 1853

Oregon Country

Louisiana Purchase

Mexican Cession

United States in 1783

Gadsden Purchase

Texas Annexation

Florida Acquisition

16.2 United States in 1783

After the Revolutionary War ended in 1783, the United States gained control from Britain of most of the territory from the Atlantic Ocean to the Mississippi River. More and more white settlers began moving west into lands where only Native Americans had been living. Some wanted to go farther, across the Mississippi River.

Several nations claimed territories that Americans wanted for themselves. In the Southeast, Florida was controlled by Spain. France claimed much of the land west of the Mississippi River. Farther west, first Spain and then Mexico controlled huge territories, including the places we know today as Texas, the Southwest, and California. Britain claimed large areas in the Northwest, including the present-day states of Oregon and Washington. Russia also claimed a part of the Northwest.

Americans wanted these lands for many reasons. The number of Americans was growing, partly because people from other countries were moving to the United States. People wanted more room, especially for farming. They wanted more opportunities to work and to build homes. Businesses wanted resources, like wood and minerals, as well as new places to sell goods. Political leaders wanted the United States to be strong and safe from attacks by other countries.

Americans were proud of their new country. Many of them believed that it was only natural and right to spread their religion, government, and way of life all the way to the Pacific Ocean. In 1845, a newspaper writer called this idea America's *Manifest Destiny*.

This painting shows Manifest Destiny represented as an angel floating westward. She is bringing the telegraph, railroads, farmers, and settlers with her. The Native Americans appear to be running away.

16.3 Louisiana Purchase (1803)

The first huge addition to the United States was the Louisiana Purchase of 1803. In a single agreement with France, the United States purchased (bought) most of the land from the Mississippi River to the Rocky Mountains.

Diplomats from the United States (standing on the left) present a French leader (seated on the right) with a map and description of the Louisiana Purchase in 1803.

The Louisiana Purchase came about because Americans wanted to be able to ship goods down the Mississippi River to the port city of New Orleans. From there, goods could be sent by ship to states on the Atlantic Coast. Moving goods in this way was easier and cheaper than shipping them over the Appalachian Mountains.

New Orleans, though, was controlled by France. To make sure that Americans could move goods freely through the city, President Thomas Jefferson offered to buy New Orleans for up to 7.5 million dollars.

At this time, France had its own problems, including worries over a possible war with England. The French wanted money for their army, and they were ready to give up their claims in North America. They surprised President Jefferson by agreeing to sell all of Louisiana Territory for 12 million dollars. This purchase was a great bargain that doubled the size of the United States overnight.

But the Louisiana Purchase was not good for everyone, especially Native Americans. For years, white settlers had wanted to push Native Americans westward. Now there was a place to put them. In the 1830s, several tribes were forced to move out of their homelands in the South to what is now Oklahoma. Thousands of Choctaws, Creeks, Chickasaws, and Cherokees were forced off their land and onto **reservations** in Oklahoma. Many starved, froze to death, or died from diseases during these terrible journeys.

reservation: an area of land set aside by the United States government for Native Americans to live on

expedition: A trip by a group of people to explore unknown places. The group itself is also called an *expedition.*

This painting shows the key members of Lewis and Clark's expedition at Three Forks, Montana. The young woman is Sacagawea. To her right is Meriwether Lewis. To his right is William Clark. The African American carrying a rifle is York, Clark's slave.

16.4 Lewis and Clark Expedition (1804 to 1806)

Shortly before the Louisiana Purchase, President Jefferson sent two former soldiers to lead an **expedition** to explore the huge territory. Jefferson asked the two men, Meriwether Lewis and William Clark, to map the Louisiana Territory and describe its soil, plants, animals, and Native American tribes. He also wanted to learn about locations for trading posts and settlements and perhaps even find the Northwest Passage.

On May 14, 1804, Lewis and Clark started up the Missouri River from St. Louis with more than 40 other men. One of them was Clark's slave, a man named York. York would become the first African American to cross North America.

The expedition traveled up the Missouri in search of another river that would take them west to the Pacific Ocean. Instead, they discovered high, cold plateaus. They spent the winter with a group of Native Americans, the Mandans, in what is now North Dakota.

One of the Native Americans they met was a young Shoshone woman named Sacagawea. In the summer, she guided the expedition over the high, steep Rocky Mountains. After crossing dry, barren land, Lewis and Clark finally found the Salmon, Snake, and Columbia Rivers. The expedition traveled down the rivers and reached the Pacific Ocean in November 1805.

On their way back from the Pacific, Lewis and Clark discovered two new routes across the Rocky Mountains. In 1806, they returned to Missouri as heroes. Now that the Louisiana Territory was better known, settlers could move even farther west.

16.5 Florida Acquisition (1819)

In the early 1800s, most of the land we know today as Florida was controlled by Spain. Americans in the Southeast wanted the United States to take over Florida. Slave owners in Georgia were angry because slaves sometimes ran away to Florida. Often, the runaway slaves hid with a tribe of Native Americans, the Seminoles. Some even became members of the tribe.

White landowners in Georgia were also upset because Seminoles sometimes raided (attacked) their settlements and then escaped back into Florida. The Seminoles made these raids because they were afraid that the white settlers would eventually attack them.

In 1817, General Andrew Jackson and his army marched into Florida. He put an end to the Seminole raids. Then he did even more. He blew up a fort that was controlled by runaway slaves. He captured two Spanish forts, including one at Pensacola, the capital of Spanish Florida. President James Monroe said he did not fully support General Jackson's attacks. But he was eager to acquire Florida so he didn't stop Jackson.

Spain realized that it could not keep the United States from taking over the territory. In 1819, Spain agreed to give Florida to the United States. In return, the United States agreed to pay 5 million dollars to the Georgian settlers. The settlers wanted money from Spain to pay for lost slaves and damaged property.

Within 10 years, many white Americans had moved to Florida. The government ordered the Seminoles to leave, but many refused. They fought one more war against the United States before most of them were either killed or forced to leave their homeland and settle in the West.

This painting shows Seminoles from Florida attacking a settlement in Georgia. General Andrew Jackson used these raids as an excuse to attack Florida.

Florida Acquisition

Texas
Annexation

16.6 Texas Annexation (1845)

In the early 1800s, Spain controlled Mexico and most of what is now the southwestern and western parts of the United States. In the 1820s, Mexico gained its independence from Spain and took control of this territory. Part of it was the region known as Texas.

Most of the people in Texas were Native Americans, such as Apaches and Comanches. The Mexican government wanted more settlers in Texas who would raise crops and animals, pay taxes, and spread the Catholic religion. Mexican officials told Americans that they could have free land if they settled in Texas. The settlers had to promise to obey Mexican laws and to accept the Catholic religion.

By 1830, more than 20,000 white Americans had settled in Texas. By this time, there were far more Americans than Mexicans living there. Soon tensions grew between the settlers and the Mexican government. Although Mexico had outlawed slavery, most of the Americans owned slaves. Even when Mexico allowed some slaves to be brought into Texas, the slave owners worried that some day Mexico might free them. Most of the American settlers wanted Texas to become part of the United States. Many of them didn't even bother to learn Spanish.

In 1833, a number of settlers asked Mexico to let Texas have its own government. Stephen Austin, who had been a loyal Mexican citizen, delivered their message to the government. Angrily, the Mexican government refused.

By 1835, fighting had broken out between groups of Texans and Mexican soldiers. In 1836, Texans declared independence. In response, the president of Mexico, Antonio López de Santa Anna, led an army into Texas to punish the American settlers for breaking their agreement with Mexico.

When Santa Anna's army reached the town of San Antonio, fewer than 200 Texans and other Americans stood in the way. They had chosen to defend an abandoned mission called the *Alamo*. Santa Anna demanded that they surrender. They answered bravely, "Victory or death!"

For more than 10 days, the tiny group of **defenders** fought off Santa Anna's army. Finally, the Mexicans were able to climb the walls and take over the Alamo. Nearly all the defenders were killed, including Jim Bowie and Davy Crockett, two famous American pioneers.

defenders: people who protect or defend against outside attack

Six weeks later, in April 1836, General Sam Houston led more than 700 Texans in a surprise attack against Santa Anna's army at San Jacinto. The Texans charged the army, shouting, "Remember the Alamo!" They won the battle and captured Santa Anna. They let him go when he promised to give Texas its independence.

Texans promptly approved a new constitution and chose Sam Houston as their president. For nine years, Texas ruled itself. Its flag showed one white star on a red, white, and blue background. People called Texas the *Lone Star Republic*. Some Mexicans moved away to Catholic, Spanish-speaking Mexico. Others stayed, marrying and doing business with American Texans and working in the government. However, in time, most Mexicans lost their lands and government positions.

Many Texans still wanted the United States to annex Texas. In 1845, their wish was granted. Congress admitted Texas as the 28th state.

In 1836, Texans declared their independence from Mexico. As a result, the Mexican army attacked a group of Texans at the Alamo. The Texans were totally defeated. In this painting, you can see the Mexican flag flying over the defeated Alamo.

Oregon Country

16.7 Acquisition of Oregon Country (1846)

Since the early 1800s, Americans had dreamed of controlling the northwestern territory known as Oregon Country. This area included the present-day states of Washington and Oregon, as well as parts of other states and western Canada. For years, Oregon Country had been jointly occupied by Britain and the United States. To the north, Russia controlled Alaska.

In 1844, James Polk was elected president. He promised to take control of all of Oregon Country, from the northern border of California to the southern edge of Alaska. This area's northern **boundary** was deep in British-controlled territory, at latitude 54°40′ north. Polk's supporters demanded, "Fifty-four forty or fight!"

Neither Britain nor the United States really wanted to fight a war over Oregon Country. Britain knew that the southern part of the territory already contained more Americans than British and Canadians. Besides, most of the British in the area trapped beavers or traded beaver furs. By the mid 1840s, few beavers were left.

In 1846, Britain agreed to a boundary drawn at latitude 49° north from the Rocky Mountains to the Pacific Ocean. The British gave up any claims to land south of this line.

The lives of Native Americans in Oregon Country soon began to change. By 1850, Congress was giving away land to American settlers. The settlers took Native American hunting lands for farming and ranching. For many years, there were wars between Native Americans and white settlers and soldiers. Eventually, most Native American tribes were forced onto reservations.

boundary: the geographic line between two places, such as two countries

Oregon City (just south of Portland), on the Willamette River, was the capital of Oregon Country until 1851.

16.8 Mexican Cession and Gadsden Purchase (1848 and 1853)

The next large addition to the United States came as a result of war with Mexico. Part of the problem with Mexico developed when the United States annexed Texas. The Mexican government wanted Texas back. In addition, Mexico knew that many Americans wanted other Mexican lands, including California.

The two countries also disagreed about the southwestern boundary of Texas. Americans wanted the boundary to be the Rio Grande ("large river," in Spanish). Mexico wanted it to be about 150 miles farther north and east.

In 1846, President Polk sent an army under General Zachary Taylor to protect the Rio Grande. A group of Mexican soldiers tried to defend the land that they believed belonged to

cession: the act of giving up ("ceding") territory, usually as the result of a treaty

American troops landed at the Mexican seaport of Vera Cruz in 1846 and began their march to Mexico City.

Mexico. Crossing the river, they fought against a small number of Americans. "American blood has been spilled," General Taylor wrote to President Polk. Now the president had an excuse to go to war with Mexico. It was Mexico, he told Congress, that started the fighting. On May 13, 1846 Congress voted to declare war.

Many Americans were against the war, saying it was a "land grab" by the United States. Others supported President Polk and cheered every victory by U.S. soldiers.

The war went on for nearly two years. At first, the United States won several battles, but Mexico refused to give in. President Polk then ordered an army to capture the capital, Mexico City.

Mexican soldiers battled fiercely to defend their country. Both sides suffered great losses. In one of the battles at Mexico City, an estimated 900 U.S. soldiers and 4,000 Mexican soldiers died. Even when U.S. soldiers captured the capital, Mexico refused to surrender. American soldiers continued to attack, rob, and kill many Mexican citizens.

Finally, the Mexicans surrendered. In February 1848, Mexico agreed to the Treaty of Guadalupe Hidalgo. In this agreement, Mexico gave up ("ceded") a huge amount of territory. It included the present-day states of California, New Mexico, Utah, and Nevada, as well as parts of four other states. Mexico also agreed to the Rio Grande as the border of Texas. For the Mexican Cession, the United States agreed to pay Mexico 15 million dollars.

Five years later, in 1853, Congress bought one last piece of Mexico. It was an area of land south of the Gila River in present-day Arizona and New Mexico. This land contained a pass through the mountains that would make it easier to build a railroad across the southern United States. This agreement became known as the *Gadsden Purchase,* after the American representative who made the purchase.

After the war with Mexico, American farmers, ranchers, and miners poured into the new territories. Their arrival changed the lives of people in the Southwest. Many of the newcomers treated the Native Americans and former Mexican citizens poorly. They often ignored previous claims on land and took it for themselves. They gave Mexicans and Native Americans poor jobs. In the years to come, they fought many wars against Apaches and other Native Americans before forcing them onto reservations.

16.9 Chapter Summary

In this chapter, you read about how the United States spread across North America between 1783 and 1853. You used a map to study the large territories that the United States gained during this time.

Many Americans believed that it was their "manifest destiny" to spread their religion, government, and way of life all the way to the Pacific Ocean. With each new gain in territory, more settlers pushed westward. Their movements and desire for land led to deadly conflicts with Native Americans and with the country of Mexico.

Although ranchers, miners, and farmers created new settlements and opportunities, their westward movement also forced Native Americans from their homelands and onto reservations. Sometimes, the new settlers took land that was claimed by others as well, including former Mexican citizens.

What kinds of people were living in the West when the settlers arrived? What were their ways of life? Who were some of the settlers who pushed westward, and what was it like to settle these new lands? You will find out in the next chapter.

In their belief that it was their "manifest destiny" to settle the new lands of the West, settlers and miners overcame unheard-of obstacles. Here miners struggle up a road leading to newly discovered mines in the Rocky Mountains.

What might these Native Americans think of the newcomers?

What is this man doing?

What kind of animals pulled the wagon?

What do you think this fire was used for?

The Diverse Peoples of the West

17.1 Introduction

In Chapter 16, you learned how the United States expanded west across North America. In this chapter, you will learn about four groups of people who moved to the West during the mid 1800s. You will also read about two groups who already lived there.

People moved to the West for different reasons. Thousands of **pioneers** were attracted by cheap land. One group, the **Mormons,** wanted to start a new religious community. Other groups of people were attracted by the discovery of gold in California. These groups included the **Forty-Niners** and **Chinese immigrants**.

Unfortunately, many new settlers did not care how their actions affected the people who already lived in the West. In this chapter, you will read about what happened to former Mexican citizens, called **Mexicanos**. You will also read about a Native American group called the **Nez Percé**.

Look at the drawing of the wagon wheel to the right. The wheel is an illustrated spoke diagram. A spoke diagram is a way to organize information. The diagram shows six groups of people who lived in the West. The hub (center) of the wheel is a reminder that all six groups lived in the same place. The spokes should remind you that each group had different experiences. As you read this chapter, think about how you can use the spoke diagram to record information about the six groups. Which groups were helped as the United States expanded westward? Which groups were harmed?

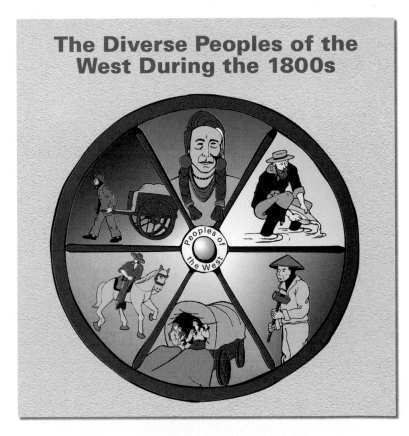

The Diverse Peoples of the West During the 1800s

HARPER'S WEEKLY.
JOURNAL OF CIVILIZATION.

VOL. XVIII.—No. 937.]   NEW YORK, SATURDAY, DECEMBER 12, 1874.   [WITH A SUPPLEMENT. PRICE TEN CENTS.

Entered according to Act of Congress, in the Year 1874, by Harper & Brothers, in the Office of the Librarian of Congress, at Washington.

17.2 The West in the Mid 1800s

In the mid 1800s, stories in books, magazines, and newspapers encouraged thousands of Americans to move westward. Western land was very cheap and sometimes free. Even families with little money could build homes and start ranches or farms.

Then, in 1848, news spread that gold had been discovered in California. Suddenly, fortune seekers were racing to the West from around the world.

Some Americans traveled to the West by ship around the tip of South America. Many chose a cheaper, but more dangerous, route. First, they sailed to the Atlantic side of the isthmus of Panama, in Central America. (An *isthmus* is a narrow strip of land.) Then, they crossed through jungles to the Pacific side. There, they boarded ships headed to California.

Most people got to the West by land (rather than by ship around the Cape of Good Hope). This was the cheapest route, but also the most difficult. Overland travelers had to cross hot deserts and climb over steep mountains. In 1849, more than 5,000 of them died, mostly from disease.

Newcomers to the West showed little concern for the people who already lived there. For example, many Spanish-speaking people lived in areas that were once controlled by Spain and Mexico. Many Americans from other parts of the country had little respect for these people or their property. Sometimes they took land away from families who had lived in the West for 100 years or more.

To gain land for settlers, the U.S. government signed treaties with Native American tribes. Often settlers broke these agreements, and, sometimes, land was taken from Native Americans without a treaty. As a result, people who had lived in the West for hundreds of years lost their homelands.

Popular magazines, such as *Harper's Weekly,* printed articles about great adventure and free land in the West. This issue, however, did not explain that white settlers were killing off the buffalo herds. As a result, Native Americans lost a major source of food, clothing, and shelter.

Mexican cowboys, called *vaqueros,* came to California to herd the cattle of the California missions and ranchos. Later they taught white settlers how to handle cattle.

17.3 Mexicanos

One group of people who lived in the West in the mid 1800s was the Spanish-speaking *Mexicanos* (MEH-he-KAH-nos).

In the 1820s, the Mexican government granted many wealthy Mexicanos in California huge plots of land called **ranchos**. Most ranchos were devoted to cattle raising. Mexicano ranchers traded cattle hides (skins) and tallow (fat) for other goods.

The cattle were looked after by highly skilled *vaqueros* (vah-KAY-rohs), or cowboys. The vaqueros used special clothes and equipment, which English-speaking newcomers learned to use as well. For example, vaqueros used a rope called *la reata* (lah-ray-AH-tah). The newcomers called it a "lariat." To protect their legs from thorny bushes, vaqueros wore leather coverings called *chaparreras* (chah-pah-RAY-rahs). English speakers called them "chaps." For protection from the sun, vaqueros wore wide-brimmed hats called *sombreros.*

Mexicanos grew all their own food. Many of their crops were fruits and other plants from Spain, including lemons, oranges, figs, and grapes. They also grew North American

rancho: an area of land granted to Spanish and Mexican citizens in North America, usually for ranching (for example, raising cattle)

crops such as corn, chiles, and beans. They loved to make a rich stew of beef spiced with chiles called *carne asada* (KAHR-nay ah-SAH-dah). And they enjoyed a flat corn bread called *tortillas* (tor-TEE-uhs).

Mexicanos adapted well to the hot, dry climate of the West and Southwest. They built houses out of thick clay bricks called *adobe* (uh-DOH-bee). Adobe stayed cooler than other materials in hot weather. To irrigate (water) their land, they dug irrigation ditches and built small dams. They told stories about current events in songs called *corridos* (koh-REE-dohs). They made music with Spanish instruments such as guitars, violins, and trumpets.

Mexicanos were citizens of Mexico until 1848, when the Mexican-American War ended. They then became U.S. citizens. But they were soon outnumbered by gold seekers and new settlers. The newcomers often saw Mexicanos as foreigners instead of fellow Americans. Many white settlers had little respect for Mexicanos and did not consider them rightful owners of the land.

The U.S. government did not protect Mexicanos' property, and many newcomers claimed rancho land for themselves. The newcomers burned Mexicanos' crops and shot their stray cattle. The new culture of the West and Southwest included many things that were learned from Mexicanos. But the rancho way of life soon disappeared.

17.4   Forty-Niners

In January 1848, gold was discovered in the Sierra Nevada mountains of California. By 1849, news of the discovery had spread to the eastern United States, to Europe, and to Asia. Suddenly, **Forty-Niners** were leaving their families, farms, and jobs to race to the gold fields. The gold rush was on!

Forty-Niners hoped to get rich quick. Some of them were former slaves and slaves who had run away. These African Americans were seeking freedom as well as gold. The luckiest ones sent money home to buy freedom for relatives.

Miners found much of the gold in rivers. Sometimes they scraped gold from river rocks with knives and spoons. Miners also learned to "pan" for gold. First, they scooped up dirt and rock from the riverbed in a pan. Then, they swished the pan around in the river. Lighter materials floated away, leaving the heavy gold in the pan.

Forty-Niner: a gold seeker in the California gold rush of 1849

To get more gold, miners used a wooden box on rockers called a *cradle*. First, they shoveled the riverbed dirt into the *cradle*. Then, they poured water over it and rocked the cradle to wash away the lighter material.

Eventually, many miners worked in larger groups. They put several boxes together to make a long, narrow box called a *sluice* (SLOOS). Men on both sides shoveled gravel into the sluice while water ran steadily through it. The water washed away the lighter particles, and the gold stayed behind.

Miners had a hard and lonely life. They lived in leaky tents and shacks far from their families. Especially in the early days of the gold rush, there were very few women in the mining towns and camps.

Storekeepers made more money than most miners by selling food, tools, and supplies at high prices. But many miners ate cheaply by making their own sourdough bread.

Two Forty-Niners, one an African American, shovel gravel into a sluice. The water running through the sluice will separate the gold from the gravel.

There was no government in the gold fields. Miners elected their own officials and made their own rules to protect their belongings and **claims**. Arguments over claim boundaries were often settled with guns. A man who stole a miner's horse or gold was likely to be hanged.

In time, gold became harder and harder to find. The gold rush did make some people millionaires. But most of the Forty-Niners eventually went home no richer than before. Some stayed in California and started businesses and farms.

claim: An area of land being worked by a miner. The miner had the right to valuable minerals found in the claim.

17.5 Chinese Immigrants

News of California gold reached China about 1851. Within a year, 25,000 Chinese immigrants sailed to California, looking for the "Golden Mountain."

Most of the Chinese hoped to earn money for their families and then return home. Many people in China were too poor to afford food or farmland. Local wars and crop failures made life even harder.

By the time Chinese immigrants arrived in California, most of the gold that was easy to mine was gone. So they worked together in mines that earlier miners had given up on. They invented new ways of finding gold using clever tools and machines.

American miners were jealous. They convinced the government to tax foreign miners. They also used threats and violence to push the Chinese away from the mines.

Many Chinese found work helping to build the first **transcontinental** railroad. The Central Pacific railroad company was laying track east from Sacramento, California. The Union Pacific company was building west from Nebraska. Eventually nearly all the Central Pacific's workers were Chinese. In fact, in one contest to see which crews could lay more track, Chinese crews won.

Chinese railroad workers were paid less than other workers. They also had to work longer hours and did more dangerous jobs. Sometimes the Chinese had to carve tunnels through solid rock. They lowered themselves down the cliffs in wicker baskets fastened to ropes. Then, they drilled holes in the rock and set gunpowder and fuses in the holes.

This was very dangerous work. Sometimes the basket

transcontinental:
Across the continent. The transcontinental railroad stretched across the continent of North America.

These Chinese laborers are digging a tunnel in the Sierra Nevada for the Central Pacific railroad company. Chinese laborers were paid less than other workers, even though they worked longer hours and under more dangerous conditions.

ropes broke, sending the workers crashing to their deaths below. Sometimes the explosives went off too soon. In winter, many workers froze.

When the transcontinental railroad was completed in 1869, Chinese found new ways to earn money, opening stores and working as farmers and fishermen. But many white Americans still saw the Chinese as "foreigners" because they looked different, had different customs, and spoke a different language. Some of them accused Chinese of taking their jobs for less pay. In some places, Chinese were forced to leave town. Some were even murdered.

In 1882, Congress responded to the anger toward Chinese by passing the Chinese Exclusion Act. (*Exclusion* means "keeping out.") This law prevented most Chinese from entering the United States. Many years passed before Chinese were allowed to enter the United States as freely as they had before.

17.6 Mormons

Most people went West to make their fortunes. The Mormons, however, were looking for religious freedom.

The Mormons were members of the Church of Jesus Christ of Latter-day Saints. (*Latter-day* means "modern.") This church was started in New York in 1830. Young Joseph Smith said that God had told him to build a new kingdom in America. There, the Mormons would lead good lives and enjoy success by working together.

An inspiring preacher, Joseph Smith attracted thousands of followers. But other people attacked the Mormons. They didn't believe that God gave special messages to Smith. They also disliked the way that Mormons were trying to create their own community.

Several times, the Mormons were forced to move—first to Ohio, then Missouri, and finally, to an Illinois town they called Nauvoo (na-VOO). Non-Mormons in Illinois were afraid that the Mormons were becoming too powerful. They also accused some Mormon men of having two or more wives, a practice called *polygamy*. During these arguments, Joseph Smith was arrested. On June 27, 1844, a mob broke into the jail and killed Smith and his brother.

In 1846, the Mormons left Illinois and later fled again to Nebraska. Their new leader, Brigham Young, said that they could only be safe if they moved farther west.

The European Mormons pictured here were too poor to buy wagons. Instead, they pushed and pulled their belongings in handcarts across the deserts and mountains. Many perished as a result of this hardship.

missionaries: representatives of a religion who try to get other people to adopt that religion

Young organized thousands of people for the move and led the first group west in 1847. Along the way, the Mormons built cabins, dug wells, and planted crops for later followers. When they reached the Great Salt Lake in Utah, Young said, "This is the right place."

The Great Salt Lake was a dry, empty plain. The Mormons irrigated the land by building dams in mountain streams and digging ditches. They planted crops and built a well-planned city.

More groups followed by wagon train. Each morning, the travelers were awakened by the sound of bugles (horns). After doing chores, they set out for another long day on the trail. They left messages in buffalo skulls for other Mormons to find.

Meanwhile, Mormon **missionaries** in Europe gained new followers who wanted to spread the Mormon religion. The European Mormons who came to America were too poor to buy wagons. Instead, they pushed and pulled their belongings in handcarts across the deserts and mountains.

The Mormons settled the territory of Utah. They organized their own political party and made their own laws. They would not be forced from their homes again.

17.7 Oregon Pioneers

In the 1840s, many Americans began catching "Oregon fever." Fur traders from Oregon Country traveled east, telling stories of thick forests and fertile land for farming. Religious leaders sent letters encouraging settlers to move there. Newspapers and books told of a place where ordinary people could have a good life farming, fishing, and trading.

In 1843, a thousand people in Missouri organized a wagon train headed for Oregon. The pioneers loaded the canvas-covered wagons with everything they would need on their journey. For food, they packed flour, salt, sugar, coffee, and dried fruit. They took cookware, clothing, rifles, tools, medicines, and cloth. Then they set out on their 2,000-mile journey along the Oregon Trail.

Every day of the trip was filled with hard work. Bugles were blown when it was time to sleep and again when it was time to wake up. Men drove wagons, herded cattle, found campsites, and guarded the wagon train at night. Women set up tents, cooked, and washed clothes. They put the heavy **yokes** on the oxen that pulled the wagons.

yoke: a wooden frame that fastens around an animal's neck

Women also cared for the sick. Many travelers caught diseases from living so close together. They suffered from hunger, heat, cold, and poisoning from bad water. Many died along the trail.

In the wide prairies, the pioneers found plenty of grass for their animals to eat. They tried to follow rivers so that they would have water. But crossing rivers with the wagons was difficult and dangerous. Sometimes, a river took as many as five days to cross. Steep mountains and hot, dry deserts brought new challenges.

This image of pioneers crossing the Great Plains on their way to Oregon highlights the role that women played during the journey. Women set up tents, cooked, washed clothes, and tended to the young.

The Oregon Trail passed through Native American lands. Some Native Americans were friendly and traded horses with the pioneers or helped them cross rivers. They rarely attacked the wagon trains. But Native Americans in the plains depended on buffalo for their food. They saw pioneers hunting buffalo and their cattle eating the buffaloes' grass. They worried that the buffalo would be killed or frightened away.

For the pioneers who survived the trip, all the difficulties were worth the chance for a new life. Each year, more wagon trains came. By 1845, close to 10,000 Americans had traveled the Oregon Trail.

Chief Joseph of the Nez Percé led a group of his followers on a 1,000-mile journey from Oregon to near the Canadian border to escape the U.S. Army. Although he fought bravely, he finally surrendered. He never again saw his homeland in Oregon.

17.8 Nez Percé

The Nez Percé (nehz-pur-SAY) were Native Americans who lived in eastern Oregon, northwestern Idaho, and southeastern Washington. There, they roamed peacefully with herds of prized horses. They enjoyed eating salmon, wild berries, and root plants. For decoration, they attached shells and feathers to their clothes and pierced their noses. (Their name is French for "pierced nose.") They treasured their relationship with nature.

In the 1840s, settlers began farming on Nez Percé land. The United States government made treaties that promised the Nez Percé certain lands while buying other land for settlers.

Chief Joseph was the leader of the Nez Percé in Oregon's Wallowa Valley. By the 1870s, settlers and gold miners wanted this land. They persuaded the government to force the Nez Percé onto a reservation. Chief Joseph refused to move. The government threatened to send soldiers to force them.

To avoid war, some Nez Percé started toward the reservation. Then, angry young warriors killed some white settlers who had mistreated Native Americans. Chief Joseph feared that the soldiers would attack. He decided to lead his people to safety in Canada.

Soldiers chased Chief Joseph and several hundred of his followers for more than 1,000 miles. The Nez Percé hid in steep mountains and deep valleys. Several times, they fought off the soldiers.

At last, the Nez Percé reached the Bearpaw Mountains in Montana, only about 30 miles from Canada. They hoped to cross the border the next day. But there the soldiers found them. For five days, the Nez Percé fought for their freedom. Many died. All of them were cold, hungry, and exhausted. Finally, Chief Joseph surrendered.

"The old men are all dead," Chief Joseph announced. *"I want to have time to look for my children.... Maybe I shall find them among the dead. Hear me, my chiefs. I am tired; my heart is sick and sad. From where the sun now stands, I will fight no more, forever."*

The soldiers had promised that the Nez Percé could return to their home country. Instead, they were taken to a reservation in far-off Oklahoma. Half or more of them died there from disease and starvation.

Eventually, some of the Nez Percé were allowed to return to reservations in Idaho and Washington. But Chief Joseph and his people never saw their beloved valley again.

17.9 Chapter Summary

In this chapter, you learned about four groups who moved to the West in the mid 1800s. You also learned about two groups who already lived there. You used a spoke diagram to compare the experiences of these groups.

Most people moved to the West in search of opportunity and fortune, like the Forty-Niners, Chinese, and Oregon pioneers. One group, the Mormons, went west to seek religious freedom. All these miners and settlers faced many hardships. The newcomers' arrival was also hard on people who already lived in the West, such as Mexicanos and the Nez Percé. Thousands of these people lost their homes, and many lost their lives.

The settlement of the West helped the United States to grow. It brought new resources and opportunities for many Americans. But it also caused conflicts between Americans over the issue of slavery in the new western lands. In the next chapter, you will discover how these conflicts led to a terrible war.

What role did these people play on the plantation?

Why is this man riding a mule?

What is this man doing?

Where is this wagon going?

chapter 18

The Causes of the Civil War

18.1 Introduction

In Chapter 17, you read about people who lived in the West. In this chapter, you will learn how Americans disagreed about how to settle the West. This disagreement helped start a bloody **Civil War** between the Northern and the Southern states.

By the 1860s, the regions of the North and South were very different. The **North** was busily building cities, factories, and railroads. Most important, workers in the North were free, not slaves.

The **South** had few factories or large cities. Most people still lived on farms. On large farms, called *plantations,* African slaves planted and harvested crops, especially cotton.

The Southern way of life depended on the labor of slaves. As the United States expanded westward, people in the North and the South disagreed bitterly over whether slaves should be allowed in new territories and states.

Look at the drawing of the brother and sister at the right. The sister has a habit that her brother does not like. She plays her music loudly and refuses to turn it down. The brother likes quiet. Think of the differences between the North and the South as being like the differences between this brother and sister. As you may remember, this kind of comparison is called a *metaphor*.

As you read this chapter, think about this metaphor of the brother and the sister arguing about loud music. Does the brother have the right to change his sister's habit? What will happen if his sister refuses?

The Causes of the Civil War: Like a Family Feud

This Colt factory, which produced weapons, was like many of the factories that began in the North.

18.2 Differences Grow Between the North and the South

In the first half of the 1800s, people in the North and the South developed very different ways of life.

In the North, cities grew large, and new industries began to appear. Busy factories made all kinds of products, including new inventions such as the sewing machine. Canals and railroads made it possible for farmers, ranchers, and business owners to move goods over long distances. Factory owners in the East made tools and supplies for farmers a thousand miles away and shipped them by railroads. Farmers sent grain and other crops to the growing cities.

All this activity provided jobs for large numbers of workers, including new **immigrants** from Ireland and Germany. Workers in the North were paid for their labor and were free to take jobs of their choice. For this reason, these workers were called "free labor."

Unlike the North, the South had few large cities and factories. Its way of life was based on farming and slave labor. While many Southern families worked their own farms, owners of large farms, called *plantations*, used slave labor.

immigrant: a person who comes to live in a country from another nation

The most important plantation crop was cotton. The South's warm weather and rich soil had always been good for growing cotton. But cotton growers made little money until Eli Whitney invented the cotton gin in 1793. Whitney's machine quickly separated the seeds from the cotton, something that used to be done by hand. The cotton gin made it easier to make money by growing large amounts of cotton. It was so successful that, by 1860, three-fourths of all the world's cotton was grown on southern plantations.

As cotton plantations spread, the South depended more than ever on large numbers of slaves. Most people in the North disliked slavery. They especially did not want to see slavery spread to new territories in the West. But white Southerners insisted on their rights to have slaves and to take them wherever they wanted.

The North and the South had other disagreements, as well. But nothing made them more suspicious of one another than their disagreement over slavery.

Plantation owners became wealthy as they used slave labor to plant and harvest cotton.

18.3 The Missouri Compromise

the Union: The United States as one country. In the Civil War, "the Union" also meant the government and the armies of the North.

compromise: a settlement of differences in which each side gives up some of its demands

In 1819, differences over slavery threatened to cause serious trouble between the North and the South. That year, the territory of Missouri asked to join **the Union** as a slave state. Settlers had been moving into Missouri and other western lands ever since the Louisiana Purchase in 1803. Many of them were Southern slave owners looking for new places to grow cotton.

When Missouri asked to join the Union, there were 11 slave states and 11 free states. Northerners did not want to upset this balance by letting in another slave state. They were afraid of giving the slave states too much power in Congress.

A fierce debate erupted in Congress. For a time, it seemed that the country might fall apart. Then, Henry Clay of Kentucky proposed a **compromise**.

Let Missouri join the Union as a slave state, Clay proposed, and, at the same time, let Maine join as a free state. That would keep the number of free and slave states equal. In addition, Clay suggested drawing a line across the map of the United States at latitude 36°30′ north. Except in Missouri, no slaves would ever be allowed north of that line.

Clay's idea became known as the *Missouri Compromise*. For 30 years, it kept the peace between North and South. But white Southerners were still afraid that, sooner or later, Northerners would try to interfere with their way of life.

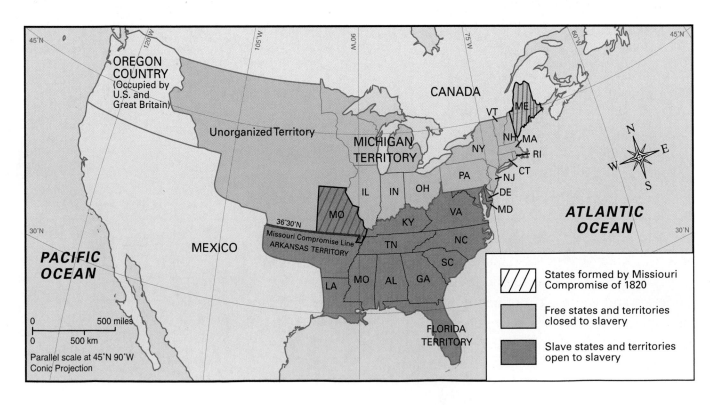

18.4 Abolitionists and the Underground Railroad

White Southerners became even more distrustful when groups of Northerners began speaking out against slavery. The fiercest opponents of slavery were called **abolitionists** because they wanted to abolish (end) slavery forever.

One of the leading abolitionists was Frederick Douglass, a former slave who had escaped to New York. Douglass gave powerful speeches against slavery. He also wrote a book telling about his terrible life as a slave. He convinced many Northerners that slavery had to end.

Opponents of slavery also organized the Underground Railroad to help slaves escape to freedom. The Underground Railroad was not really a railroad, and it was not under the ground. The name *Underground Railroad* was a metaphor for people who secretly helped escaping slaves when they reached a free state. They provided safe houses, called *stations*, where runaway slaves could hide and rest. They gave the slaves food and clothing. Then they guided them to the next station.

Many slaves traveled from station to station all the way to Canada. They were safer there, because even in free states they could be tracked down by Southern slave hunters and brought back to slavery.

One of the bravest "conductors" on the Underground Railroad was a former slave named Harriet Tubman. After escaping to the North herself, she risked her life by going back to the South 19 times and guiding hundreds of other slaves to freedom.

Most Northerners were not abolitionists or members of the Underground Railroad. But people who openly opposed slavery made white Southerners angry and fearful. More and more, the North and the South saw each other as enemies.

abolitionist: a person who wanted to see slavery ended (abolished) everywhere

The Underground Railroad helped runaway slaves escape to free territory.

18.5 The Compromise of 1850

The fight between the North and the South over western lands started again after the Mexican American War in the 1840s. As a result of the war, the United States gained a huge amount of territory in the West and Southwest, including California. In 1849, California asked to enter the Union as a free state. Southerners were furious because that would mean having more free states than slave states in Congress. Also, much of California was south of the 36°30′ line, where slavery should have been allowed. Some Southerners began to talk about removing their states from the Union.

Once again, Senator Henry Clay suggested a compromise. Called the *Compromise of 1850,* Clay's proposal included several laws.

To please the North, Congress admitted California into the Union as a free state and stopped the sale of slaves in the nation's capital, Washington, D.C.

To please the South, Congress said that people in New Mexico and Utah could vote on whether to allow slavery in their territories. In addition, Congress passed the Fugitive Slave Law. According to this law, officials in the North would help capture runaway ("fugitive") slaves.

The Fugitive Slave Law surprised and angered many Northerners. In Illinois, a rising political leader named Abraham Lincoln was "thunderstruck" (stunned) by the law. Some states passed laws forbidding officials to help the slave hunters. Opponents of slavery broke into jails to free captured runaways. And the Underground Railroad was busier than ever.

The Compromise of 1850 left many people unhappy. Southerners accused the North of wanting to destroy slavery. Northerners accused the South of wanting to spread slavery. Later, Abraham Lincoln would warn that the United States could not go on forever "half-slave and half-free."

In 1850, Henry Clay proposed a second compromise to keep peace between the North and the South.

18.6 "Bleeding Kansas"

Tensions between the North and the South became even worse as the territories of Kansas and Nebraska prepared to become states. Both territories were north of latitude 36°30′. According to the Missouri Compromise, both should have become free states. But, in 1854, Congress changed the rules by passing the Kansas-Nebraska Act.

This new law allowed people in the two territories to elect representatives to write state constitutions. The constitutions could either permit or forbid slavery.

Congress's action turned Kansas, the more southern territory, into a battleground over slavery. Both pro-slavery and anti-slavery settlers raced to Kansas so that they could vote in the election. The two sides attacked each other with weapons as well as words. For the first time, Americans were killing each other over slavery.

On election day, the pro-slavery settlers won by a huge margin. But those who were against slavery refused to accept the results. They claimed that slavery support-ers from Missouri had crossed into Kansas and voted illegally. Ignoring the election, they set up their own government in the town of Topeka.

The Kansas-Nebraska Act caused bitter fighting in Kansas between pro-slavery and anti-slavery forces.

In 1856, a pro-slavery mob entered the town of Lawrence in Kansas to arrest anti-slavery leaders. The mob burned a hotel and wrecked much of the town. This attack enraged an abolitionist named John Brown. Armed with swords, Brown and a small band of followers attacked and killed five settlers at Pottawatomie Creek.

The fighting in Kansas continued throughout the summer. Abolitionists called the conflict "Bleeding Kansas." By the time federal troops restored order, 200 people had died. For many Northerners and Southerners alike, "Bleeding Kansas" showed that the time for compromise was over.

Abraham Lincoln opposed the spread of slavery into new territories. When he was elected president, the South seceded from the Union.

secede: to reject the government of the United States and leave the Union

Confederates: supporters of the Confederacy, especially soldiers in the Confederate armies

18.7 The Election of Abraham Lincoln

By the time Americans voted for president in 1860, the Union was close to splitting apart over slavery. The Republican Party's candidate, Abraham Lincoln, promised to leave slavery alone in the South. But he was firmly against letting it spread into new territories. For most white Southerners, that was enough to make Lincoln an enemy. Disagreement over slavery helped to split the other major party, the Democrats, in two. With the vote against him divided among other candidates, Lincoln won the election without winning a single Southern state.

Lincoln's election alarmed Southern leaders. One by one, seven Southern states **seceded** from the Union without even waiting to see what Lincoln would do as president. To protect the right to own slaves, they joined together as the Confederate States of America, also called the *Confederacy*. Early in 1861, the Confederacy selected its own president, Jefferson Davis of Mississippi.

The Confederacy moved quickly to take over federal forts and other property in the South. Still, President Lincoln and many other Americans hoped that somehow the Union could be put back together.

Then, on April 12, 1861, **Confederates** attacked Fort Sumter, a federal fortress in the harbor of Charleston, South Carolina. For 33 hours, Southern cannons shelled the fort. Finally, the Union commander surrendered. The Civil War had begun.

In the South, church bells rang out in celebration. Soon, four more states joined the Confederacy. Most Southerners believed that the United States would let the South go without putting up much of a fight. Not many imagined how long, bloody, and terrible the Civil War would turn out to be.

18.8 Chapter Summary

In this chapter, you learned about the major events that led to the Civil War. You used the metaphor of a feuding brother and sister and compared their disagreement over loud music with the tensions between the North and the South.

The North and the South were especially divided over slavery. Most people in the North disliked slavery and wanted to keep it out of western lands. But white Southerners insisted on their right to keep slaves and to bring them into the West.

Twice, Congress tried to keep the peace through compromises. In the end, compromise failed because of events like the passage of the Fugitive Slave Law, the fighting in Kansas, and Abraham Lincoln's election as president.

After Lincoln's election, 11 Southern states formed a new country, the Confederacy. The Confederate attack on Fort Sumter shattered hopes that the Union could be restored peacefully. The Civil War was underway.

What was it like to be a soldier fighting in the bloody battles of the Civil War? How did the war affect people throughout the United States? You will find out in the next chapter.

On April 12, 1861, the South attacked Fort Sumter and the Civil War began.

For which side are these soldiers fighting?

For which side are these soldiers fighting?

What kind of weapon is this?

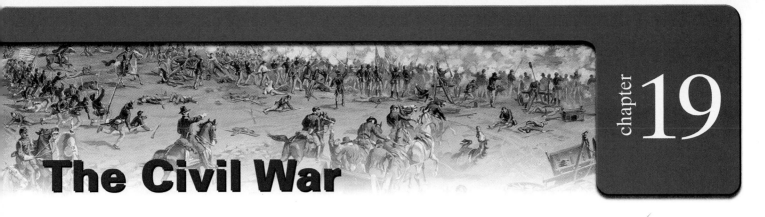

chapter 19

The Civil War

19.1 Introduction

In Chapter 18, you learned about the causes of the Civil War. In this chapter, you will learn about the war itself.

The Civil War killed more Americans than any other war in the history of the United States. What was it like to be involved in this terrible conflict? To find out, you will visit one of the war's most important battlefields.

In July, 1863, about 160,000 soldiers of the **Union** and the **Confederacy** fought at **Gettysburg** in Pennsylvania. This battle was one of the turning points in the war. As you visit this famous battlefield, you will discover how the two armies fought the Civil War. You will learn about the soldiers, the weapons they used, and the food they ate. You will read about the

horrors of combat (fighting) and the poor medical treatment that soldiers received. You will also find out what was happening on the **home front,** or areas away from the fighting.

Look at the figures of the Union and Confederate soldiers (right). You will use them to create character collages. Character collages are outlines of historical figures with words and drawings showing added details. As you read this chapter, think about what details you could add to the character collages to answer this question: What was life like for soldiers in the Civil War?

Gettysburg: A Soldier's Experience

19.2 The Union and Confederate Armies

In 1861, neither the North nor the South was ready to fight a war. Both faced the task of building strong armies.

Some men on both sides eagerly signed up to fight for money, adventure, or glory. Others needed more patriotic reasons to fight.

In the North, President Abraham Lincoln asked men to fight for the Union—in other words, to keep the United States

Each army in the war adopted special uniforms to prevent confusion on the battlefield.

together as one country. Later on, in 1863, Lincoln announced an order that freed slaves in states that were fighting against the Union. This order, called the **Emancipation Proclamation,** made many Northerners feel that they were fighting for freedom as well as for the Union.

White Southerners also felt that they were fighting for freedom—the freedom of states to leave the Union, and the freedom from control by the North. In addition, Confederate president Jefferson Davis called on Southerners to defend their homeland and way of life.

Even these reasons weren't enough. Before the war was over, both sides used unpopular **drafts** to get enough soldiers. In the end, millions of men fought in this conflict.

Most Union soldiers were poor farmers. About one-fourth were immigrants from Europe. In addition, about 180,000 African Americans fought for the Union. The Confederate armies consisted mostly of farmers and poor white men.

At first, groups of Civil War soldiers chose their own uniforms. This variety in clothing was confusing on the battlefield, and soldiers often shot at the wrong men. Soon, both armies adopted official uniforms. Union soldiers wore dark blue jackets, light blue pants, a blue cap, and black shoes. Confederate soldiers wore long gray shirts, light blue pants, and gray jackets.

Early in the war, new soldiers received little training. Some went into battle with no training at all. Gradually, training improved. Soldiers performed hundreds of hours of drills, learning how to march, to change directions on command, and to obey orders instantly.

Besides needing soldiers, both sides needed leaders for their troops (soldiers). Many of the nation's leading generals were Southerners who chose to fight for the Confederacy. The most famous was Robert E. Lee of Virginia. Out of loyalty to his home state, Lee turned down an offer to command the Union armies. Instead, he eventually took command of the Confederate armies. In the North, President Lincoln spent the early years of the war trying one general after another, looking for someone who could lead the Union armies to victory.

When the war began, soldiers on both sides looked forward to the coming battles. They thought that the war would be short and that little blood would be shed. They were wrong.

Emancipation Proclamation: A special order by President Lincoln that freed (emancipated) slaves in states that were fighting against the Union. After the Civil War, slavery was ended everywhere in the United States.

draft: the selection of people to serve in an army whether they wish to serve or not

19.3 The Battle of Gettysburg

During the first two years of the war, the Confederacy won many battles in the East. These victories kept the Union army from capturing the Confederate capital at Richmond, Virginia. Still, the fighting went on.

In 1863, Robert E. Lee decided that a Confederate victory in the North might convince the Union to ask for peace. Taking most of his army, Lee left Virginia and invaded Pennsylvania. A large Union army followed at a distance.

On July 1, a group of Confederate soldiers entered the town of Gettysburg, looking for a supply of shoes. To their surprise, Union soldiers were also in town. When fighting broke out, both armies rushed to Gettysburg.

Most of the Union army, commanded by General George G. Meade, lined up on a strip of high ground near Gettysburg. For two days, Meade's army beat back furious Confederate attacks.

On the third day, Lee decided on a brave gamble. He sent General George Pickett, with about 15,000 troops, to attack the middle of General Meade's defensive line. This was where the Union army was strongest.

Yelling and waving flags, Pickett's men crossed 400 yards of open fields and charged up the strip of high ground. Union bullets and cannonballs tore into them. Soon, the ground was covered with dead bodies. A few Confederates reached the top of the ridge, but Union soldiers drove them back. Pickett's Charge had failed.

The Battle of Gettysburg was a turning point of the war. Lee lost almost one-third of his army and was forced to return to Virginia. The Confederacy never again invaded the North.

On the third day of the Battle of Gettysburg, Confederate forces charged the Union lines. At the end of the fighting, thousands lay dead and wounded.

Rifles like this one were more accurate from greater distances than the old muskets. These new guns changed the tactics of war.

19.4 Military Tactics and Technology

Civil War armies suffered terrible losses in battles like Gettysburg. That was partly because of new technology (machines and weapons) and partly because of military tactics (ways of fighting).

In earlier wars, generals had often tried to win battles by attacking enemies head-on with larger armies. Both sides used this tactic during the Civil War. But new tactics and technology helped defenders to fight off large numbers of attackers. For example, defending troops usually chose high ground, from where they could fire down on attackers. For protection, defenders fired from trenches (ditches) or from behind walls made of earth. In contrast, attackers had to cross open ground under the deadly fire of the enemy's guns.

New weapons also helped defenders. As the war went on, more soldiers used rifles instead of muskets. Rifles were more accurate over longer distances. Now, defenders could shoot down attackers before they got close. Large, heavy guns like cannons, called *artillery,* were also deadlier against attackers than against defenders who had the protection of walls and trenches. For all these reasons, many bloody battles had no clear winner.

Other new technologies made this one of the bloodiest wars in American history. Railroads allowed armies to move quickly, especially in the North. The South was the first to use the telegraph to communicate over long distances. Union spies in hot-air balloons watched enemy movements. Finally, for the first time, Union and Confederate ships with iron sides battled each other at sea.

Pointed bullets like these punched through their targets more effectively than the old, round musket balls.

Shells from artillery guns shattered the lines of attacking troops.

19.5 Combat Conditions

Civil War combat (fighting) was a nightmare of horrors that is difficult to imagine.

Attacks on enemy positions usually started with fierce artillery shelling (bombing) that filled the air with deafening noise and clouds of stinging, black smoke. Soldiers could not see one another or their enemies. One soldier at Gettysburg told how, "the air, thick with smoke...almost suffocated the troops. ... Through the murk [darkness] we heard hoarse commands, the bursting of shells, cries of agony."

Then the order came to move forward. Soldiers walked or ran in rows, elbow to elbow, 13 inches from the row in front. Drums beat a pace of 110 steps per minute. Bullets and artillery shells tore into the attackers, ripping off arms, legs, and heads. Troops stumbled over the fallen bodies of their fellow soldiers.

Near the enemy lines, the attacking troops paused to fasten bayonets (long blades) onto their rifles. Then, they dashed toward men who were firing at them from trenches or from behind walls and fences. When they got close, men fought face-to-face, firing their guns from just a few feet away. They usually had time for only one shot. Then, they used their bayonets and the butts of their rifles to spear or club their enemy. If they lost their rifles or ran out of bullets, they beat the enemy with stones, fence posts, or fists.

When battles ended, thousands of soldiers on both sides lay dead. Wounded men cried out in thirst and pain. Many of them died before they could be helped.

19.6 Medical Care

Medical care during the Civil War was very poor. More than 200,000 soldiers died from injuries they received in battle. More than twice as many died from disease.

Civil War doctors had too little knowledge to cure many of the wounded and sick soldiers. They had little understanding of what caused infections. **Surgeons** operated in dirty tents and rarely washed their hands or medical instruments (tools). As a result, infections spread from one man to another. Often, surgeons ran out of medicine and anesthetics (drugs used to make patients unconscious during operations). Many screaming soldiers had wounded legs sawed off with only a swallow of whiskey to ease the pain.

Civil War surgeons had only simple instruments in their medical kits. They used bone saws for removing wounded arms and legs before infections could spread and kill the injured soldiers. They used a tool called a *bullet probe* to remove bullets, a *scalpel* (a razor-sharp knife) to cut through flesh, and tight bandages called *tourniquets* to stop bleeding. Devices called *splints* kept broken bones from moving. Special pill molds were used to make pills.

Sometimes, especially in the South, doctors didn't have even basic tools and medicines. They used tree bark for splints, treated burns with cucumbers, and prescribed geranium—a flowering plant—for soldiers with diarrhea.

Diseases spread rapidly in the soldiers' crowded, filthy camps. No one knew about germs. Soldiers threw their garbage on the ground, attracting rats and flies. They drank dirty water. Sometimes they camped near germ-infested swamps.

Doctors often did not know how to treat certain kinds of sickness. Some doctors gave soldiers poisonous "medicines."

Thousands of women in both the North and South tried to ease the suffering of sick and wounded soldiers. Clara Barton, who started the American Red Cross, was one of the many women whose bravery and kindness won the soldiers' respect.

surgeon: a doctor who performs operations, such as cutting into the body to remove a bullet, or removing an infected leg

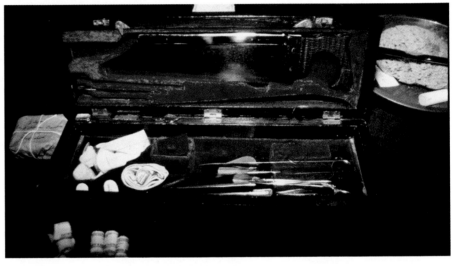

Equipped with only simple surgical instruments like these, doctors tried bravely to save the lives of badly wounded soldiers.

19.7 Food and Drink

Poor food may have helped to cause some of the men's health problems. It certainly made soldiers on both sides unhappy.

Soldiers had to carry food that would not quickly spoil. Usually, they ate beef and pork that was pickled (preserved) in salt water. Pickled meat could last for a very long time, but it was so salty that men had to soak it in water for several hours. Then, they fried the meat in thick grease.

For vegetables, soldiers carried cakes of dried beans, onions, turnips, carrots, and beets. Sometimes these cakes contained roots, stalks, and leaves.

Union soldiers were given dry biscuits made of flour and water, called *hardtack*. Hardtack was like a thick, unsalted, hard cracker. Often, it was filled with worms and weevils (a type of beetle). Union soldiers also carried coffee beans for making their favorite hot drink. Confederates often boiled a root called *chicory* to make a coffee-like drink.

Men on both sides foraged (searched) for fresh food and water in the countryside. When Confederate armies ran short of supplies, soldiers had to find their own food to keep from starving. Both Union and Confederate soldiers hunted, picked berries, and took fruit from orchards. They stole cows, pigs, and chickens. When they could, they raided each other's supplies.

Bad food only increased the misery of the soldiers on the battlefield.

19.8   Conditions on the Home Front

In letters and newspapers, soldiers learned about hardships and unhappiness on the home front.

In the North, many people were angry about the draft. Draft laws allowed rich men to hire other men to take their places in the army. Wealthy men could also escape the draft by paying the government $300. This seemed so unfair that draft riots (violent protests) broke out.

In 1863, a mob of white workers destroyed the draft offices in New York City, burned many other buildings, and attacked innocent African Americans. The rioters did not want to go to war to free slaves. They also believed that African Americans were taking their jobs. More than 100 people died in the New York riots.

Southerners were especially affected by the war because most of the fighting took place in the South. As the war went on, the South suffered shortages of food and other goods. In addition, many Southerners lost property when Union armies marched through the territory. Sometimes, soldiers stole books, silver, and jewelry. Sometimes they burned houses, killed farm animals, and set crops on fire. To survive, some families had to eat meat from mules and rats.

Despite causing hardships, the war opened up new opportunities for women in both the North and the South. With so many men in the army, women took on jobs as schoolteachers, nurses, and secretaries. Many worked in factories, making equipment for the armies. But men and women alike missed each other and hoped for the day when families would be together again.

General William Sherman marched through the South, ruining much of the property that lay in his path. This destruction caused terrible shortages on the Southern home front.

On April 9, 1865, General Robert E. Lee surrendered to General Ulysses S. Grant at Appomattox Court House.

19.9   From Gettysburg to Appomattox

At almost the same time as the Battle of Gettysburg, the Union also won an important victory in the West. Soldiers under General Ulysses S. Grant captured Vicksburg, a Confederate fort that overlooked the Mississippi River. The capture of Vicksburg gave the Union control of the river, splitting the Confederacy in half. It also made General Grant a hero throughout the North.

In 1864, President Lincoln asked Grant to take over command of the entire Union army. Grant planned to end the war by attacking the South from two directions. He ordered General William Sherman to march from Tennessee through Georgia to the Atlantic Ocean. Meanwhile, Grant led an army into Virginia to defeat Robert E. Lee and capture Richmond.

Grant knew that the North had more men and equipment than the South. He believed that the way to win the war was to keep attacking, no matter how many men he lost.

So many men were killed in Grant's attacks that some people called him a "butcher." But his idea worked. Many Confederates began to feel that the war was lost and left the army to go home. On April 3, 1865, the Union army marched into Richmond.

Six days later, on April 9, Lee surrendered to Grant at Appomattox Court House in Virginia. Grant was generous in victory. He allowed Confederate soldiers to return home with their horses. He also ordered Union troops to share their food with starving Southerners.

After four years of terrible fighting, the soldiers finally laid down their weapons. The Civil War was over.

19.10 Chapter Summary

In this chapter, you learned about the Civil War. You used character collages of Union and Confederate soldiers to describe what life was like for those who fought in this terrible war.

By visiting the battlefield at Gettysburg, you learned about the lives of Civil War soldiers. You learned about their weapons, their food, and the poor medical care they received. You learned about how they fought and why so many of them died. You also learned about some of the hardships that people suffered on the home front. Finally, you learned how the Union won the war.

The Civil War made the United States one country again, and it brought an end to slavery. But there were many more changes ahead for the reunited nation. And African Americans' journey toward equality was only beginning.

The United States today is a far different place than it was when the Civil War ended in 1865. In the next chapter, you will read about some of the changes that brought the United States into the 20th century.

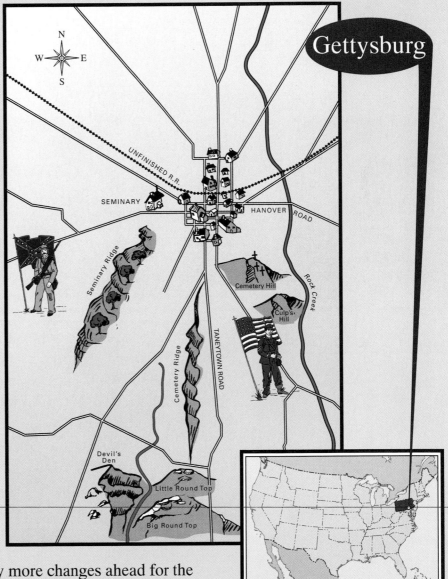

The Battle of Gettysburg was the turning point of the Civil War. The Confederates lost. Never again was the South able to seriously threaten to invade the North.

Map.(1961) by Jasper Johns. Oil on Canvas 8'6"x10'3"x3 1/", The Museum of Modern Art, New York. Gift of Mr. & Mrs. Robert C. Scull. Photograph
© 1999 The Museum of Modern Art. © Jasper Johns/Licensed by VAGA, New York, NY

How did the United States
gain this territory?

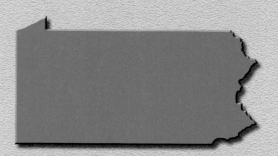

What famous documents were
signed in a city located in this state?

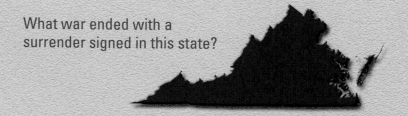

What war ended with a
surrender signed in this state?

Industrialization and Modern America

20.1 Introduction

In Chapter 19, you read about the Civil War. In this chapter, you will learn about events that have dramatically changed the United States since the end of the Civil War.

In the 1800s, most Americans still lived in the countryside. Often, their lives were very similar to those of their grandparents. Then, the **Industrial Revolution** brought hundreds of new inventions and new ways of making products. As a result, more and more Americans lived in cities and worked in factories and offices instead of working on farms.

Changes came even faster during the **20th century**. Telephones, cars, and airplanes became common. Radio and television were invented. By the end of the century, computers and other inventions had created the **Information Age**. Now people all over the world could share news and information instantly. The world was becoming a "global village."

The 20th century was also a time of great wars. Millions of people died in the conflicts known as **World War I, World War II,** and the **Cold War**.

Besides changes and wars, two other events helped to shape America in the 20th century. These events were the **Great Depression** and the **Civil Rights movement**.

Look at the timeline on this page. As you read this chapter, think about how you might use a timeline to organize the events you read about. When did each event happen? Which one is still going on right now?

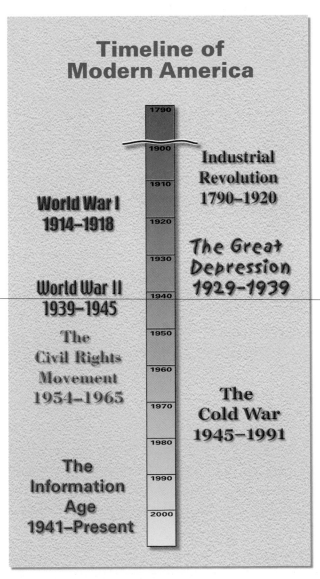

Timeline of Modern America

1790

1900

World War I
1914–1918

Industrial Revolution
1790–1920

1910

1920

The Great Depression
1929–1939

1930

World War II
1939–1945

1940

The Civil Rights Movement
1954–1965

1950

1960

The Cold War
1945–1991

1970

1980

The Information Age
1941–Present

1990

2000

20.2 The Industrial Revolution

Huge cities and great construction projects, like this bridge, were part of the Industrial Revolution.

After the Civil War, the Industrial Revolution changed the way Americans lived and worked. The Industrial Revolution refers to a time of new inventions and new ways of making products. During this time, new industries, or businesses, caused such dramatic changes that together they are called a "revolution."

The Industrial Revolution began in the early 1800s, but it picked up speed after the Civil War. Before the Industrial Revolution, most Americans lived on farms or in small towns. They rarely traveled far from home. When they did, they were likely to walk or to ride a horse.

By the mid 1800s, this slow pace of life was already changing. Canals, steamboats, and railroads allowed people and goods to move faster over longer distances. Many of Americans moved to cities and took jobs in factories and offices.

Changes came faster and faster after the Civil War. The first transcontinental railroad was completed in 1869. Now people and goods could travel across the entire United States in a week. Most Americans used to grow their own food and make their own clothes. Now they bought products that were made in huge quantities by machines and sold in stores. More and more workers spent long days in dirty, unsafe factories.

The Industrial Revolution continued into the 20th century, bringing inventions such as electric lights and telephones into people's homes. Cars replaced horses and carriages. Huge buildings called *skyscrapers* were built in cities. Everything seemed to be getting bigger and faster.

20.3 World War I

In the summer of 1914, World War I broke out in Europe. Because of the Industrial Revolution, armies were bigger than ever before, and weapons were more deadly. When the war ended four years later, more than nine million soldiers were dead. So were five million ordinary citizens.

The war started because of competition and mistrust between several European countries. For years, various nations had built up their armies and navies. As tensions grew, allies promised to fight together if war broke out. One group of allies included Germany, Italy, and Austria-Hungary. Another included Russia, France, and Great Britain. In 1914, a disagreement between Russia and Austria-Hungary led to threats of war. Soon, the fight between Austria and Russia involved their allies as well. Eventually, more than 30 countries, including the United States, fought in World War I.

Soldiers on both sides fought from ditches called *trenches*. Armies fought for weeks and months just to move their trenches a few yards and claim a little more land. New types of weapons, such as machine guns, tanks, and poison gas, killed soldiers by the thousands.

During World War I, men spent endless months in muddy trenches, waiting for orders to attack.

In 1917, the United States entered the war and helped France and Great Britain to defeat Germany and its allies. After the war, France and Great Britain insisted on a treaty that blamed and punished Germany. The treaty took land away from Germany and demanded that Germany pay huge amounts of money for the damage caused by the war. This treaty led to great anger in Germany. In time, it would help to cause World War II.

During the Great Depression, families lost almost everything they had.

20.4 The Great Depression

After World War I, the U.S. economy grew steadily. Suddenly, the good times came to an end. Beginning in 1929, America entered the period of hardship known as the Great Depression.

During the 1920s, the strong economy encouraged many Americans to put their money into stocks. Stocks are shares in the ownership of companies. When companies do well, the value of stocks goes up. Then, when people sell their stocks, they make money. Stocks are bought and sold on the stock market.

On October 29, 1929, the stock market "crashed." Prices of stocks suddenly dropped sharply. People tried to get rid of their stocks. That only made prices drop even faster. And when people went to banks to take their money out, it wasn't there. The banks had loaned the money out and had no way of getting it back. As a result, many Americans lost all of their savings. Soon, banks were closing everywhere.

The disaster continued throughout the 1930s. Workers lost their jobs because companies had no money to pay them. People lost their homes and ended up living in tents and shacks. In addition, much of the farmland in the central United States was ruined by a terrible drought (a long period without rain). With no crops to sell, farmers couldn't keep their farms. More than a million families lost their land.

In fighting the Great Depression, the national government grew dramatically. Today, it continues to play a much larger role in the economy than it did in the 1920s. In addition, programs like Social Security, which helps to protect older people from being poor, began as a result of the Great Depression.

20.5 World War II

In 1939, war again broke out in Europe. This new war, World War II, eventually involved more than 50 countries. It also changed the role of the United States in the world.

World War II began when the leader of Germany, Adolf Hitler, tried to take over other countries in Europe. Hitler told Germans that the treaty that ended World War I was unfair. He said that Germany should take back the land it had lost and gain new territory besides. Hitler also preached hatred against people whom he saw as enemies. Among them were the Jewish people of Europe.

Within three years, Germany had conquered almost all of Europe and North Africa. Hitler still wanted to defeat both the Soviet Union and Great Britain.

Meanwhile, one of Germany's allies, Japan, wanted to conquer lands in Asia as well as islands in the Pacific Ocean. In December 1941, Japan launched a surprise attack on American ships and planes in Hawaii, at Pearl Harbor. The attack brought the United States into the war on the side of Britain and the Soviet Union.

By 1945, Hitler was defeated. Japan surrendered after the United States used a terrible new weapon, the atomic bomb, on two Japanese cities.

World War II was the most terrible war in history. More than 50 million people died, including 6 million Jews who were murdered by Hitler's followers. Much of Europe was in ruins.

The war left the United States and the Soviet Union as the world's most powerful nations. From now on, the United States would remain involved in events all around the world.

During World War II, the United States had to fight on two fronts. The country fought Germany in Europe and Japan in Asia. Here, U.S. soldiers raise the flag on Iwo Jima, after a terrible battle against the Japanese.

Throughout the Cold War, the United States and the Soviet Union each raced to produce the most nuclear weapons.

nuclear weapons: Weapons that release huge amounts of energy contained in the nuclei (centers) of atoms. Nuclear weapons also release deadly *radiation* (a form of energy).

20.6 The Cold War

A new kind of war began after 1945. It involved the two "superpowers": the United States and the Soviet Union. Both countries supported allies around the world who fought "hot" wars with weapons, but the United States and the Soviet Union never fought each other directly. As a result, their tension was called the *Cold War*.

The Cold War was a struggle over types of government and ways of life. The United States favored a democratic form of government and economic freedom. The Soviet Union favored a system called *Communism*. Communism involves control of the economy by the government. In addition, the Soviet style of government gives people very little freedom.

Both sides wanted other countries to follow their example. The Soviet Union supported Communists who tried to take power in other countries. The United States was determined to keep Communism from spreading.

Many people died in wars between Communists and non-Communists around the world, such as in Viet Nam in Southeast Asia. In these wars, the United States and the Soviet Union supported opposite sides with money, weapons, and sometimes, soldiers.

In addition, both superpowers feared an attack from the other. So, they raced to build up their supplies of **nuclear weapons**. Eventually, the two countries had enough of these weapons to destroy the world many times.

The Cold War ended when the Soviet Union fell apart in 1991. But its effects are still felt today. Nuclear weapons have spread to several countries. There is still a danger that they will be used someday. And the money and lives that were spent on the Cold War cannot be recovered.

20.7 The Civil Rights Movement

The Civil War ended slavery in the United States, but African Americans continued to face discrimination, or unfair treatment. In the 1950s and 1960s, more and more people joined together to end discrimination. This struggle for equal rights is called the *Civil Rights movement*.

The Civil Rights movement began as a fight against **segregation** in the South. Since the late 1800s, laws and customs in southern states segregated, or separated, whites and blacks. Whites had their own schools, restaurants, hotels, and parks. African Americans couldn't drink from whites' water fountains or use the same swimming pools. They were forced to sit in the backs of buses and theaters. And the facilities that were reserved for them were never as good as those that whites used.

In the 1950s, civil rights leaders organized protests against segregation. African Americans marched in the streets. They demanded to be served in restaurants. They refused to ride in the backs of buses. Often, civil rights workers were attacked by whites who supported segregation. Some were even killed.

Martin Luther King, Jr. was one of the most important civil rights leaders. King believed in nonviolent, or peaceful, protest. His bravery and powerful speeches touched the hearts of millions of people. In 1963, King led more than 250,000 people in a march on Washington. He thrilled many Americans by describing his dream of a day when would be treated equally and with respect.

The Civil Rights movement resulted in a number of laws that protect the rights of all Americans. It also inspired other groups to fight against unfair treatment, such as Mexican Americans) and women.

segregation: The separation of people, especially by race. Segregation in the South was enforced partly by laws and partly by customs.

Martin Luther King, Jr. (left) and Malcolm X (right) devoted their lives to ending discrimination against African Americans.

20.8 The Information Age

After World War II, new inventions, such as television and computers, changed the way people communicate and share information. This change was so dramatic that the period from 1941 to today has been called the start of the Information Age.

During the 1950s, television replaced radio as the most popular form of entertainment in people's homes. It also became a major source of information. By the 1990s, more Americans got their news by watching TV than by reading newspapers.

Information from around the world is available to anyone with a computer and Internet access.

The invention of computers added to the changes of the Information Age. At first, computers were huge machines that filled entire rooms. By the 1960s, many businesses were using large computers to do the work of many people accurately and quickly.

Engineers kept working to make computers smaller, faster, and more powerful. In the 1980s, companies began selling personal computers that could fit on top of a desk. Now, ordinary people could use the power of computers to access information at work and at home. Tiny computers also made their way into thousands of other products, such as video-cassette recorders (VCRs).

In the 1990s, the Information Age picked up speed with the development of the Internet and the World Wide Web. The Internet allowed computers to communicate and share information. The Web brought pictures and sounds to the Internet and made using it easier. Now people could send instant messages around the world and obtain information from millions of sources. Many new jobs were created in which people use computers to work with information. No one knows what other changes everyone will see as the Information Age continues.

20.9 Chapter Summary

In this chapter, you learned about major events that changed the lives of Americans since the end of the Civil War. You used a timeline to organize these events from the Industrial Revolution through the 20th century.

The Industrial Revolution introduced new inventions and changed the way products were made. It also changed where Americans lived and worked.

Partly because of the Industrial Revolution, wars became more terrible than ever before. In the 20th century, two great wars involved countries all around the world. During the Cold War, the United States and the Soviet Union developed weapons that were powerful enough to destroy the world.

Between the two world wars, the Great Depression created great hardship for millions of Americans. The national government became larger and more important as a result of the Great Depression.

Beginning in the 1950s, two other events changed American life. The Civil Rights movement promoted equality for all Americans. The start of the Information Age brought instant communication and the power to work quickly with large amounts of information. The Information Age will continue to change American life in the years to come.

Space exploration helped change the way Americans saw themselves and the world.

The Declaration of Independence

In Congress, July 4, 1776
The unanimous Declaration of the
thirteen united States of America

Preamble (Introduction)

The Preamble explains why the Declaration was written. The Delaration is a statement to the world that explains why the colonies believe they should be independent.

Statement of Human Rights

This section boldly states that all people have rights that no government can take away. Three of these rights are life, liberty, and the pursuit of happiness. If a government does not respect these rights, the people have the right to change the government. By his actions, the King has failed to respect the colonists' rights.

Statement of Charges Against the King

This section lists more than 20 ways that the King has violated the colonists' rights. By interfering with laws, the King has taken away the colonists' right to govern themselves. Some of his laws have prevented the colonists from pursuing happiness in their own way. And by sending soldiers to fight the colonists, he has even threatened their right to life.

When in the Course of human events it becomes necessary for one people to dissolve the political bands which have connected them with another and to assume among the powers of the earth, the separate and equal station to which the Laws of Nature and of Nature's God entitle them, a decent respect to the opinions of mankind requires that they should declare the causes which impel them to the separation.

We hold these truths to be self-evident, that all men are created equal, that they are endowed by their Creator with certain unalienable Rights, that among these are Life, Liberty and the pursuit of Happiness. —That to secure these rights, Governments are instituted among Men, deriving their just powers from the consent of the governed, —That whenever any Form of Government becomes destructive of these ends, it is the Right of the People to alter or to abolish it, and to institute new Government, laying its foundation on such principles and organizing its powers in such form, as to them shall seem most likely to effect their Safety and Happiness. Prudence, indeed, will dictate that Governments long established should not be changed for light and transient causes; and accordingly all experience hath shewn that mankind are more disposed to suffer, while evils are sufferable than to right themselves by abolishing the forms to which they are accustomed. But when a long train of abuses and usurpations, pursuing invariably the same Object evinces a design to reduce them under absolute Despotism, it is their right, it is their duty, to throw off such Government, and to provide new Guards for their future security. —Such has been the patient sufferance of these Colonies; and such is now the necessity which constrains them to alter their former Systems of Government. The history of the present King of Great Britain is a history of repeated injuries and usurpations, all having in direct object the establishment of an absolute Tyranny over these States. To prove this, let Facts be submitted to a candid world.

He has refused his Assent to Laws, the most wholesome and necessary for the public good.

He has forbidden his Governors to pass Laws of immediate and pressing importance, unless suspended in their operation till his Assent should be obtained; and when so suspended, he has utterly neglected to attend to them.

He has refused to pass other Laws for the accommodation of large districts of people, unless those people would relinquish the right of Representation in the Legislature, a right inestimable to them and formidable to tyrants only.

He has called together legislative bodies at places unusual, uncomfortable, and distant from the depository of their Public Records, for the sole purpose of fatiguing them into compliance with his measures.

He has dissolved Representative Houses repeatedly, for opposing with manly firmness his invasions on the rights of the people.

He has refused for a long time, after such dissolutions, to cause others to be elected, whereby the Legislative Powers, incapable of Annihilation, have returned to the People at large for their exercise; the State remaining in the mean time exposed to all the dangers of invasion from without, and convulsions within.

He has endeavoured to prevent the population of these States; for that purpose obstructing the Laws for Naturalization of Foreigners; refusing to pass others to encourage their migrations hither, and raising the conditions of new Appropriations of Lands.

He has obstructed the Administration of Justice by refusing his Assent to Laws for establishing Judiciary Powers.

He has made Judges dependent on his Will alone for the tenure of their offices, and the amount an payment of their salaries.

He has erected a multitude of New Offices, and sent hither swarms of Officers to harass our people and eat out their substance.

He has kept among us, in times of peace, Standing Armies without the Consent of our legislatures.

He has affected to render the Military independent of and superior to the Civil Power.

He has combined with others to subject us to a jurisdiction foreign to our constitution, and unacknowledged by our laws; giving his Assent to their Acts of pretended Legislation:

For quartering large bodies of armed troops among us:

For protecting them, by a mock Trial from punishment for any Murders which they should commit on the Inhabitants of these States:

For cutting off our Trade with all parts of the world:

For imposing Taxes on us without our Consent:
For depriving us in many cases, of the benefit of Trial by Jury:

For transporting us beyond Seas to be tried for pretended offences:

For abolishing the free System of English Laws in a neighbouring Province, establishing therein an Arbitrary government, and enlarging its Boundaries so as to render it at once an example and fit instrument for introducing the same absolute rule into these Colonies

For taking away our Charters, abolishing our most valuable Laws and altering fundamentally the Forms of our Governments:

For suspending our own Legislatures, and declaring themselves invested with power to legislate for us in all cases whatsoever.
He has abdicated Government here, by declaring us out of his Protection and waging War against us.

He has plundered our seas, ravaged our Coasts burnt our towns, and destroyed the lives of our people.

He is at this time transporting large Armies of foreign Mercenaries to compleat the works of death, desolation, and tyranny, already begun with circumstances of Cruelty & Perfidy scarcely paralleled in the most barbarous ages, and totally unworthy the Head of a civilized nation.

He has constrained our fellow Citizens taken Captive on the high Seas to bear Arms against their Country, to become the executioners of their friends and Brethren, or to fall themselves by their Hands.

He has excited domestic insurrections amongst us, and has endeavoured to bring on the inhabitants of our frontiers, the merciless Indian Savages whose known rule of warfare, is an undistinguished destruction of all ages, sexes and conditions.

In every stage of these Oppressions We have Petitioned for Redress in the most humble terms: Our repeated Petitions have been answered only by repeated injury. A Prince, whose character is thus marked by every act which may define a Tyrant, is unfit to be the ruler of a free people.

Nor have We been wanting in attentions to our British brethren. We have warned them from time to time of attempts by their legislature to extend an unwarrantable jurisdiction over us. We have reminded them of the circumstances of our emigration and settlement here. We have appealed to their native justice and magnanimity, and we have conjured them by the ties of our common kindred. to disavow these usurpations, which would inevitably interrupt our connections and correspondence. They too have been deaf to the voice of justice and of consanguinity. We must, therefore, acquiesce in the necessity, which denounces our Separation, and hold them, as we hold the rest of mankind, Enemies in War, in Peace Friends.

We, therefore, the Representatives of the United States of America, in General Congress, Assembled, appealing to the Supreme Judge of the world for the rectitude of our intentions, do, in the Name, and by Authority of the good People of these Colonies, solemnly publish and declare, That these United Colonies are, and of Right ought to be Free and Independent States, that they are Absolved from all Allegiance to the British Crown, and that all political connection between them and the State of Great Britain, is and ought to be totally dissolved; and that as Free and Independent States, they have full Power to levy War, conclude Peace contract Alliances, establish Commerce, and to do all other Acts and Things which Independent States may of right do. —And for the support of this Declaration, with a firm reliance on the protection of Divine Providence, we mutually pledge to each other our Lives, our Fortunes and our sacred Honor.

John Hancock

New Hampshire:
Josiah Bartlett, William Whipple, Matthew Thornton

Massachusetts:
John Hancock, Samuel Adams, John Adams, Robert Treat Paine, Elbridge Gerry

Rhode Island:
Stephen Hopkins, William Ellery

Connecticut:
Roger Sherman, Samuel Huntington, William Williams, Oliver Wolcott

New York:
William Floyd, Philip Livingston, Francis Lewis, Lewis Morris

The Government's Failure to Answer the Colonists' Complaints

This section states that the colonists have tried many times to solve their problems with Britain peacefully. Both the King and the British government have failed to answer their complaints. For this reason, the colonists have no choice except to break away from Britain.

Statement of Independence

This section declares the colonies' independence. The writers of the Declaration emphasize that they are acting as the representatives of the people. As the Preamble stated, it is the people who have the right to form a new government. The colonies are now separate countries that have all the powers and rights of other nations.

New Jersey:
Richard Stockton, John Witherspoon, Francis Hopkinson, John Hart, Abraham Clark

Pennsylvania:
Robert Morris, Benjamin Rush, Benjamin Franklin, John Morton, George Clymer, James Smith, George Taylor, James Wilson, George Ross

Delaware:
Caesar Rodney, George Read, Thomas McKean

Maryland:
Samuel Chase, William Paca, Thomas Stone, Charles Carroll of Carrollton

Virginia:
George Wythe, Richard Henry Lee, Thomas Jefferson, Benjamin Harrison, Thomas Nelson, Jr., Francis Lightfoot Lee, Carter Braxton

North Carolina:
William Hooper, Joseph Hewes, John Penn

South Carolina:
Edward Rutledge, Thomas Heyward, Jr., Thomas Lynch, Jr., Arthur Middleton

Georgia:
Button Gwinnett, Lyman Hall, George Walton

Constitution of the United States

Preamble
The Preamble says that the Constitution receives its authority from the people of the United States. The people agree to form a government to protect their rights and provide for safety and order.

Article I: The Legislative Branch
The government's lawmaking branch is Congress, made up of a Senate and a House of Representatives. The comments below point out some of the specific powers of this branch.

Representation in the House: In the House, the number of representatives for each state depends on the number of people who live in the state.

Checks and balances: Impeachment. Only the House has the power to impeach federal officials.
Representation in the Senate: Each state is represented by two Senators.

W e the People of the United States, in Order to form a more perfect Union, establish Justice, insure domestic Tranquility, provide for the common defence, promote the general Welfare, and secure the Blessings of Liberty to ourselves and our Posterity, do ordain and establish this Constitution for the United States of America.

ARTICLE I
Section 1. All legislative Powers herein granted shall be vested in a Congress of the United States, which shall consist of a Senate and House of Representatives.

Section 2. The House of Representatives shall be composed of Members chosen every second Year by the People of the several States, and the Electors in each State shall have the Qualifications requisite for Electors of the most numerous Branch of the State Legislature.

No Person shall be a Representative who shall not have attained to the Age of twenty five Years, and been seven Years a Citizen of the United States, and who shall not, when elected, be an Inhabitant of that State in which he shall be chosen.

[Representatives and direct Taxes shall be apportioned among the several States which may be included within this Union, according to their respective Numbers, which shall be determined by adding to the whole Number of free Persons, including those bound to Service for a Term of Years, and excluding Indians not taxed, three fifths of all other Persons.][1] The actual Enumeration shall be made within three Years after the first Meeting of thc Congress of the United States, and within every subsequent Term of ten Years, in such Manner as they shall by Law direct. The number of Representatives shall not exceed one for every thirty Thousand, but each State shall have at Least one Representative; and until such enumeration shall be made, the State of New Hampshire shall be entitled to choose three, Massachusetts eight, Rhode-Island and Providence Plantations one, Connecticut five, New-York six, New Jersey four, Pennsylvania eight, Delaware one, Maryland six, Virginia ten, North Carolina five, South Carolina five, and Georgia three.

When vacancies happen in the Representation from any State, the Executive Authority thereof shall issue Writs of Election to fill such Vacancies.

The House of Representatives shall choose their Speaker and other Officers; and shall have the sole Power of Impeachment.

Section 3. The Senate of the United States shall be composed of two Senators from each State, [chosen by the Legislature thereof,][2] for six Years; and each Senator shall have one Vote.

Immediately after they shall be assembled in Consequence of the first Election, they shall be divided as equally as may be into three Classes. The Seats of the Senators of the first Class shall be vacated at the Expiration of thc second Year, of the second Class at the Expiration of the fourth Year, and of the third Class at the Expiration of the sixth Year, so that one third may be chosen every second Year; [and if Vacancies happen by Resignation, or otherwise, during the Recess of the Legislature of any State, the Executive thereof may make temporary Appointments until the next Meeting of the Legislature, which shall then

1. Changed by Section 2 of the Fourteenth Amendment
2. Changed by the Seventeenth Amendment

fill such Vacancies.] [3]

No Person shall be a Senator who shall not have attained to the Age of thirty Years, and been nine Years a Citizen of the United States, and who shall not, when elected, be an Inhabitant of that State for which he shall be chosen.

The Vice President of the United States shall be President of the Senate, but shall have no Vote, unless they be equally divided.

The Senate shall choose their other Officers, and also a President pro tempore, in the Absence of the Vice President, or when he shall exercise the Office of President of the United States.

The Senate shall have the sole Power to try all Impeachments. When sitting for that Purpose, they shall be on Oath or Affirmation. When the President of the United States is tried, the Chief Justice shall preside: And no Person shall be convicted without the Concurrence of two thirds of the Members present.

Checks and balances: Impeachment. Only the Senate has the power to put impeached officials on trial.

Judgment in Cases of Impeachment shall not extend further than to removal from Office, and disqualification to hold and enjoy any Office of honor, Trust or Profit under the United States: but the Party convicted shall nevertheless be liable and subject to Indictment, Trial, Judgment and Punishment, according to Law.

Section 4. The Times, Places and Manner of holding Elections for Senators and Representatives, shall be prescribed in each State by the Legislature thereof; but the Congress may at any time by Law make or alter such Regulations, except as to the Places of choosing Senators.

The Congress shall assemble at least once in every Year, and such Meeting shall be [on the first Monday in December,][4] unless they shall by Law appoint a different Day.

Section 5. Each House shall be the Judge of the Elections, Returns and Qualifications of its own Members, and a Majority of each shall constitute a Quorum to do Business, but a smaller Number may adjourn from day to day, and may be authorized to compel the Attendance of absent Members, in such Manner, and under such Penalties as each House may provide.

Each House may determine the Rules of its Proceedings, punish its Members for disorderly Behaviour, and, with the Concurrence of two thirds, expel a Member.

Each House shall keep a Journal of its Proceedings, and from time to time publish the same, excepting such Parts as may in their Judgment require Secrecy; and the Yeas and Nays of the Members of either House on any question shall, at the Desire of one fifth of those Present, be entered on the Journal.

Neither House, during the Session of Congress, shall, without the Consent of the other, adjourn for more than three days, nor to any other Place than that in which the two Houses shall be sitting.

Section 6. The Senators and Representatives shall receive a Compensation for their Services, to be ascertained by law, and paid out of the Treasury of the United States. They shall in all Cases, except Treason, Felony and Breach of the Peace, be privileged from Arrest during their Attendance at the Session of their respective Houses, and in going to and returning from the same; and for any Speech or Debate in either House, they shall not be questioned in any other Place.

No Senator or Representative shall, during the Time for which he was elected, be appointed

4. Changed by Section 2 of the Twentieth Amendment

to any civil Office under the Authority of the United States, which shall have been created, or the Emoluments whereof shall have been encreased during such time; and no Person holding any Office under the United States, shall be a Member of either House during his Continuance in Office.

Proposing laws: Either house of Congress can propose and vote on new laws. Only the House can propose new taxes.

Section 7. All Bills for raising Revenue shall originate in the House of Representatives; but the Senate may propose or concur with Amendments as on other Bills.

Every Bill which shall have passed the House of Representatives and the Senate, shall, before it becomes a Law, be presented to the President of the United States; If he approve he shall sign it, but if not he shall return it, with his Objections to that House in which it shall have originated, who shall enter the Objections at large on their Journal, and proceed to reconsider it. If after such Reconsideration two thirds of that House shall agree to pass the Bill, it shall be sent, together with the Objections, to the other House, by which it shall likewise be reconsidered, and if approved by two thirds of that House, it shall become a Law. But in all such Cases the Votes of both Houses shall be determined by Yeas and Nays, and the Names of the Persons voting for and against the Bill shall be entered on the Journal of each House respectively. If any Bill shall not be returned by the President within ten Days (Sundays excepted) after it shall have been presented to him, the Same shall be a Law, in like Manner as if he had signed it, unless the Congress by their Adjournment prevent its Return, in which Case it shall not be a Law.

Checks and balances: Overriding the President's veto. Bills passed by Congress become laws when the President signs them. If the President vetoes (rejects) a bill, Congress can overrule the President's veto by a two-thirds vote of both houses.

Every Order, Resolution, or Vote to which the Concurrence of the Senate and House of Representatives may be necessary (except on a question of Adjournment) shall be presented to the President of the United States, and before the Same shall take Effect, shall be approved by him, or being disapproved by him, shall be repassed by two thirds of the Senate and House of Representatives, according to the Rules and Limitations prescribed in the Case of a Bill.

Creating and collecting taxes: Congress has the power to create and collect taxes.

Section 8. The Congress shall have Power To lay and collect Taxes, Duties, Imposts and Excises, to pay the Debts and provide for the common Defence and general Welfare of the United States; but all Duties, Imposts and Excises shall be uniform throughout the United States

To borrow Money on the credit of the United States;

To regulate Commerce with foreign Nations, and among the several States, and with the Indian Tribes;

To establish an uniform Rule of Naturalization, and uniform Laws on the subject of Bankruptcies throughout the United States;

Creating a system of money: Congress has the power to create a national currency (system of money).

To coin Money, regulate the Value thereof, and of foreign Coin, and fix the Standard of Weights and Measures;

To provide for the Punishment of counterfeiting the Securities and current Coin of the United States;

To establish Post Offices and post Roads;

To promote the Progress of Science and useful Arts, by securing for limited Times to Authors and Inventors the exclusive Right to their respective Writings and Discoveries;

Creating federal courts: Congress has the power to create new federal courts.

To constitute Tribunals inferior to the supreme Court;

To define and punish Piracies and Felonies committed on the high Seas, and Offenses against the Law of Nations;

To declare War, grant Letters of Marque and Reprisal, and make Rules concerning Captures on land and Water;

To raise and support Armies, but no Appropriation of Money to that Use shall be for a longer Term than two Years;

To provide and maintain a Navy;

To make Rules for the Government and Regulation of the land and naval Forces;

To provide for calling forth the Militia to execute the Laws of the Union, suppress Insurrections and repel Invasions;

To provide for organizing, arming, and disciplining, the Militia, and for governing such Part of them as may be employed in the Service of the United States, reserving to the States respectively, the Appointment of the Officers, and the Authority of training the Militia according to the discipline prescribed by Congress;

To exercise exclusive Legislation in all Cases whatsoever, over such District (not exceeding ten Miles square) as may, by Cession of particular States, and the Acceptance of Congress, become the Seat of the Government of the United States, and to exercise like Authority over all Places purchased by the Consent of the Legislature of the State in which the Same shall be, for the Erection of Forts, Magazines, Arsenals, dock-Yards and other needful Buildings;—And

To make all Laws which shall be necessary and proper for carrying into Execution the foregoing Powers, and all other Powers vested by this Constitution in the Government of the United States, or in any Department or Officer thereof.

Section 9. The Migration or Importation of such Persons as any of the States now existing shall think proper to admit, shall not be prohibited by the Congress prior to the Year one thousand eight hundred and eight, but a Tax or duty may be imposed on such Importation, not exceeding ten dollars for each Person.

The Privilege of the Writ of Habeas Corpus shall not be suspended, unless when in Cases of Rebellion or Invasion the public Safety may require it.

No Bill of Attainder or ex post facto Law shall be passed.

No Capitation, or other direct, Tax shall be laid, unless in Proportion to the Census or Enumeration herein before directed to be taken.[5]

No Tax or Duty shall be laid on Articles exported from any State.

No Preference shall be given by any Regulation of Commerce or Revenue to the Ports of one State over those of another: nor shall Vessels bound to, or from, one State, be obliged to enter, clear, or pay Duties in another.

No Money shall be drawn from the Treasury, but in Consequence of Appropriations made by Law; and a regular Statement and Account of the Receipts and Expenditures of all public Money shall be published from time to time.

No Title of Nobility shall be granted by the United States: And no Person holding any Office of Profit or Trust under them, shall, without the Consent of the Congress, accept of any present, Emolument, Office, or Title, of any kind whatever, from any King, Prince, or foreign State.

Declaring war: Only Congress can declare war on another country.

Creating and paying for armed forces: Congress has the power to create an army and navy, and to raise the money to pay for them.

Making other laws: Congress has the power to make all laws that are needed to carry out the government's powers under the Constitution.

5. See Sixteenth Amendment

Section 10. No State shall enter into any Treaty, Alliance, or Confederation; grant Letters of Marque and Reprisal; coin Money; emit Bills of Credit; make any Thing but gold and silver Coin a Tender in Payment of Debts; pass any Bill of Attainder, ex post facto Law, or Law impairing the Obligation of Contracts, or grant any Title of Nobility;

No State shall, without the Consent of the Congress, lay any Imposts or Duties on Imports or Exports, except what may be absolutely necessary for executing it's inspection Laws: and the net Produce of all Duties and Imposts, laid by any State on Imports or Exports, shall be for the Use of the Treasury of the United States; and all such Laws shall be subject to the Revision and Controul of the Congress.

No State shall, without the Consent of Congress, lay any Duty of Tonnage, keep Troops, or Ships of War in time of Peace, enter into any Agreement or Compact with another State, or with a foreign Power, or engage in War, unless actually invaded, or in such imminent Danger as will not admit of delay.

Article II: The Executive Branch

The head of the Executive Branch is the President. The comments below point out some of the specific powers of this branch.

ARTICLE II

Section 1. The executive Power shall be vested in a President of the United States of America. He shall hold his Office during the Term of four Years, and, together with the Vice President, chosen for the same Term, be elected, as follows

Each State shall appoint, in such Manner as the Legislature thereof may direct, a Number of Electors, equal to the whole Number of Senators and Representatives to which the State may be entitled in the Congress: but no Senator or Representative, or Person holding an Office of Trust or Profit under the United States, shall be appointed an Elector.

[The Electors shall meet in their respective States, and vote by Ballot for two Persons, of whom one at least shall not be an Inhabitant of the same State with themselves. And they shall make a List of all the Persons voted for, and of the Number of Votes for each; which List they shall sign and certify, and transmit sealed to the Seat of the Government of the United States, directed to the President of the Senate. The President of the Senate shall, in the Presence of the Senate and House of Representatives, open all the Certificates, and the Votes shall then be counted. The Person having the greatest Number of Votes shall be the President, if such Number be a Majority of the whole Number of Electors appointed; and if there be more than one who have such Majority, and have an equal Number of Votes, then the House of Representatives shall immediately choose by Ballot one of them for President; and if no Person have a Majority, then from the five highest on the List the said House shall in like Manner choose the President. But in choosing the President, the Votes shall be taken by States, the Representation from each State having one Vote; A quorum for this Purpose shall consist of a Member or Members from two thirds of the States, and a Majority of all the States shall be necessary to a Choice. In every Case, after the Choice of the President, the Person having the greatest Number of Votes of the Electors shall be the Vice President. But if there should remain two or more who have equal Votes, the Senate shall choose from them by Ballot the Vice President.][6]

The Congress may determine the Time of choosing the Electors, and the Day on which they shall give their Votes; which Day shall be the same throughout the United States.

No Person except a natural born Citizen, or a Citizen of the United States, at the time of the Adoption of this Constitution, shall be eligible to the Office of President; neither shall any person be eligible to that Office who shall not have attained to the Age of thirty five Years, and been fourteen Years a Resident within the United States.

[In Case of the Removal of the President from Office, or of his Death, Resignation, or Inability to discharge the Powers and Duties of the said Office, the Same shall devolve on the Vice President, and the Congress may be Law provide for the Case of Removal, Death, Resignation or Inability, both of the President and Vice President, declaring what Officer

6. Changed by the Twelfth Amendment
7. Changed by the Twenty-Fifth Amendment

shall then act as President, and such Officer shall act accordingly, until the Disability be removed, or a President shall be elected.][7]

The President shall, at stated Times, receive for his Services, a Compensation, which shall neither be increased nor diminished during the Period for which he shall have been elected, and he shall not receive within that Period any other Emolument from the United States, or any of them.

Before he enter on the Execution of his Office, he shall take the following Oath or Affirmation:—"I do solemnly swear (or affirm) that I will faithfully execute the Office of President of the United States, and will to the best of my Ability, preserve, protect and defend the Constitution of the United States."

Section 2. The President shall be Commander in Chief of the Army and Navy of the United States, and of the Militia of the several States, when called into the actual Service of the United States; he may require the Opinion, in writing, of the principal Officer in each of the executive Departments, upon any Subject relating to the Duties of their respective Offices, and he shall have Power to grant Reprieves and Pardons for Offenses against the United States, except in Cases of Impeachment.

Commanding the armed forces: The President is Commander-in-Chief of the armed forces of the United States.

Granting pardons: The President can grant pardons for federal crimes, except in cases of impeachment.

He shall have Power, by and with the Advice and Consent of the Senate, to make Treaties, provided two thirds of the Senators present concur; and he shall nominate, and by and with the Advice and Consent of the Senate, shall appoint Ambassadors, other public Ministers and Consuls, Judges of the supreme Court, and all other Officers of the United States, whose Appointments are not herein otherwise provided for, and which shall be established by Law: but the Congress may by law vest the Appointment of such inferior Officers, as they think proper, in the President alone, in the Courts of Law, or in the Heads of Departments.

Checks and balances: Treaties and appointments. The President can sign treaties with other countries. But the Senate must approve treaties by a two-thirds vote. The President can name certain officials and federal judges, but the Senate must approve the President's choices.

The President shall have Power to fill up all Vacancies that may happen during the Recess of the Senate, by granting Commissions which shall expire at the End of their next Session.

Section 3. He shall from time to time give to the Congress Information of the State of the Union, and recommend to their Consideration such Measures as he shall judge necessary and expedient; he may, on extraordinary Occasions, convene both Houses, or either of them and in Case of Disagreement between them with Respect to the Time of Adjournment, he may adjourn them to such Time as he shall think proper; he shall receive Ambassadors and other public Ministers; he shall take Care that the Laws be faithfully executed, and shall Commission all the Officers of the United States.

Powers of leadership: The President can propose ideas for new laws and reports to Congress on the State of the Union. In emergencies, the President can call Congress into special session.

Section 4. The President, Vice President and all civil Officers of the United States, shall be removed from Office on Impeachment for, and Conviction of, Treason, Bribery, or other high Crimes and Misdemeanors.

Checks and balances: Impeachment. Presidents and other federal officials can be removed from office if they misuse their powers.

Article III
Section 1. The judicial Power of the United States, shall be vested in one supreme Court, and in such inferior Courts as the Congress may from time to time ordain and establish. The Judges, both of the supreme and inferior Courts, shall hold their Officer during good Behaviour, and shall at stated Times, receive for their Services, a Compensation, which shall not be diminished during their Continuance in Office.

Article III: The Judicial Branch
The judicial branch consists of the Supreme Court and other federal courts. The comments below point out some of the specific powers of this branch.

Section 2. The judicial Power shall extend to all Cases, in Law and Equity, arising under this Constitution, the Laws of the United States, and Treaties made, or which shall be made, under their Authority, —to all Cases affecting Ambassadors, other public Ministers and Consuls; —to all Cases of admiralty and maritime Jurisdiction, —to Controversies to which the United States shall be a Party; —to Controversies between two or more States, —[between a State and Citizens of another State;][8] between Citizens of different States, —

Checks and balances: Interpreting the Constitution. The judicial branch has the power to decide whether laws and treaties are constitutional.

Resolving disputes: Federal courts have the power to settle disputes involving the federal government, different states, or citizens of different states.

8. Changed by the Eleventh Amendment
9. Changed by the Eleventh Amendment

between Citizens of the same State claiming Lands under Grants of different States, [and between a State or the Citizens thereof, and foreign States, Citizens or Subjects.][9]

In all Cases affecting Ambassadors, other public Ministers and Consuls, and those in which a State shall be Party, the supreme Court shall have original Jurisdiction. In all the other Cases before mentioned, the supreme Court shall have appellate Jurisdiction, both as to Law and Fact, with such Exceptions, and under such Regulations as the Congress shall make.

The Trial of all Crimes, except in Cases of Impeachment; shall be by Jury, and such Trial shall be held in the State where the said Crimes shall have been committed but when not committed within any State, the Trial shall be at such Place or Places as the Congress may by Law have directed.

Section 3. Treason against the United States, shall consist only in levying War against them, or in adhering to their Enemies, giving them Aid and Comfort. No Person shall be convicted of Treason unless on the Testimony of two Witnesses to the same overt Act, or on Confession in open Court.

The Congress shall have Power to declare the Punishment of Treason, but no Attainder of Treason shall work Corruption of Blood, or Forfeiture except during the Life of the Person attainted.

Article IV: Relations Between the States

This article says that each state must honor the laws and authority of other states, as well as the rights of their citizens. The article also describes how new states can be added to the Union.

ARTICLE IV
Section 1. Full Faith and Credit shall be given in each State to the public Acts, Records, and judicial Proceedings of every other State; And the Congress may by general Laws prescribe the Manner in which such Acts, Records and Proceedings shall be proved, and the Effect thereof.

Section 2. The Citizens of each State shall be entitled to all Privileges and Immunities of Citizens in the several States.

A Person charged in any State with Treason, Felony, or other Crime, who shall flee from Justice, and be found in another State, shall on Demand of the executive Authority of the State from which he fled, be delivered up, to be removed to the State having Jurisdiction of the Crime.

[No Person held to Service or Labour in one State, under the Laws thereof, escaping into another, shall, in Consequence of any Law or Regulation therein, be discharged from such Service or Labour, but shall be delivered up on Claim of the party to whom such Service or Labour may be due.][10]

Section 3. New States may be admitted by the Congress into this Union; but no new State shall be formed or erected within the Jurisdiction of any other State; nor any State be formed by the Junction of two or more States, or Parts of States, without the Consent of the Legislatures of the States concerned as well as of the Congress.

The Congress shall have rower to dispose of and make all needful Rules and Regulations respecting the Territory or other Property belonging to the United States; and nothing in this Constitution shall be construed as to Prejudice any Claims of the United States, or of any particular State.

Section 4. The United States shall guarantee to every State in this Union a Republican Form of Government, and shall protect each of them against Invasion; and on Application of the Legislature, or of the Executive (when the Legislature cannot be convened) against domestic Violence.

10. Changed by the Thirteenth Amendment

ARTICLE V

The Congress, whenever two thirds of both houses shall deem it necessary, shall propose Amendments to this Constitution, or, on the Application of the Legislatures of two thirds of the several States, shall call a Convention for proposing Amendments, which in either Case, shall be valid to all Intents and Purposes, as Part of this Constitution, when ratified by the Legislatures of three fourths of the several States, or by Conventions in three fourths thereof, as the one or the other Mode of Ratification may be proposed by the Congress; Provided that no Amendment which may be made prior to the Year One thousand eight hundred and eight shall in any Manner affect the first and fourth Clauses in the Ninth Section of the first Article; and that no State, without its Consent, shall be deprived of it's equal Suffrage in the Senate.

ARTICLE VI

All Debts contracted and Engagements entered into, before the Adoption of this Constitution, shall be as valid against the United States under this Constitution, as under the Confederation.

This Constitution, and the Laws of the United States which shall be made in Pursuance thereof; and all Treaties made, or which shall be made, under the Authority of the United States, shall be the supreme Law of the Land; and the Judges in every State shall be bound thereby, any Thing in the Constitution or Laws of any State to the Contrary notwithstanding.

The Senators and Representatives before mentioned, and the Members of the several State Legislatures, and all executive and judicial Officers, both of thc United States and of the several States, shall be bound by Oath or Affirmation, to support this Constitution; but no religious Test shall ever be required as a Qualification to any Office or public Trust under the United States.

ARTICLE VII

The Ratification of the Conventions of nine States, shall be sufficient for the Establishment of this Constitution between the States so ratifying the Same.

Done in Convention by the Unanimous Consent of the States present the Seventeenth Day of September in the Year of our Lord one thousand seven hundred and Eighty seven and of the Independence of the United States of America the Twelfth In Witness whereof We have hereunto subscribed our Names,

G. Washington — Presdent and deputy from Virginia

New Hampshire		**Delaware**	
John Langdon	Nicholas Gilman	Geo. Read	Gunning Bedford jun
Massachusetts		John Dickenson	Richard Bassett
Nathaniel Gorham	Rufus King	Jaco. Broom	
Connecticut		**Maryland**	
Wm. Saml. Johnson	Roger Sherman	James McHenry	Dan. of St. Thos. Jenifer
New York		Danl. Carroll	
Alexander Hamilton		**Virginia**	
New Jersey		John Blair	James Madison, Jr.
Wil. Livingston	David Brearley	**North Carolina**	
Wm. Paterson	Jona: Dayton	Wm. Blount	Richd. Dobbs Spaight
Pennsylvania		Hu Williamson	
B. Franklin	Thomas Mifflin	**South Carolina**	
Robt. Morris	Geo. Clymer	J. Rutledge	Pierce Butler
Thos. FitzSimons	Jared Ingersoll	Charles Cotesworth Pinckney	
James Wilson	Gouv. Morris	**Georgia**	
		William Few	Abr Baldwin

Article V: Amending the Constitution
This article describes how the Constitution can be amended, or changed. Amendments must be ratified (approved) by three-fourths of the states.

Article VI: The Constitution as the Supreme Law of the Land
This article makes the Constitution the supreme (highest) law of the nation. No federal or state law can contradict the Constitution.

Article VII: Ratifying the Constitution
This article says that the Constitution must be ratified (approved) by 9 of the original 13 states.

Bill of Rights and Later Amendments

Original Ten Amendments: The Bill of Rights
Passed by Congress September 25, 1789.
Ratified December 15, 1791.

Congress cannot make laws that violate Americans' basic freedoms, including freedom of speech, religion, and the press. Citizens have the right to gather peacefully and to ask the government to correct wrongs.

AMENDMENT 1
BASIC FREEDOMS
Congress shall make no law respecting an establishment of religion, or prohibiting the free exercise thereof; or abridging the freedom of speech, or of the press, or the right of the people peaceably to assemble, and to petition the Government for a redress of grievances.

Citizens have the right to own and carry weapons for use in state militias.

AMENDMENT 2
RIGHT TO BEAR ARMS
A well regulated Militia, being necessary to the security of a free State, the right of the people to keep and bear Arms, shall not be infringed.

In peacetime, the government cannot force citizens to let soldiers stay in their homes.

AMENDMENT 3
QUARTERING OF SOLDIERS
No Soldier shall, in time of peace be quartered in any house, without the consent of the Owner, nor in time of war, but in a manner to be prescribed by law.

Government officials cannot search citizens or their property, or seize their belongings, without good reason. Normally, searches and seizures require a warrant approved by a judge.

AMENDMENT 4
SEARCH AND ARREST
The right of the people to be secure in their persons, houses, papers, and effects, against unreasonable searches and seizures, shall not be violated, and no Warrants shall issue, but upon probable cause, supported by Oath or affirmation, and particularly describing the place to be searched, and the persons or things to be seized.

Citizens who are accused of crimes have certain basic rights. They cannot be tried twice for the same crime, or be forced to testify against themselves. They cannot be jailed or lose their property except through proper legal actions.

AMENDMENT 5
RIGHTS IN CRIMINAL CASES
No person shall be held to answer for a capital, or otherwise infamous crime, unless on a presentment or indictment of a Grand Jury, except in cases arising in the land or naval forces, or in the Militia, when in actual service in time of War or public danger; nor shall any person be subject for the same offence to be twice put in jeopardy of life or limb, nor shall be compelled in any criminal case to be a witness against himself, nor be deprived of life, liberty, or property, without due process of law; nor shall private property be taken for public use, without just compensation.

Citizens who are accused of crimes have the right to a trial by jury that is fair and public. They have the right to question witnesses, and they have the right to a lawyer.

AMENDMENT 6
RIGHT TO A FAIR TRIAL
In all criminal prosecutions, the accused shall enjoy the right to a speedy and public trial, by an impartial jury of the State and district wherein the crime shall have been committed; which district shall have been previously ascertained by law, and to be informed of the nature and cause of the accusation; to be confronted with the witnesses against him; to have compulsory process for obtaining witnesses in his favor, and to have the assistance of counsel for his defence.

Citizens have the right to demand a jury trial to settle disputes over things of value.

AMENDMENT 7
RIGHTS IN CIVIL CASES
In Suits at common law, where the value in controversy shall exceed twenty dollars, the right of trial by jury shall be preserved, and no fact tried by a jury shall be otherwise re-examined in any Court of the United States, than according to the rules of the common law.

AMENDMENT 8
BAIL, FINES, PUNISHMENT
Excessive bail shall not be required, nor excessive fines imposed, nor cruel and unusual punishments inflicted.

Bail and fines that are set by a court must be reasonable. Punishments for crimes cannot be cruel or unusual.

AMENDMENT 9
RIGHTS RETAINED BY THE PEOPLE
The enumeration in the Constitution of certain rights shall not be construed to deny or disparage others retained by the people.

The government must respect all the rights of Americans, including rights that are not listed in the Constitution.

AMENDMENT 10
STATES' RIGHTS
The powers not delegated to the United States by the Constitution, nor prohibited by it to the States, are reserved to the States respectively, or to the people.

The states, and the people, keep any powers that the Constitution does not specifically give to the federal government.

Later Amendments

AMENDMENT 11
LAWSUITS AGAINST STATES
The Judicial power of the United States shall not be construed to extend to any suit in law or equity, commenced or prosecuted against one of the United States by Citizens of another State, or by Citizens or Subjects of any Foreign State.
Ratified February 7, 1795.

People cannot sue a state in federal court if they are citizens of a different state, or of a foreign country.

AMENDMENT 12
PRESIDENTIAL ELECTIONS
The Electors shall meet in their respective states, and vote by ballot for President and Vice-President, one of whom, at least, shall not be an inhabitant of the same state with themselves; they shall name in their ballots the person voted for as President, and in distinct ballots the person voted for as Vice-President, and they shall make distinct lists of all persons voted for as President, and of all persons voted for as Vice-President, and of the number of votes for each, which lists they shall sign and certify, and transmit sealed to the seat of the government of the United States, directed to the President of the Senate;—The President of the Senate shall, in the presence of the Senate and House of Representatives, open all the certificates and the votes shall then be counted;—The person having the greatest number of votes for President, shall be the President, if such number be a majority of the whole number of Electors appointed; and if no person have such majority, then from the persons having the highest numbers not exceeding three on the list of those voted for as President, the House of Representatives shall choose immediately, by ballot, the President. But in choosing the President, the votes shall be taken by states, the representation from each state having one vote; a quorum for this purpose shall consist of a member or members from two-thirds of the states, and a majority of all the states shall be necessary to a choice. [And if the House of Representatives shall not choose a President whenever the right of choice shall devolve upon them, before the fourth day of March next following, then the Vice-President shall act as President, as in the case of the death or other constitutional disability of the President.]* The person having the greatest number of votes as Vice-President, shall be the Vice-President, if such number be a majority of the whole number of Electors appointed, and if no person have a majority, then from the two highest numbers on the list, the Senate shall choose the Vice-President; a quorum for the purpose shall consist of two-thirds of the whole number of Senators, and a majority of the whole number shall be necessary to a choice. But no person constitutionally ineligible to the office of President shall be eligible to that of Vice-President of the United States.
Ratified June 15, 1804. Superseded by Section 3 of the Twentieth Amendment

The Vice President will be elected separately from the President. In the original Constitution, the candidate who finished second in the voting for President automatically became Vice President. Under that system, the President and Vice President were likely to be political enemies. The 12th Amendment allows the same political party to win the elections for both President and Vice President.

AMENDMENT 13
END OF SLAVERY
Section 1. Neither slavery nor involuntary servitude, except as a punishment for crime whereof the party shall have been duly convicted, shall exist within the United States, or

No person in the United States can be kept as a slave. No person can be forced to work for someone else, except as a legal punishment for a crime.

any place subject to their jurisdiction.

Section 2. Congress shall have power to enforce these article by appropriate legislation.

Ratified December 6, 1865.

AMENDMENT 14
CIVIL RIGHTS

Section 1. All persons born or naturalized in the United States and subject to the jurisdiction thereof, are citizens of the United States and of the State wherein they reside. No State shall make or enforce any law which shall abridge the privileges or immunities of citizens of the United States; nor shall any State deprive any person of life, liberty, or property, without due process of law; nor deny to any person within its jurisdiction the equal protection of the laws.

All Americans, including former slaves, have the right to be treated as citizens. For example, states must respect the constitutional rights of all citizens. States must give all their citizens equal protection in their laws. In addition, they cannot deny the right of eligible men to vote in federal elections. If they do, they will lose some of their representatives in Congress.

Section 2. Representatives shall be apportioned among the several States according to their respective numbers, counting the whole number of persons in each State, excluding Indians not taxed. But when the right to vote at any election for the choice of electors for President and Vice President of the United States, Representatives in Congress, the Executive and Judicial officers of a State, or the members of the Legislature thereof, is denied to any of the male inhabitants of such State, being twenty-one years of age, and citizens of the United States, or in any way abridged, except for participation in rebellion, or other crime, the basis of representation therein shall be reduced in the proportion which the number of such male citizens shall bear to the whole number of male citizens twenty-one years of age in such State.

The 14th Amendment also deals with other questions that arose because of the Civil War. For instance, it prevents people from being elected to office who have rebelled against the United States. It also says that the federal government is not responsible for Confederate debts.

Section 3. No person shall be a Senator or Representative in Congress, or elector of President and Vice President, or hold any office, civil or military, under the United States, or under any State, who, having previously taken an oath, as a member of Congress, or as an officer of the United States, or as a member of any State legislature, or as an executive or judicial officer of any State, to support the Constitution of the United States, shall have engaged in insurrection or rebellion against the same, or given aid or comfort to the ene-mies thereof. But Congress may by a vote of two-thirds of each House, remove such disability.

Section 4. The validity of the public debt of the United States, authorized by law, including debts incurred for payment of pensions and bounties for services in suppressing insurrection or rebellion, shall not be questioned. But neither the United States nor any State shall assume or pay any debt or obligation incurred in aid of insurrection or rebellion against the United States, or any claim for the loss or emancipation of any slave; but all such debts, obligations and claims shall be held illegal and void.

Section 5. The Congress shall have power to enforce, by appropriate legislation, the provisions of this article.

Ratified July 9, 1868

AMENDMENT 15
VOTING RIGHTS

States cannot deny anyone the right to vote simply because of the person's race or color, or because the person used to be a slave.

Section 1. The right of citizens of the United States to vote shall not be denied or abridged by the United States or by any State on account of race, color, or previous condition of servitude.

Section 2. The Congress shall have power to enforce this article by appropriate legislation.

Ratified February 3, 1870.

AMENDMENT 16
INCOME TAXES

Congress has the power to collect taxes from individual citizens based on their income (wealth).

The Congress shall have power to lay and collect taxes on incomes, from whatever source derived, without apportionment among the several States, and without regard to any census or enumeration.

Ratified February 3, 1913.

AMENDMENT 17
SENATORIAL ELECTIONS
The Senate of the United States shall be composed of two senators from each State, elected by the people thereof, for six years; and each Senator shall have one vote. The electors in each State shall have the qualifications requisite for electors of the most numerous branch of the State legislature.

When vacancies happen in the representation of any State in the Senate, the executive authority of such State shall issue writs of election to fill such vacancies: Provided, That the legislature of any State may empower the executive thereof to make temporary appointments until the people fill the vacancies by election as the legislature may direct.

This amendment shall not be so construed as to affect the election or term of any Senator chosen before it becomes valid as part of the Constitution.
Ratified April 8, 1913.

Members of the Senate will be elected directly by voters. Previously, Senators were elected by state legislatures.

AMENDMENT 18
PROHIBITION OF LIQUOR
Section 1. After one year from the ratification of this article, the manufacture, sale, or transportation of intoxicating liquors within, the importation thereof into, or the exportation thereof from the United States and all territory subject to the jurisdiction thereof for beverage purposes is hereby prohibited.

Section 2. The Congress and the several States shall have concurrent power to enforce this article by appropriate legislation.

Section 3. This article shall be inoperative unless it shall have been ratified as an amendment to the Constitution by the legislatures of the several States, as provided in the Constitution, within seven years from the date of the submission hereof to the States by the Congress.
Ratified January 16, 1919. Repealed by the Twenty-First, December 5, 1933

This amendment outlawed the making and selling of liquor (alcohol) in the United States. The 21st Amendment removed this amendment from the Constitution.

AMENDMENT 19
WOMEN'S SUFFRAGE
The right of citizens of the United States to vote shall not be denied or abridged by the United States or by any States on account of sex.

Congress shall have power to enforce this article by appropriate legislation.
Ratified August 18, 1920.

Neither the federal government nor the states can deny people the right to vote because of their sex. This amendment guaranteed the right of women to vote.

AMENDMENT 20
TERMS OF OFFICE
Section 1. The terms of the President and Vice President shall end at noon the 20th day of January, and the terms of Senators and Representatives at noon on the 3d day of January, of the years in which such terms would have ended if this article had not been ratified; and the terms of their successors shall then begin.

Section 2. The Congress shall assemble at least once in every year, and such meeting shall begin at noon on the 3d day of January, unless they shall by law appoint a different day.

Section 3. If, at the time fixed for the beginning of the term of the President, the President elect shall have died, the Vice President elect shall become President. If a President shall not have been chosen before the time fixed for the beginning of his term, or if the President elect shall have failed to qualify, then the Vice President elect shall act as President until a President shall have qualified; and the Congress may by law provide for the case wherein neither a President elect nor a Vice President elect shall have qualified, declaring who shall then act as President, or the manner in which one who is to act shall be selected, and such person shall act accordingly until a President or Vice President shall have qualified.
Section 4. The Congress may by law provide for the case of the death of any of the persons

This amendment changes the dates when elected federal officials began serving their terms. It also deals with special situations, such as the death of a President-elect before the start of the President's term in office.

from whom the House of Representatives may choose a President whenever the right of choice shall have devolved upon them, and for the case of the death of any of the persons from whom the Senate may choose a Vice President whenever the right of choice shall have devolved upon them.

Section 5. Sections 1 and 2 shall take effect on the 15th day of October following the ratification of this article.

Section 6. This article shall be inoperative unless it shall have been ratified as an amendment to the Constitution by the legislatures of three-fourths of the several States within seven years from the date of its submission.
Ratified January 23, 1933.

AMENDMENT 21
REPEAL OF PROHIBITION
Section 1. The eighteenth article of amendment to the Constitution of the United States is hereby repealed.

Section 2. The transportation or importation into any State, Territory, or possession of the United States for delivery or use therein of intoxicating liquors, in violation of the laws thereof, is hereby prohibited.

Section 3. The article shall be inoperative unless it shall have been ratified as an amendment to the Constitution by conventions in the several States, as provided in the Constitution, within seven years from the date of the submission hereof to the States by the Congress.
Ratified December 5, 1933.

AMENDMENT 22
TERM LIMITS FOR THE PRESIDENCY
Section 1. No person shall be elected to the office of the President more than twice, and no person who has held the office of President, or acted as President, for more than two years of a term to which some other person was elected President shall be elected to the office of the President more than once. But this Article shall not apply to any person holding the office of President when this Article was proposed by the Congress, and shall not prevent any person who may be holding the office of President, or acting as President, during the term within which this Article becomes operative from holding the office of President or acting as President during the remainder of such term.

Section 2. This article shall be inoperative unless it shall have been ratified as an amendment to the Constitution by the legislatures of three-fourths of the several States within seven years from the date of its submission to the States by the Congress.
Ratified February 27, 1951.

AMENDMENT 23
WASHINGTON, D.C., SUFFRAGE
Section 1. The District constituting the seat of government of the United States shall appoint in such manner as the Congress may direct:

A number of electors of President and Vice President equal to the whole number of Senators and Representatives in Congress to which the District would be entitled if it were a state, but in no event more than the least populous State; they shall be in addition to those appointed by the States, but they shall be considered, for the purposes of the election of President and Vice President, to be electors appointed by a State; and they shall meet in the District and perform such duties as provided by the twelfth article of amendment.

Section 2. The Congress shall have power to enforce this article by appropriate legislation.
Ratified March 29, 1961.

The 18th Amendment is repealed (removed from the Constitution).

Presidents cannot serve more than two full terms in office.

This amendment gives the District of Columbia the right to participate in electing the President and Vice President. The District of Columbia is the nation's capital and is not part of any state.

AMENDMENT 24
ABOLITION OF POLL TAXES
Section 1. The right of citizens of the United States to vote in any primary or other election for President or Vice President, for electors for President or Vice President, or for Senator or Representative in Congress, shall not be denied or abridged by the United States or any State by reason of failure to pay any poll tax or other tax.

Section 2. The Congress shall have power to enforce this article by appropriate legislation. Ratified January 23, 1964.

No state can deny someone the right to vote because the person failed to pay a special voting tax. Before this amendment, some states used a tax to prevent African Americans from voting.

AMENDMENT 25
PRESIDENTIAL SUCCESSION
Section 1. In case of the removal of the President from office or of his death or resignation, the Vice President shall become President.

Section 2. Whenever there is a vacancy in the office of the Vice President, the President shall nominate a Vice President who shall take office upon confirmation by a majority vote of both Houses of Congress.

Section 3. Whenever the President transmits to the President pro tempore of the Senate and the Speaker of the House of Representatives his written declaration that he is unable to discharge the powers and duties of his office, and until he transmits to them a written declaration to the contrary, such powers and duties shall be discharged by the Vice President as Acting President.

Section 4. Whenever the Vice President and a majority of either the principal officers of the executive departments or of such other body as Congress may by law provide, transmit to the President pro tempore of the Senate and the Speaker of the House of Representatives their written declaration that the President is unable to discharge the powers and duties of his office, the Vice President shall immediately assume the powers and duties of the office as Acting President.

This amendment deals with situations in which the President dies or is unable to carry out his duties. It spells out when the Vice President should act for the President or take over as President. It also says how a new Vice President should be elected if the Vice President dies or leaves office between elections.

Thereafter, when the President transmits to the President pro tempore of the Senate and the Speaker of the House of Representatives his written declaration that no inability exists, he shall resume the powers and duties of his office unless the Vice President and a majority of either the principal officers of the executive department or of such other body as Congress may by law provide, transmit within four days to the President pro tempore of the Senate and the Speaker of the House of Representatives their written declaration that the President is unable to discharge the powers and duties of his office. Thereupon Congress shall decide the issue, assembling within forty-eight hours for that purpose if not in session. If the Congress, within twenty-one days after receipt of the latter written declaration, or, if Congress is not in session, within twenty-one days after Congress is required to assemble, determines by two-thirds vote of both Houses that the President is unable to discharge the powers and duties of his office, the Vice President shall continue to discharge the same as Acting President; otherwise, the President shall resume the powers and duties of his office. Ratified February 10, 1967.

AMENDMENT 26
18-year-old suffrage
Section 1. The right of citizens of the United States, who are eighteen years of age or older, to vote shall not be denied or abridged by the United States or by any State on account of age.

Section 2. The Congress shall have power to enforce this article by appropriate legislation. Ratified June 30, 1971.

The federal government and the states cannot deny citizens who are 18 years and older the right to vote.

AMENDMENT 27
CONGRESSIONAL PAY RAISES
No law, varying the compensation for the services of the Senators and Representatives, shall take effect, until an election of Representatives shall have intervened. Ratified May 7, 1992

Congress cannot change the pay of Senators and Representatives who are serving in that session of Congress. Changes in pay will take

The Pledge of Allegiance

I pledge allegiance to the Flag
of the United States of America,
and to the Republic
for which it stands,
one Nation under God, indivisible,
with liberty and justice for all.

The Star-Spangled Banner

September 20, 1814
By Francis Scott Key

Oh, say can you see, by the dawn's early light,
What so proudly we hailed at the twilight's last gleaming?
Whose broad stripes and bright stars, through the perilous fight,
O'er the ramparts we watched, were so gallantly streaming?
And the rockets' red glare, the bombs bursting in air,
Gave proof thought the night that our flag was still there.
O say, does that star-spangled banner yet wave
O'er the land of the free and the home of the brave?

On the shore, dimly seen through the mists of the deep,
Where the foe's haughty host in dread silence reposes,
What is that which the breeze, o'er the towering steep,
As it fitfully blows, now conceals, now discloses?
Now it catches the gleam of the morning's first beam,
In full glory reflected now shines on the stream:
'Tis the star-spangled banner! O long may it wave
O'er the land of the free and the home of the brave.

And where is that band who so vauntingly swore
That the havoc of war and the battle's confusion
A home and a country should leave us no more?
Their blood has wiped out their foul footstep's pollution.
No refuge could save the hireling and slave
From the terror of flight, or the gloom of the grave:
And the star-spangled banner in triumph doth wave
O'er the land of the free and the home of the brave.

Oh! thus be it ever, when freemen shall stand
Between their loved homes and the war's desolation!
Blest with victory and peace, may the heaven-rescued land
Praise the Power that hath made and preserved us a nation.
Then conquer we must, for our cause it is just,
And this be our motto: "In God is our trust."
And the star-spangled banner forever shall wave
O'er the land of the free and the home of the brave!

The World: Political

160° 120° 80° 40°

ARCTIC OCEAN

80°

Arctic Circle

GREENLAND

ALASKA (U.S.)

CANADA

ALEUTIAN ISLANDS

NORTH AMERICA

Newfoundland

40°

UNITED STATES OF AMERICA

NORTH ATLANTIC OCEAN

Tropic of Cancer

Gulf of Mexico

HAWAIIAN ISLANDS

MEXICO

CUBA

HAITI

DOMINICAN REPUBLIC

PUERTO RICO

BELIZE

HONDURAS

JAMAICA

GUATEMALA

EL SALVADOR

NICARAGUA

TRINIDAD & TOBAGO

COSTA RICA

VENEZUELA

GUYANA

SURINAM

PANAMA

FRENCH GUIA

0°

PACIFIC OCEAN

GALAPAGOS ISLANDS

ECUADOR

COLOMBIA

PERU

SOUTH AMERICA

BRAZIL

FIJI

BOLIVIA

PARAGUAY

Tropic of Capricorn

CHILE

URUGUAY

ARGENTINA

FALKLAND/MALVINAS ISLAN

South Georgia

Cape Horn

80° 40°

EUROPE

N W E S

SWEDEN

FINLAND

NORWAY

ESTONIA

RUSSIA

LATVIA

DENMARK

LITHUANIA

UNITED KINGDOM

RUSSIA

IRELAND

BELARUS

NETHERLANDS

POLAND

BELGIUM

GERMANY

UKRAINE

LUXEMBOURG

CZECH REP.

SLOVAK REP.

AUSTRIA

MOLDOVA

SWITZERLAND

HUNGARY

SLOVENIA

ROMANIA

FRANCE

CROATIA

BOSNIA

ANDORRA

ITALY

YUGOSLAVIA

BULGARIA

PORTUGAL

SPAIN

ALBANIA

MACEDONIA

GREECE

TURKEY

0°　　　40°　　　80°　　　120°　　　160°

SVALBARD　ARCTIC OCEAN　SEVERNAYA ZEMLYA　ARCTIC OCEAN　80°

ZEMLYA FRANTSA IOSIFA

ELAND　Novaya Zemlya　Arctic Circle

Area of Inset　RUSSIA

EUROPE　ASIA

KAZAKHSTAN　MONGOLIA

GEORGIA　UZBEKISTAN　KYRGYZSTAN　NORTH　40°
ARMENIA　AZERBAIJAN　TAJIKISTAN　KOREA
TURKMENISTAN　　SOUTH　JAPAN
CYPRUS　SYRIA　CHINA　KOREA
LEBANON　IRAQ　AFGHANISTAN
ISRAEL　IRAN
TUNISIA　JORDAN　PAKISTAN　NEPAL　BHUTAN
CANARY　MOROCCO　SAUDI　QATAR　BANGLADESH　TAIWAN　Tropic of Cancer
ISLANDS　ALGERIA　LIBYA　ARABIA　U.A.E.　INDIA　BURMA　PACIFIC
WESTERN　EGYPT　LAOS　OCEAN
SAHARA　AFRICA　ERITREA　OMAN　VIETNAM
MAURITANIA　MALI　NIGER　CHAD　YEMEN　THAILAND
SENEGAL　SUDAN　CAMBODIA　PHILIPPINES
BURKINA　NIGERIA　CENTRAL　ETHIOPIA　SRI
GUINEA　FASO　AFRICAN REPUBLIC　LANKA　BRUNEI
SIERRA　IVORY　CAMEROON　SOMALIA　MALAYSIA
LEONE　COAST　UGANDA　EAST INDIES　MELANESIA
LIBERIA　GHANA　CONGO　SINGAPORE　PAPUA
GUINEA-BISSAU　GABON　RWANDA　KENYA　INDONESIA　NEW　SOLOMON
GAMBIA　TOGO　REPUBLIC　BURUNDI　GUINEA　ISLANDS
BENIN　OF CONGO　TANZANIA
EQUATORIAL　　INDIAN
GUINEA　ANGOLA　OCEAN　Coral Sea　VANUATU　FIJI
SOUTH　ZAMBIA　MALAWI
ATLANTIC　MOZAMBIQUE　MAURITIUS　AUSTRALIA　Tropic of Capricorn
OCEAN　NAMIBIA　ZIMBABWE　MADAGASCAR　AUSTRALIA
BOTSWANA　RÉUNION
SWAZILAND　North I.　40°
SOUTH　NEW
AFRICA　LESOTHO　ZEALAND
South I.

N　0　2000　4000 miles (at equator)
W　E
S　0　2000　4000　6000 kilometres (at equator)
Gall Projection　Antarctic Circle

ANTARCTICA

0°　　40°　　80°　　120°　　160°

Maps　237

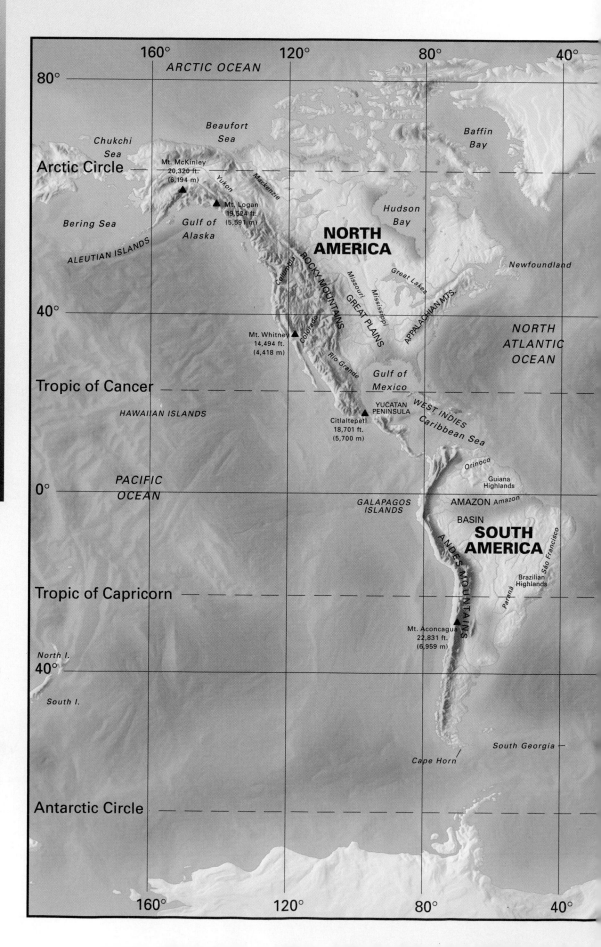

ARCTIC OCEAN

160°   120°   80°   40°

80°

Chukchi
Sea

Beaufort
Sea

Baffin
Bay

Arctic Circle

Mt. McKinley
20,320 ft.
(6,194 m)

Yukon

Mackenzie

Hudson
Bay

Bering Sea

Gulf of
Alaska

NORTH
AMERICA

Newfoundland

ALEUTIAN ISLANDS

Columbia

ROCKY MOUNTAINS

Missouri

Mississippi

Great Lakes

APPALACHIAN MTS.

40°

Mt. Whitney
14,494 ft.
(4,418 m)

Colorado

GREAT PLAINS

NORTH
ATLANTIC
OCEAN

Rio Grande

Tropic of Cancer

Gulf of
Mexico

HAWAIIAN ISLANDS

YUCATAN
PENINSULA

Citlaltepetl
18,701 ft.
(5,700 m)

WEST INDIES

Caribbean Sea

Orinoco

Guiana
Highlands

PACIFIC
OCEAN

0°

GALAPAGOS
ISLANDS

AMAZON   Amazon

BASIN

SOUTH
AMERICA

ANDES MOUNTAINS

São Francisco

Brazilian
Highlands

Tropic of Capricorn

Paraná

Mt. Aconcagua
22,831 ft.
(6,959 m)

North I.

40°

South I.

South Georgia

Cape Horn

Antarctic Circle

160°   120°   80°   40°

ARCTIC OCEAN
SVALBARD
ZEMLYA FRANTSA IOSIFA
Novaya Zemlya
Barents Sea
Kara Sea
SEVERNAYA ZEMLYA
Laptev Sea
East Siberian Sea
Chukchi Sea
Arctic Circle

Norwegian Sea
Dvina
Nizhnyaya Tunguska
Lena
Indigirka
Kolyma
Bering Sea

North Sea
Baltic Sea
NORTH EUROPEAN PLAIN
Volga
URAL MTS
Ob
Yenisey
Angara
Lena
Aldan
Sea of Okhotsk
ALEUTIAN ISLANDS

EUROPE
Don
Ural
Tobol
Ishim
Irtysh
LAKE BAIKAL
ASIA

ALPS
Black Sea
Caspian Sea
Aral Sea
GOBI (DESERT)
Sea of Japan
40°

Mediterranean Sea
K2 28,250 ft. (8,611 m)
Huang He
Yellow Sea
East China Sea

ATLAS MTS.
CANARY ISLANDS
SAHARA
Nile
Red Sea
THAR DESERT
Indus
Ganges
HIMALAYAS
Mt. Everest 29,028 ft. (8,848 m)
Chang Jiang
Tropic of Cancer

SAHEL
ARABIAN PENINSULA
DECCAN PLATEAU
PACIFIC OCEAN

Niger
AFRICA
White Nile
Uele
Mt. Kenya 17,058 ft. (5,199 m)
Bay of Bengal
South China Sea
Philippine Sea

CONGO BASIN
Congo
Mt. Kilimanjaro 19,340 ft. (5,985 m)
INDIAN OCEAN
Celebes Sea
EAST INDIES
MELANESIA
0°

SOUTH ATLANTIC OCEAN
KALAHARI DESERT
Orange
Coral Sea
AUSTRALIA
GREAT VICTORIA DESERT
Tropic of Capricorn

Tasman Sea
North I.
South I.
40°

N
W E
S

0   2000   4000 miles (at equator)

0   2000   4000   6000 kilometres (at equator)

Gall Projection

Antarctic Circle

ANTARCTICA

0°   40°   80°   120°   160°

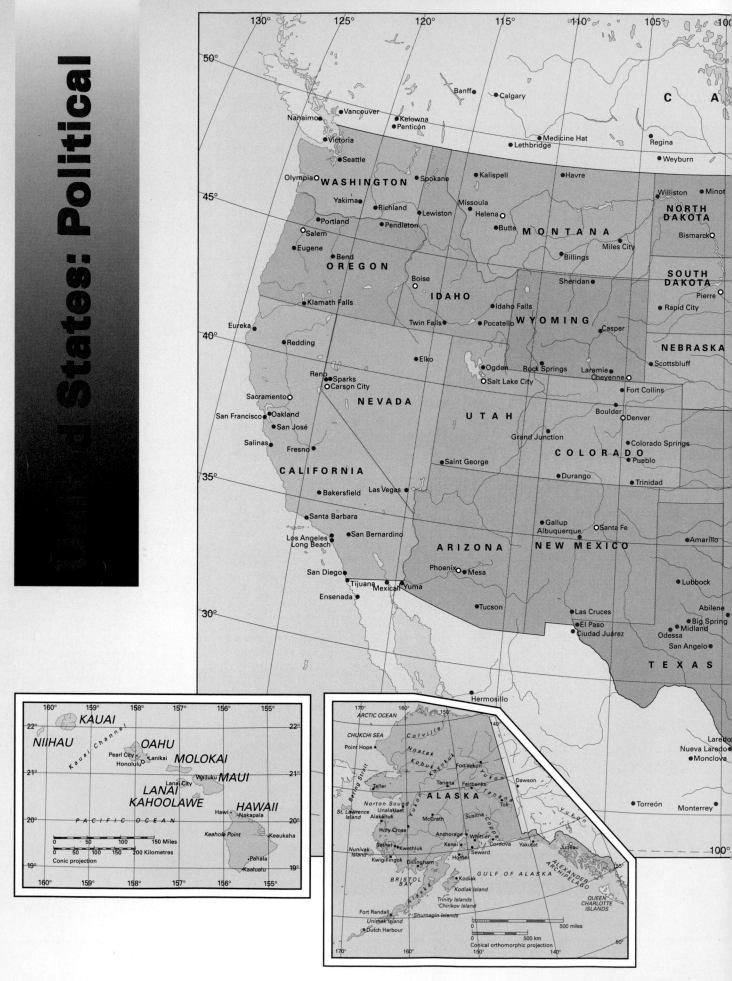

WASHINGTON

Vancouver Island

C. Flattery

Mt. Rainier ▲

Columbia

OREGON

Klamath

C. Medocino

Sacramento

SIERRA NEVADA

NEVADA

CALIFORNIA

Pt. Arguello

CHANNEL ISLANDS

GULF OF SANTA CATALINA

ARIZONA

Colorado

Gila

IDAHO

Snake

Great Salt Lake

UTAH

Colorado

NEW MEXICO

Rio Grande

ROCKY

Missouri

MONTANA

Mt.

WYOMING

Powder

N. Platte

S. Platte

▲ Mt. Elbert

COLORADO

Arkansas

Cimar

Canadian

Pecos

Conch

Rio Grande

NORTH DA

SOUTH DA

NEB

K

TE

Lake Winnipeg

C

50°

45°

40°

35°

30°

130°   125°   120°   115°   110°   105°   10

▲ Mt. Whitney

160°   159°   158°   157°   156°   155°

22°   22°

Mt. Kawaikini ▲   KAUAI

NIIHAU   Kauai Channel   OAHU

21°   MOLOKAI   21°

MAUI

LANAI   ▲ Kolekole

KAHOOLAWE

HAWAII

PACIFIC   OCEAN

Mauna Kea ▲

Keahole Point

20°   Mauna Loa ▲   20°

0   50   100   150 Miles

0   50   100   150   200 Kilometres

Conic projection

19°   19°

160°   159°   158°   157°   156°   155°

170°   160°   150°

ARCTIC OCEAN   ARCTIC COASTAL PLAIN

CHUKCHI SEA   Colville   140°

Ngatuk   BROOKS RANGE

Kotzebue Sound   Kobuk

Koyukuk

Bering Strait

Yukon

Norton Sound   Tanana   Yukon

St. Lawrence Island   ALASKA

Mt. McKinley ▲

Susitna   ▲ Mt. Bona

Nunivak Island   ▲ Mt. Logan

Illiamna Lake

Cape Newenham

BRISTOL BAY   GULF OF ALASKA

ALEXANDER ARCHIPELAGO

Kodiak Island

Trinity Islands

Chirikov Island   QUEEN CHARLOTTE ISLANDS

Unimak Island   Shumagin Islands

0   500 miles

0   500 km

Conical orthomorphic projection

170°   160°   150°   140°

100

Glossary

Teal words are defined in the margins of *History Alive! America's Past.*
Red words (key terms) found inside definitions are defined in the Glossary.

abolitionist   **Civil Rights movement**

A

abolitionist: A person who wanted to see slavery ended (abolished) everywhere.

acts: Laws created or passed by a **government**. For example, the Stamp Act was a law that was passed by the **British Parliament**.

adapt: To change ideas and ways of living to fit a new situation, such as a new **environment**.

adaptations: Changes in a way of life that allow people (or organisms) to survive in a particular **environment**.

Age of Exploration: A time in history when people from Europe traveled to faraway and unfamiliar places, such as Africa and the Americas, in order to learn about them and make maps of them. The Age of Exploration began in the late 1400s and continued through the 1500s.

allies: People or countries who help each other (for example, by fighting on the same side in a war).

amendments: Changes that have been approved and made part of the **Constitution**.

Americas: The continents of North and South America (connected by Central America), along with nearby islands, like those in the Caribbean Sea.

annex: To add new land to a country by taking control of it.

archeologists: Scientists who study human **artifacts** to learn about past cultures.

Articles of Confederation: The document that described a new national government for the former American colonies. (*Confederation* means "a joining together.") The Articles were approved by the states in 1781. They were replaced in 1789 by the **Constitution**.

artifacts: Objects made by groups of humans, such as tools and clothes. Artifacts help us understand the ways of life of the groups who made them.

Assembly: A group of **government** officials who meet to make laws.

B

bayonet: A sharp blade, like a sword, attached to the end of a rifle.

big game: Large animals that are hunted for their flesh, skins, and other valuable body parts. (*Game* is another word for hunted animals.)

Bill of Rights: The first 10 changes, or **amendments,** to the **Constitution.** These amendments list basic rights and freedoms of Americans that the **government** cannot take away.

boundary: The geographic line between two places, such as two countries.

branches: Parts of **government** with different kinds of responsibilities and powers. In the United States government, the **legislative branch** makes laws, the **executive branch** carries them out, and the **judicial branch** interprets them.

British: Coming from, located in, or related to Great Britain (for example, the British government or the British army). The most important part of Great Britain is the country of England. For this reason, *British* and *English* are often used to mean the same thing.

C

cabinet: A group of advisers to the president, including the heads of important departments in the executive branch.

capital: The town or city where government leaders do their work.

capitol: The main government building, where lawmakers meet.

cash crop: A crop that is grown in large quantities for sale to other people.

cession: The act of giving up ("ceding") **territory,** usually as the result of a **treaty**.

checks and balances: In the **Constitution,** ways of limiting the powers of the three parts (**branches**) of the **government**. The Constitution gives one branch the ability to "check," or stop, the action of another branch. It also divides, or balances, powers so that no one branch becomes too powerful.

Chinese immigrants: People from China who moved to the United States in the 1800s. (**Immigrants** are people who move to another country or part of the world and make their homes there.)

Civil Rights movement: The organized efforts by African Americans and other citizens to force individuals and states to honor their rights as Americans. The

244   Glossary

Civil Rights movement began in the 1950s as a fight against segregation and other forms of unfair treatment in the **South**.

Civil War: The war that divided America in the 1860s. (A *civil war* is a war between citizens of the same country.) The war was fought between the states of the **North** and those of the **South** (or between the **Union** and the **Confederacy**).

claim: An area of land being worked by a miner. The miner had the right to valuable minerals found in the claim.

Cold War: The struggle between the "superpowers" (the United States and the Soviet Union) in the years following **World War II.** Although both sides piled up huge stores of weapons, they never fought each other directly, as countries do in "hot wars."

colonial regions: Areas in North America where different kinds of **colonies** developed because of differences in climate and natural features, or **geography.** The three colonial regions were the New England, Middle, and Southern regions.

colonies: Places ruled by another country, not by their own people.

colonists: People who settle in colonies.

Common Sense: A short, powerful book by Thomas Paine that argued plainly and simply that the American colonies should break away from Great Britain. *Common Sense* was printed in 1776 and helped to persuade many **colonists** to favor **independence** for the **colonies**.

compass: An instrument (tool) for finding directions. A magnetic compass has a needle that always points north.

compromise: A settlement of differences in which each side gives up some of its demands. For example, before the **Civil War**, the **North** and the **South** tried to settle their differences through compromises.

Confederacy: The new country that was formed by southern states in 1861. The Confederacy had its own **government,** laws, money, and army. It fought against the **Union** in the **Civil War**.

Confederates: Supporters of the **Confederacy**, especially soldiers in the Confederate armies.

conquistadors: Spanish **explorers** who came to the Americas in the 1500s and claimed large areas of land for Spain. *Conquistador* means "conqueror." The conquistadors often conquered native peoples (ruled over them in the name of Spain).

Constitution: The document that describes the government of the United States. The Constitution is the "supreme law of the land," which means that no other laws can contradict it.

Constitutional Convention: The meeting of delegates in Philadelphia in 1787 that made plans for a new and stronger government for the United States. The convention proposed the **Constitution** to replace the **Articles of Confederation**.

contagious diseases: Sicknesses that can pass from one person to another as germs are spread by touch or through the air. For example, influenza ("the flu") is a contagious disease.

Continental Army: The army of volunteers led by General George Washington that fought the **British** in the **Revolutionary War**. The army was formed by the **Second Continental Congress**.

craftsmen: Highly skilled workers who usually specialize in one kind of work, or craft.

cultural regions: Areas of the world where people develop similar ways of life, or **cultures**. For example, Native Americans in North America lived in several cultural regions. The groups within each region had similar cultures.

cultures: Ways of living of different groups of people. A group's culture includes such things as its language, beliefs, tools, types of homes, and ways of working and playing.

D

debts: Money that is owed to someone else. People (and organizations, such as **governments**) have debts when they have borrowed money and promised to pay it back.

Declaration of Independence: The document that announced that the American **colonies** were breaking away from Great Britain. The Declaration was approved by the **Second Continental Congress** on July 4, 1776. This date is considered the "birthday" of the United States.

defenders: People who protect or defend against outside attack.

democratic: Controlled or run by the people themselves, with each person having an equal say. In democratic **governments,** people usually elect representatives to make laws for them, and every person's vote counts equally. In some other kinds of governments, one person or a few people have the power to rule over everyone else without being elected.

dilemmas: Situations in which a person is forced to make a choice, even though there is no good choice to make. For example, millions of **enslaved Africans** had to choose between dying on the voyage to America or working for the rest of their lives as slaves.

diverse: Different from each other. For example, the

people who settled in the Middle **colonies** were very diverse.

draft: The selection of people to serve in an army whether they wish to serve or not.

driftwood: Wood that has washed up onto the shores of rivers or oceans.

E

East Indies: Southeast Asia, including India, Indonesia, and Malaysia.

economy: The way that a particular region or country organizes the manufacture and exchange of such things as money, food, products, and services. An *economy* includes a system of money and all the businesses, industries, farms, and so on that help to produce, sell, or trade things of value.

Emancipation Proclamation: A special order by President Lincoln that freed (emancipated) slaves in states that were fighting against the **Union.** After the **Civil War,** slavery was ended everywhere in the United States.

enslaved Africans: People from Africa who were forced to give up their freedom and spend their lives obeying and working for their "owners," or masters. Enslaved Africans were treated as property that could be bought and sold.

environments: Places with different types of natural surroundings, including land, water, air, plants, and animals. For example, grasslands and deserts are two very different types of environments.

executive branch: The branch of **government** that carries out ("executes") laws.

expedition: A trip by a group of people involving some danger or risk, for example, to explore unknown places. The group itself is also called an *expedition.*

explorers: People who travel to new and unfamiliar places in order to learn what these places are like and describe them with words, pictures, and maps.

F

Forty-Niners: Gold seekers from around the world who rushed to California beginning in 1849.

G

geographic terms: Words that name different land-forms and bodies of water. Examples of geographic terms include *bay, sea, peninsula,* and *island.*

geography: The study of our physical surroundings and how humans interact with them. Often, *geography* is used to mean the physical surroundings themselves, such as "the geography of the United States." People who study geography are called *geographers.*

Gettysburg: A small town in Pennsylvania where one of the greatest battles of the **Civil War** was fought. The Battle of Gettysburg was a major turning point that helped the **Union** win the war.

globe: A sphere (ball) that shows a map of the Earth's features.

goddesses: Female spirits or gods who control parts of the world.

gorge: A narrow, deep valley with steep sides.

government: The people and groups who are in charge of a country or area (such as a town, a colony, or a state). The government makes rules and laws, and it has the power to see that they are obeyed.

grant: To give to someone something he or she has asked for. For example, the king granted William Penn the land called *Pennsylvania.*

Great Depression: A time of great hardship during the 1930s when millions of people lost their jobs and even their homes. (A *depression* is a long period when an **economy** suffers and businesses are forced to shrink or even to close.)

guerilla tactics: Tactics used by *guerillas* (fighters outside of a regular army), such as shooting at soldiers from hiding places in the woods.

H

home front: In a war, the areas away from the fighting. A "front" is a place where fighting is taking place. On the "home front," people can help to win the war by ways other than fighting. For example, they can make supplies for their armies and send letters and gifts to encourage their soldiers.

I

immigrant: A person who comes to live in a country from another nation.

impeachment: The act of accusing a **government** official of serious crimes, as defined by the **Constitution**.

indentured servants: Individuals who agreed to work for a period of time in exchange for free passage from Europe.

independence: Freedom, especially from control by another country or **government**.

Industrial Revolution: A time of great change in business, industry, and transportation that lasted from about 1790 to about 1920. The Industrial Revolution changed the way people lived and worked by introducing hundreds of new inventions, machines, and ways of making products.

Information Age: A time of great change in the way people communicate and work with information. The Information Age began with the spread of television and computers in the second half of the **20th century,** and it continues to this day.

J

Jamestown: The name of the second English **settlement,** or new community, in North America. Jamestown was started in 1607 in present-day Virginia.

judicial branch: The branch of **government** that interprets laws and settles disagreements about them. (*Judicial* is related to the word *judge.*)

jury: A group of citizens who decide the outcome of a trial.

L

landforms: Masses of land, such as continents, islands, and peninsulas.

latitude: How far a place on Earth is from the equator, measured in degrees. Latitude is measured with the help of imaginary lines around the Earth called *parallels of latitude.*

legislative branch: The branch of **government** that makes laws. (Another word for "make laws" is *legislate.*)

liberties: The freedoms of citizens, such as freedom of speech and freedom of religion. In the United States, these freedoms are protected by the **Bill of Rights**.

longitude: How far a place on Earth is from an imaginary line called the *prime meridian,* measured in degrees. Longitude is measured with the help of imaginary lines called *meridians of longitude* that are drawn from the North Pole to the South Pole.

Loyalists: People in the American **colonies** who wanted the colonies to remain under the control of the king and Great Britain. Loyalists were loyal to the king and opposed **independence**.

M

Manifest Destiny: "Obvious fate." In the 1800s, many Americans believed that it was natural and right for the United States to expand westward to the Pacific Ocean. This belief in the "obvious fate" of the United States was called *Manifest Destiny.*

mesa: A flat-topped hill area with steep sides.

Mexicanos: In the 1800s, Spanish-speaking people who lived in parts of the United States that previously belonged to Mexico.

Middle Passage: The voyage ("passage") of slave traders and **enslaved Africans** across the Atlantic Ocean from Africa to the Americas.

migrants: People who move (migrate) from one country or area of the world to a new home in another country or area.

migration: A movement of people from one country or area of the world to a new home in another country or area.

migration routes: The path followed by a group of people when they move from one country or area of the world to another.

militia: A small army made up of ordinary citizens.

missionaries: Representatives of a religion who try to get other people to adopt that religion.

Mormons: Members of the Church of Jesus Christ of Latter-day Saints. The Mormon church was started by Joseph Smith in 1830. In the 1800s, Mormon **pioneers** settled in the American West, especially Utah.

N

Neutralists: American colonists who did not support either side (**Loyalist** or **Patriot**) in the fight for **independence** from Great Britain.

New World: The European name for lands in the Western Hemisphere, including North and South America. The Americas were a "new" world for Europeans, but not for the native peoples who already lived there.

Nez Percé: A group of Native Americans who lived in the northwestern part of the United States in the 1800s. French explorers called them *Nez Percé,* which means "pierced nose."

nomadic: Moving from place to place, often with changes in the seasons. For example, some Native American groups were nomadic, while others stayed in the same place year-round.

North, the: The northern region of the United States. In the 1800s, this region's **culture** and **economy** were very different from those of the **South**. In particular, most of the states in the North did not permit slavery. During the **Civil War,** "the North" meant the states that were loyal to the **Union.**

Northwest Passage: The supposed route across the northern part of North America that Europeans were looking for but never found. The explorers had hoped to find a northwest passage from the Atlantic Ocean to the Pacific Ocean so that they could get to Asia more quickly.

nuclear weapons: Weapons that release huge amounts of energy contained in the nuclei (centers) of atoms. Nuclear weapons also release deadly *radiation* (a form of energy).

O

ore: Rock or earth from which metal can be taken.

origin stories: Tales that a group of people tell about where they came from and how the Earth came to be.

overseer: A person who was put in charge of the work of slaves. The overseer had great power over the slaves and could punish them for disobeying him.

P

Parliament: The lawmaking part of the **British** government, similar to the Congress in the United States. The American colonists did not have the right to elect representatives to Parliament.

Patriots: People in the American colonies who wanted the colonies to break away from Great Britain. Such people favored **independence** for the colonies.

physical features: Important parts of the Earth's surface, such as mountains, rivers, plains, and oceans. Physical features of the United States include the Rocky Mountains, the Mississippi River, and the Great Plains.

pioneers: The first people from a particular group to move to a new place and begin living there. In the 1800s, the settlers who moved to the West were pioneers. But they were not the first people to make their homes in the West. Other groups of people already lived there, including Native Americans and **Mexicanos.**

plantation: A usually large area of privately owned land where crops were grown with the labor of workers or slaves who lived on the land.

Plymouth: A town started in 1620 by early English settlers, called *Pilgrims.* Plymouth was located in present-day Massachusetts.

prejudiced: Having a negative judgment or opinion without knowledge of the facts.

professional: To be well-trained and paid for one's work. For example, a professional army is made up of soldiers who are taught how to be skilled fighters and who are paid for their service.

protest: To complain publicly about something that people believe is wrong or unfair.

R

rancho: An area of land granted to Spanish and Mexican citizens in North America, usually for ranching (for example, raising cattle).

ratified: Approved; to have made a written document official by signing it.

repeal: To take back, or to cancel, a law.

reservation: An area of land set aside by the United States government for Native Americans to live on.

Revolutionary War: The war between the American colonies and Great Britain from 1775 until 1783. *Revolutionary* means "completely new and different." American revolutionaries wanted **independence** and a new and different **government**.

rights of the accused: The protections that the **Constitution** guarantees to citizens who are accused of crimes. Among these protections are the right to a lawyer and the right to a trial by jury.

Roanoke: The name of the island where the first English **settlement** (new community) was started in North America in 1587. Roanoke is located near the coast of present-day North Carolina.

S

secede: A Southern state's action in rejecting the **government** of the United States and leaving the **Union.**

Second Continental Congress: The meeting of delegates from the American colonies that began in Philadelphia in 1775. The Congress approved the **Declaration of Independence** and acted as the colonies' **government** during the **Revolutionary War.**

segregation: The separation of people, especially by race. Segregation in the **South** was enforced partly by laws and partly by customs.

settlements: Small communities that are started in a new place.

slave auction: A sale in which slaves were sold to buyers who bid (offered prices) for them. Usually a slave was sold to the person making the highest bid.

South, the: The southern region of the United States. In the 1800s, this region's **culture** and **economy** were very different from those of the **North.** In particular, the states in the South allowed slavery. During the **Civil War,** "the South" meant the states that were part of the **Confederacy.**

strategies: Plans for winning a war, such as how and where to use an army or navy.

surgeon: A doctor who performs operations, such as cutting into the body to remove a bullet, or removing an infected leg.

T

tactics: Specific ways of carrying out a plan, such as ways of fighting battles.

taxation without representation: Forcing people to pay taxes when they have had no say in making the law that created the tax. American colonists were angry about paying taxes that were passed by the **British Parliament,** where they had no representatives (people who could vote on the tax).

territories: Large regions of land. Within the United States, *territories* often refers to areas that have not yet been organized into states.

tobacco: A plant whose leaves are dried and turned into material for smoking or sniffing, or chewing.

traitor: A person guilty of acting against his or her own country.

transcontinental: Across the continent. The transcontinental railroad stretched across the continent of North America.

treason: The crime of disloyalty toward a ruler or **government**.

treaty: A formal agreement between two or more nations.

20th century: The 1900s, a time of great change in technology and ways of life. The 20th century was also a time of huge wars involving countries from all over the world.

U

unconstitutional: In conflict with the **Constitution**. Laws that do not conflict with the Constitution are called *constitutional.*

Union: The United States as one country that is made up of the individual states. For example, a new state is said to join "the Union." In **Civil War** times, *the Union* referred to the **government** in Washington, D.C., and the states that remained loyal to it. In this meaning, *the Union* refers to the **North.**

V

veto: To reject a bill and prevent it from becoming a law. Only the president has the power to veto bills.

volunteers: People who freely perform a service.

W

Williamsburg: The capital town of the British colony of Virginia, where the colony's government met.

World War I: The first huge war in the **20th century** that involved countries from all over the world. World War I was fought from 1914 to 1918 and involved more than 30 countries.

World War II: The second huge war in the **20th century** that involved countries from all over the world. World War II was fought from 1939 to 1945 and involved more than 50 countries.

Y

yoke: A wooden frame that fastens around an animal's neck.

Index

Page references for illustrations and photographs are in italics. An italic *m* indicates a map. Red words are key terms, with a red page number to show where the term is introduced. Teal words are margin definitions, with a teal page number to show where the term is found.

Acknowledgments

Table of Contents (top to bottom)
Page **6B**, Library of Congress
Page **6C**, National Musem of American Art, Washington, DC/Art Resource, Detail from *Comanche Village, Women Dressing Robes and Drying Meat,* by George Catlin
Page **6D**, Bates Littlefield/National Geographic Image Collection
Page **6E**, Huntington Library
Page **7A**, Library of Congress
Page **7B**, Library of Congress
Page **7C**, The Granger Collection, New York
Page **7D**, Colonial Williamsburg Foundation
Page **7E**, North Wind Pictures
Page **7F**, Library of Congress
Page **8A**, Library of Congress
Page **8B**, Library of Congress
Page **8C**, The Granger Collection, New York
Page **8D**, The Granger Collection, New York
Page **8E**, The Granger Collection, New York
Page **8F**, The Granger Collection, New York
Page **9A**, Library of Congress
Page **9B**, Library of Congress

Chapter 2
page **20**, Library of Congress; **21**, Library of Congress; **22**, Corbis/Bettmann; **24 L**, Gary Milburn/Tom Stack & Associates; **24 R**, Terry Donnelly/Tom Stack & Associates; **25 L**, John Shaw/Tom Stack & Associates; **25 R**, Stan Osolinski/FPG; **26**, Library of Congress

Chapter 3
28, National Museum of American Art, Washington DC/Art Resource, NY *Comanche Village, Women Dressing Robes and Drying Meat* . by George Catlin(including details from painting); **29**, National Musem of American Art, Washington, DC/Art Resource, NY Detail from *Comanche Village, Women Dressing Robes and Drying Meat,* by George Catlin; **30**, Smithsonian Institution; **31**, R. Berenholtz/The Stock Market; **32**, Smithsonian Institution; **33**, James Blank/FPG; **34**, Library of Congress; **35**, Eastcott-Momatiuk/Woodfin Camp; **36-37**, J. Greenberg/The Image Works

Chapter 4
38, Bates Littlefield/National Geographic Image Collection; **39**, Bates Littlefield/National Geographic Image Collection; **40**, Prit J. Vesilind/National Geographic Image Collection; **41**, The Pierpont Morgan Library/Art Resource, NY; **43**, Bill Strode/Woodfin Camp & Associates; **44**, Scala/Art Resource, NY; **45**, Corbis/The Academy of Natural Sciences, Philadelphia

Chapter 5
46, Huntington Library; **47**, Huntington Library; **49**, The Granger Collection, New York; **50**, Stock Montage; **51**, Giraudon/Art Resource, NY; **52**, American Musem of Natural History; **53**, Giraudon/Art Resource, NY; **54**, The Granger Collection, New York; **55**, Library of Congress; **56**, North Wind Pictures; **57**, The Granger Collection, New York

Chapter 6
58 T, Virginia Museum of Fine Arts; **58 B**, Library of Congress; **59**, Library of Congress; **60**, North Wind Pictures; **61**, The Granger Collection, New York; **62**, National Portrait Gallery, Smithsonian Institution/Art Resource, NY; **63**, The Pilgrim Society; **64**, The Granger Collection, New York

Chapter 7
66, Library of Congress; **67**, Library of Congress; **69**, Corbis/Bettmann; **70**, Stock Montage; **71**, Library of Congress; **72**, Library of Congress; **73**, *The Founding of Maryland* by Emmanuel Leutze/The Maryland Historical Society; **74**, Library of Congress; **75**, Library of Congress

Chapter 8
76, The Granger Collection, New York; **77T**, The Granger Collection, New York; **78**, Corbis/Bettmann; **79**, North Wind Pictures; **80**, Library of Congress; **81**, Library of Congress; **82**, Library of Congress; **83**, Library of Congress; **84**, Library of Congress; **85**, Library of Congress

Chapter 9
All; Colonial Williamsburg Foundation

Chapter 10
102, North Wind Pictures; **103**, North Wind Pictures; **104**, Library of Congress; **106**, Library of Congress; **107**, Massachusetts Historical Society; **108**, Library of Congress; **109**, Library of Congress; **110**, North Wind Pictures; **111**, Library of Congress

Chapter 11
112, Library of Congress; **113**, Library of Congress; **114**, Colonial Williamsburg Foundation; **115**, Massachusetts Historical Soceity; **116**, The Granger Collection, New York; **117**, The Granger Collection, New York; **118**, The Granger Collection, New York; **119**, *Mrs. James Warren (Mercy Otis) about 1763;* by John Singleton Copley/Museum of Fine Arts, Boston; **120**, *Samuel Adam, about 1772;* by John Singleton Copley/Museum of Fine Arts, Boston; **121**, The Granger Collection, New York

Chapter 12
122 T, Historical Society of Pennsylvania, *The Congress Voting Independence* by Robert Edge Pine and/or Edward Savage (Accession #1904.1); **122 B**, Library of Congress; **123**, Library of Congress; **124**, *A View of the South Part of Lexington* by Amos Doolittle/Connecticut Historical Society; **125**, Library of Congress; **126**, Art Resource, NY; **127**, Yale University Art Gallery; **128**, Library of Congress; **129**, The Granger Collection, New York

Chapter 13
130 T, Yale University Art Gallery; **130 B**, Library of Congress; **131**, Library of Congress; **132**, The Granger Collection, New York; **133**, The Granger Collection, New York; **134**, The Granger Collection, New York; **135**, Library of Congress; **136**, Metropolitan Museum of Art; **137**, The Granger Collection, New York; **138**, *Peace Treaty Commissioners* by Benjamin West/Courtesy, Winterthur Museum; **139**, Library of Congress

Chapter 14
140, The Granger Collection, New York; **141**, The Granger Collection, New York; **142**, North Wind Pictures; **143**, Library of Congress; **145**, Peter Gridley/FPG; **146**, Peter Gridley/FPG; **147**, Peter Gridley/FPG; **149**, The Granger Collection, New York

Chapter 15
150, The Granger Collection, New York; **151**, The Granger Collection, New York; **152**, Library of Congress; **153**, Holbrooke/The Stock Market; **154**, The Granger Collection, New York; **155 T**, North Wind Pictures; **155 B**, Spencer Grant/Stock Boston; **157**, Stacy Pick/Stock Boston; **158**, Bob Daemmrich/The Image Works

Chapter 16
160, The Granger Collection, New York; **161**, The Granger Collection, New York; **162**, Library of Congress; **163**, Library of Congress; **164**, Montana Historical Society; **165**, Library of Congress; **167**, Library of Congress; **168**, The Granger Collection, New York; **169**, Library of Congress; **171**, Library of Congress

Chapter 17
172, The Granger Collection, New York; **173**, The Granger Collection, New York; **174**, Library of Congress; **175**, Bancroft Library/University of California, Berkeley; **177**, California State Library; **178**, Library of Congress; **180**, *Handcart Pioneers,* by C. C. A. Christensen © by Intellectual Reserve, Inc., Courtesy of the Museum of Church History and Art, Used by Permission; **181**, Library of Congress; **182**, Denver Public Library, Western History Collection

Chapter 18
184, Library of Congress; **185**, Library of Congress; **186**, Library of Congress; **187**, Library of Congress; **189**, Library of Congress; **190**, The Granger Collection, New York; **191**, Library of Congress; **192**, The Granger Collection, New York; **193**, The Granger Collection, New York

Chapter 19
194, Library of Congress; **195**, Library of Congress; **196 R**, The Museum of the Confederacy; **196 L**, Corbis / Bettmann; **198**, The Granger Collection, NY; **199 T**, Ron Van Meir Collection /Cheryl Fenton Photography*; **198 B**, Sanchez/Vetter Collection/Cheryl Fenton Photography*; **200**, The Granger Collection, New York; **201**, National Museum of Civil War Medicine; **202**, The Granger Collection, New York; **203**, The Granger Collection, New York; **204**, Tom Lovell/National Geographic Image Collection

Chapter 20
214, The Museum of Modern Art; **216**, *Brooklyn Bridge, circa 1883.* Photoengraving by Shugg Brothers/Museum of the City of New York, 34.401, Bequest of Mrs. J. Insley Blair; **217**, Corbis /Bettmann; **218**, Copyright, The Dorothea Lange Collection, The Oakland Museum of California, The City of Oakland. Gift of Paul S. Taylor; **219**, Library of Congress; **220**, Library of Congress; **221**, Library of Congress; **222**, Frank Pedrick//The Image Works; **223**, NASA

*Photographed expressly for the publisher.